Metaphysics and Nihilism

Martin Heidegger

Metaphysics and Nihilism

1. The Overcoming of Metaphysics
2. The Essence of Nihilism

Edited by Hans-Joachim Friedrich

Translated by Arun Iyer

polity

Originally published in German as *Metaphysik und Nihilismus. 1. Die Überwindung der Metaphysik. 2. Das Wesen der Nihilismus* © Vittorio Klostermann GmbH, Frankfurt am Main, 1999. 2nd revd. edn. 2018.

This English edition © Polity Press, 2022

Polity Press
65 Bridge Street
Cambridge CB2 1UR, UK

Polity Press
111 River Street
Hoboken, NJ 07030, USA

ISBN-13: 978-1-5095-4004-4

A catalogue record for this book is available from the British Library.

Library of Congress Control Number: 2022939601

Typeset in 10.5 on 12 pt Times New Roman
by Cheshire Typesetting Ltd, Cuddington, Cheshire
Printed and bound by CPI Group (UK) Ltd, Croydon, CR0 4YY

The publisher has used its best endeavors to ensure that the URLs for external websites referred to in this book are correct and active at the time of going to press. However, the publisher has no responsibility for the websites and can make no guarantee that a site will remain live or that the content is or will remain appropriate.

Every effort has been made to trace all copyright holders, but if any have been overlooked the publisher will be pleased to include any necessary credits in any subsequent reprint or edition.

For further information on Polity, visit our website:
politybooks.com

Contents

Translator's Introduction   *page* xiii

THE OVERCOMING OF METAPHYSICS
THE OVERCOMING OF METAPHYSICS

1. The Overcoming of Metaphysics   5
2. The Overcoming of Metaphysics   7
3. The History of Beyng and the Overcoming of
   Metaphysics   8
4. The Vanishing of Being   9
5. Metaphysics and the Predominance of Beings: The
   Impotence and the Vanishing of Beyng   9
6. "Overcoming"   10
7. On the Formation of the Text   17
8. On the Correct Grasp of the Whole   18
9. The Overcoming of Metaphysics through Beyng   18
10. The Overcoming as the History of Beyng   19
11. The Other Inception   20
12. The Transition   20
13. Metaphysics and the Question of Possibility   21
14. The Question of Possibility as the Mode of the Question
    of Essence   22
15. The Truth of Beyng   26
16. "Truth" (Cf. Winter Semester 37/38)   27
17. Truth [Clearing of Beyng (Event) and the Correctness of
    Representing]   27
18. The Essence of History   28
19. On the Overcoming of Metaphysics   28

20. Correctness   28
21. The Overcoming of Metaphysics   29
22. The Overcoming of "Metaphysics"   29
23. Overcoming   31
24. "Overcoming" and "the Human"   32
25. The Overcoming of Metaphysics   32
26. The Overcoming of Metaphysics   33
27. The Overcoming of Metaphysics at its End   33
28. The Overcoming of Metaphysics   34
29. Over-coming is only in the Other Inception   34
30. "Worldview" – "Ideology"   35
31. The End of Metaphysics   36
32. The End of Metaphysics   37
33. The Clearing of Beyng   38
34. Nietzsche and the End of Western Metaphysics   38
35. The End of Metaphysics as Consummation in the
    Unconditional Corrupted Essence. (The Metaphysics of
    Nietzsche)   39
36. The Metaphysics of Nietzsche as the Consummation of
    Metaphysics   41
37. The Consummation of Metaphysics: The Positing of Value
    as Nihilism   42
38. The Consummation of Metaphysics Comes to Fruition   44
39. Beyng – (Event)   44
40. Metaphysics   45
41. Metaphysics   45
42. The Consummation of Modern Metaphysics   45
43. Metaphysics as the History of Beyng   45
44. Metaphysical Errancy   46
45. Metaphysics and the "Universal"   46
46. Metaphysics (cf. "Basic Words")   47
47. Basic concepts (*of Metaphysics*)   47
48. The Essence of Metaphysics in Terms of the History of
    Beyng   48
49. Metaphysics and "Physics"   49
50. The History of Being (The Overcoming of Metaphysics) –
    Being and Time (The Question of Being)   49
51. Metaphysics   49
52. "The Metaphysical"   50
53. The Role of "Science" and Philosophy as Metaphysics   50
54. On *What is Metaphysics?*   51
55. On *What is Metaphysics?* The Nothing   53

56. *On the Essence of Ground:* Ground – Freedom – Truth –
    Beyng   53
57. "Ground" and "Truth"   54
58. Projection and Eventuation [*Er-eignung*]   55
59. "Ground"   56
60. "Ground"   56
61. On the Essence of Ground   56
62. The Differentiation   58
63. Metaphysics and the Differentiation   58
64. Metaphysics   58

THE OVERCOMING OF METAPHYSICS

I. SEQUEL

I. THE DIFFERENTIATION

65. The Differentiation   63
66. The Differentiation (and the Question concerning the
    Nothing)   65
67. The Differentiation (Beyng is the Nothing)   66
68. Being and Beings – Metaphysics – the Differentiation   66
69. Differentiation and Event   67
70. Differentiating Being from Beings and the Distinctness of
    the Two   67
71. The Differentiation and What is Borne Out   67
72. Metaphysics ("Being" – an Empty Word)   68
73. The Differentiation   68
74. Being and Beyng   68
75. The Differentiation – What is Borne Out   69
76. The Differentiation   70

II. ON THE CONCEPT OF METAPHYSICS

77. Metaphysics and the Thinking that is Responsive to the
    History of Beyng   73
78. The Overcoming of "Metaphysics"   73
79. The Transition of Metaphysics within the History of
    Beyng into the Other Inception of the Truth of Beyng   74
80. The A priori   75
81. Metaphysics and the A priori   75
82. The "A priori" – Character of "Being"   76
83. Metaphysics and the Differentiation   76

84. Metaphysics   77
85. "Metaphysics"   78
86. Being Conscious and Being (Modern Metaphysics)   79
87. Metaphysics and "Theology"   79
88. The Relation to Being within the History supported by
    Metaphysics   80
89. "Metaphysics" and the Thinking of Beyng   80
90. Metaphysics as Theology   81
91. Metaphysics and Modern Humanity   81
92. Metaphysics and "Theology"   82
93. Nietzsche and Heraclitus ("Metaphysics" and the First
    Inception of Philosophy)   83
94. The History of Beyng: "Overcoming"   84
95. Kant and Metaphysics   84
96. "Metaphysics" ("Subjectivity" and Substantiality)   85
97. The Overcoming of Metaphysics   85
98. The Essence of Metaphysics and its Overcoming   86
99. The Consummation of Metaphysics   86
100. The Overcoming of Metaphysics   87
101. The Consummation of Metaphysics   88
102. Metaphysics – Consummation (Inversion into the most
     Extreme)   89
103. The Interpretation of the Cogito   89

III. ART AND METAPHYSICS

104. In the Lectures on the *Origin of the Work of Art*   91
105. "Art"   92
106. When Metaphysics Ends, so too does Art   92

IV. METAPHYSICS AND "WORLDVIEW"

107. Metaphysics and Worldview   95
108. Worldview is the Perishing of Metaphysics   95
109. The Consummation of Metaphysics (Nietzsche)   96
110. "Worldview"   97
111. "Worldview" and "Philosophy"   98
112. "World-view" ("Life")   99
113. Metaphysics – Worldview: The True, the Good, the
     Beautiful   99
114. Metaphysics and Worldview and the Thinking Responsive
     to the History of Beyng.   100

115. Metaphysics and Worldview   101
116. Metaphysics and Worldview   102

V. *BEING AND TIME* IN THE HISTORY OF BEYNG
INSOFAR AS THIS HISTORY IS EXPERIENCED AS THE
OVERCOMING OF METAPHYSICS

117. *Being and Time* and Metaphysics   103
118. Time and Eternity   104
119. On the History of the Concept of Time   104
120. The Essence of Time   105
121. Time and Being   105
122. Being and Time   106
123. *Being and Time*   106
124. Being and Time   108
125. "The Sense of Being"   109
126. Being and Time   109
127. *Being and Time*   110
128. Being, the Understanding of Being and Beyng   110
129. Da-sein and "Care" – "Attunement"   111
130. Being and Time   111

THE OVERCOMING OF METAPHYSICS

II. SEQUEL

I. THE CONSUMMATION OF METAPHYSICS
THE ABANDONMENT BY BEING AND DEVASTATION

131. Metaphysics and "Science"   119
132. At the End of Metaphysics   119
133. Inception and Metaphysics   119
134. The Essence of the Consummation of Metaphysics in
     terms of the History of Beyng   120
135. The Consummation of "Modernity" within the History of
     Beyng   120
136. The Nothing and Devastation   120
137. Abandonment by Being   121
138. Abandonment by Being   121
139. The Abandonment of Beings by Being   121
140. Manipulation – Technology – Beyng   122

141. "Technology"   123
142. Manipulation   123

II. THE ORIGIN OF METAPHYSICS IN
THE HISTORY OF BEYNG
THE ORIGIN OF METAPHYSICS AND THE ESSENCE OF
TRUTH IN THE FIRST INCEPTION

143. Overcoming   125
144. One of the Characteristic Features of Metaphysics   126
145. The Age of "Theologies"   127
146. The Essence of Metaphysics: Theology and Mathematics   127
147. "Truth" and Metaphysics (Grades of the True)   128
148. On the Essential Determination of Modern Metaphysics in
     its Consummation   129
149. If Being is "Will" . . .   130
150. Metaphysics and "System"   131
151. The A priori   132
152. The First Inception and the Origin of Metaphysics   132
153. Being as ἰδέα and the Collapse of ἀλήθεια   133
154. ἡ τοῦ ἀγαθοῦ ἰδέα: The Beginning of Metaphysics and the
     Crash and Collapse of the Ungrounded ἀλήθεια   133
155. How Metaphysics Begins and Peters Out   134
156. "Watching" and "Thinking" (The End of Metaphysics)   135
157. The History of Being and Metaphysics   135
158. "Worldview" and "Metaphysics"   136
159. Animal rationale – absolutum (causa)   136
160. Truth as Certainty: Modern Metaphysics (Leibniz)   137

III. METAPHYSICS
THE INDIVIDUAL BASIC POSITIONS OF METAPHYSICS

161. From Whence the Appearance that the Thinking
     Responsive to the History of Beyng is Only a Modification
     of Hegel's Metaphysics?   139
162. Hegel's Concept of History   140
163. Beyng – Event – Inception (Meant from the Standpoint of
     "Metaphysics")   140
164. Beings as a Whole and their Entirety (Metaphysics and
     Beyng)   142

THE ESSENCE OF NIHILISM   145

APPENDIX

Addendum to: The Essence of Nihilism   211

Editor's Afterword   219

Translator's Introduction

This book in front of you is a translation of the second revised edition of volume 67 of Martin Heidegger's *Gesamtausgabe* titled *Metaphysics and Nihilism*. The volume contains two texts spanning ten years: *The Overcoming of Metaphysics* (1938/39) and *The Essence of Nihilism* (1946–1948).

It is clear for us to see, even as the editor informs us, that the two texts constituting this volume are formally different. The first text written in 1938/39 is part of the *Ereignis*-writings accompanying *The Contributions to Philosophy (Of the Event)*, which exhibit the immediacy of thought in its emergence and do not possess the polish of a finished written text. We cannot say that of the second text, which is a polished piece of writing, two-thirds of which, as the editor points out, was revised by Heidegger and published under the title "Nihilism as Determined by the History of Being" in the second of the two Nietzsche volumes from 1961.

In abiding by Heidegger's wish to have the reader confront his text directly, this translation has eschewed any mediation in the form of a critical apparatus. There is no index. The only interventions made in this translation are to provide English translations of Heidegger's foreign language citations in footnotes in curly brackets, indicated by the abbreviation TN for Translator's Note, and the original German pagination, which is inserted into the text in square brackets.

A translation is a set of decisions that can always be challenged. In this sense, it is like a performance of a piece of classical music. Just like every performance of a piece, every translation of a text is different, and yet, all the different translations of a text, like all the different performances of a piece, are one and the same. For they are translations of one and the same text and performances of one and the same piece. Every translation has to take some decisions and follow the linguistic consequences of those decisions in the conviction that they render the text being translated into the language of the translation, as it is meant to be read, in much the same way as every musical performance has to take decisions and abide by the musical consequences of those decisions in the conviction that they render the piece as it is meant to be heard.

The following are some of the important decisions I have made as a translator:

1. *Ereignis and Er-eignis* and related words: Both words have been translated as "event," with the hyphenated German placed in brackets next to its English translation. I have avoided terms like "appropriative event" or "appropriating event" to translate *Er-eignis* for they end up misleading the reader into seeing acquisition and possession as the primary sense of these words, when in fact they are not. In addition to this, there are reasons of elegance and readability, which I believe are important virtues that aid the understanding of a text, especially a difficult text like this one.

2. *Wesen* and *Wesung: Wesen* has been translated as "to essence" and *Wesung* as the gerund "essencing." In this, I believe I have followed Heidegger's own directions in *The Essence of Nihilism* (p. 192):

> ... "[E]ssence" does not mean here what previous reflections unthinkingly assumed. "Essence" does not mean an essentiality, which as something non-sensuous and abstract floats over the actual understood as the sensibly perceptible. "Essence" thought verbally, and, that is to say, experienced in thinking, is the essencing of being itself, which leads all beings into becoming beings as such.

The translations are awkward, as the English language does not grant any conventional space to verbalize the noun essence or to use it as a gerund. The word, as we know, comes from the Latin *essentia*, which in turn renders the Greek οὐσία. The prefix "esse-" comes from the Latin *esse* meaning "to be" and the suffix "-ence," according to *Klein's Comprehensive Etymological Dictionary of the English Language (1971)*, denotes action, process, state or quality and comes from the Latin *-entia*. So, one can see a verbal sense in the English word "essence" if one notes that the suffix "-ence" does also denote action and process in addition to a state and quality. The *Deutsches*

---

[1] *Deutsches Wörterbuch von Jacob Grimm und Wilhelm Grimm*, digitized version in *Wörterbuchnetz* of Trier Center for Digital Humanities.

Wörterbuch von Jacob Grimm und Wilhelm Grimm[1] tells us that the verbal meaning of *wesen* is *leben und weben*, which means "to exist, to be there (often concretely elaborated) in a broadly inclusive sense of an intensive and concept-specific life-expression and activity." Now, *Leben* means "to live" and *weben*, it tells us, has three connotations: "to move back and forth," "to show oneself and be active" and "to waft or wave." In fact, this mellifluous combination of the words *leben* and *weben* was introduced by Luther in his translation of the Acts of the Apostles 17: 28, which in English reads: "For in him, we live, move, and have our being."[2] Luther uses *weben* to translate the Greek κινούμεθα. Heidegger in these texts being translated makes it clear that he wishes to use the word *wesen* in a way that reminds us of the Latin noun *essentia*, understood as essentiality but, at the same time, shows us what is overlooked when we are transfixed by the static nature of the noun, namely, the essential moment of beings becoming beings. He does this by verbalizing the very same noun, which in the English language can be executed only in all its awkwardness.

3. *Seyngeschichtliches/geschichtliches Denken: Seynsgeschichte* translates to "history of beyng." *Geschichtliches Denken* is easily translated as "historical thinking," which means thinking in terms of history or thinking in a manner that is responsive to history. However, the transition from *geschichtliches Denken* to *seynsgeschichtliches Denken* is not grammatically and semantically possible in the English language. Moreover, it is necessary to translate *seynsgeschichtliches Denken* in a way that preserves the translation of *Seynsgeschichte* as "history of beyng," if the translation has to convey to an English-speaking reader, the meaning it possesses in German. I have done this by translating *seynsgeschichtliches Denken* as "thinking responsive to the history of beyng." Yes, one can legitimately complain that this is an inelegant paraphrase of a compact and self-evident term. But in this particular case, I believe that the need to convey the precise meaning of the term outweighs the need for elegance.

4. *Machenschaft* has been translated as "manipulation." It is usually translated as "machination." But, in the English language, "machination" always carries a morally negative connotation. Hence it is always used in English as a term of moral condemnation. But the German word *Machenschaft*, on the other hand, does not always carry

---

[2] The Holy Bible: King James Version (Oxford, New York: Oxford University Press, 2010).

a negative connotation. The *Deutsches Wörterbuch von Jacob Grimm und Wilhelm Grimm* tells us that *Machenschaft* is a southern German word meaning making, ordering, determining, erecting, which requires further qualifications to give it an explicitly morally negative sense. Moreover, Heidegger is adamant that the terms that he employs in his writings on being do not carry any moral connotation and are not used for the purposes of moral judgment. It is for these reasons that I have used the English word "manipulation" to translate *Machenschaft*. Manipulation does carry a morally negative connotation but it does not possess only such a connotation. It can also be used in a morally neutral sense to mean adjusting, operating, and working on something in order to make it work for our purpose. Heidegger's use of the word *Machenschaft* carries precisely this sense of being able to work on things and transform them into things that serve our needs, and viewing all beings as that which can be transformed into serving our needs without any explicit moral judgment on our needs and on our capacity to transform things to suit our needs.

In keeping with the wishes of the publisher, I have attempted to make the translation stand as a text on its own, which can be read and understood without referring to the original German text. This is of course particularly difficult to do in the case of Heidegger, who uses every resource the German language provides him with to express his difficult and highly original intuitions. However, this translation has, as far as possible, avoided the practice of placing the original German words next to their English counterparts in brackets, except in those cases where it is absolutely necessary for the reader to see the etymological kinship between the German words not reflected in the English words chosen to translate them, and there are quite a few instances where this has been done. But, in most instances, I have wagered that the specific significance that attaches to the etymological kinship between the German words will come through in the English language in the way that I have translated those words and the sentences containing those words.

Mumbai, July 2022
Arun Iyer

The Overcoming of Metaphysics

The Overcoming of Metaphysics

"Transition" and "overcoming"
are inadequate determinations
of the history of beyng (conceived
historiographically and technically)
even though in what follows
"overcoming" is construed historically.

1. The Overcoming of Metaphysics[1]

We must be able to experience: The abandonment of beings by being in the primacy given to beings; the groundlessness of truth (of its essence as the truth of beyng); the necessity of grounding its essence; the abolition of the "human" (οὐσία and animal rationale; *subjectivity* and the human being as "*subject*," the will to power, anthropomorphism – that anthropology is to be first grasped as that which is no longer equal to anthropomorphism and which employs it only superficially); truth as clearing of beyng; the history of beyng.

*

Introduction as Preview of the Individual Parts (cf. p. 19f.)

1. What is metaphysics?
2. On the essence of ground (truth and the differentiation)
3. On the essence of truth
4. On the origin of the *work of art* understood from the standpoint of metaphysics comprehended in terms of the history of beyng. ("art" –possible only within metaphysics, "art" and "poetry")
5. Laying the ground for the modern world-picture through metaphysics (the metaphysics of subjectivity) (cf. the guiding statements on the essence of modern science)[2]
6. The dominance of logic (essence of logic, summer semester 1935),[3] cf. 1.
7. Metaphysics as physics (Aristotle, *Physics* B. 1).

---

[1] In the transcription Heidegger strikes out the word "overcoming" and in its stead inserts the word "consummation" in brackets. He then again reverses his first emendation.

[2] *Leitgedanken zur Entstehung der Metaphysik, der neuzeitlichen Wissenschaft und der modernen Technik* [Guiding Ideas on the Emergence of Metaphysics, Modern Science and Modern Technology], GA 76, ed. Claudius Strube (Frankfurt am Main: Vittorio Klostermann, 2009), 117–125.

[3] *Einführung in die Metaphysik*, Freiburg Lecture of Summer Semester 1935, GA 40, ed. P. Jaeger (Frankfurt am Main: Vittorio Klostermann, 1983), 127–131. {TN: Translated into English as *Introduction to Metaphysics*, trans. Gregory Fried and Richard Polt (New Haven and London: Yale University Press, 2000), 176–183.}

7.a The beginning of metaphysics
[6] 8. The inceptual φύσις, Anaximander – Heraclitus ((πόλεμος aphorism), Aristotle *Metaphysics*, Θ 10 (τὸ ὂν ὡς ἀληθές),[4] Parmenides τὸ αὐτό
9. The inversion of metaphysics (will to power, Nietzsche's metaphysics)
10. The essence of technology (τέχνη – machine technology), *"end of art"*
11. The overcoming and Da-sein (*Being and Time* and the concept of existence)
12. The history of beyng

*

Who are we? We are the ones who, having our inception in the history of beyng, experience the overcoming [*Überwindung*] of metaphysics, join into the winch of this overcoming in order to get over [*verwinden*] what is ungrounded and disjointed in the transition.

What all of us experience but none of us can know is this: Unleashing beings into being as unconditional manipulability with unlimited reach. Unleashing them brings about the total abandonment of beings by the truth of beyng, a truth that can be grounded.

The metaphysical differentiation: that is to say, the *differentiation that joins together* everything that pertains to the essence of meta-physics – this *differentiation* and the *"truth"* of beyng.

The differentiation (cf. basic words) – of beings and being. Its ground and its truth.

The decision: whether we are made appropriate for the overcoming through beyng or whether *we*, fixating on beings, unleashed into unconditional manipulability, also become fully *forgetful* of being.

Whether this *un*grounded differentiation and what it passes off as [7] decided, has ungrounded and ungrasped predominance and power or the truth of beyng is grounded as the tranquillity of the event.

The tranquil grounding of tranquillity, which does not exude power and does not even reign.

The separation of beings and being, to which all metaphysics is subordinated without decision, till it reaches the fulfillment and

[4] Cf. *Vom Wesen der menschlichen Freiheit. Einleitung in die Philosophie*, Freiburg Lecture of Summer Semester 1930, GA 31, 2nd revd. edn., ed. H. Tietjen (Frankfurt a. Main: Vittorio Klostermann 1994), 73–109. {TN: Translated into English as *The Essence of Human Freedom: An Introduction to Philosophy*, trans. Ted Sadler (London, New York: Continuum, 2002), 51–76.}

consummation of its own essence: in keeping with this separation, beings gain primacy and being is allowed to become something supplemental and merely general.

Subjectivity and *anthropomorphism* (cf. *Mindfulness*;[5] the grounding of the modern world picture through metaphysics, Remark 8 on Protagoras and Descartes;[6] cf. basic words: *Subjectum*).

Truth as "unconditional" assuring of beings as such – the empowering of beings as a whole and the predominance of manipulation. Subjectivity and anthropomorphism (cf. Schelling lecture, summer semester 36, Addendum).[7]

The abandonment of beings by being – the forgottenness of beyng – *blindness*.

To simply speak of the *overcoming* as the *history* of beyng (essencing of truth – Da-sein).

To allow one to see *indirectly* the hidden coherence and the grades and aberrations of what is inevitably metaphysical, from the history of beyng.

Overcoming becomes commensurate to Dasein historically in an *abandoning* of metaphysics (*de-tachment*), but this abandonment is in itself a placing-back of metaphysics into its essence founded in the history of beyng.

Abandoning on the basis of being eventuated [*Er-eignung*] into the other inception; no *bridges*.

[8] 2. The Overcoming of Metaphysics

The essence of history can only be experienced "historically" by belonging to it, that is to say, in the impoverishment from poverty, that is to say, the essence of history can be eventuated [*er-eignet*] only by

---

[5] *Besinnung* (1938/39), GA 66, ed. F.-W. von Hermann (Frankfurt am Main: Vittorio Klostermann, 1997), IX, Anthropomorphism, 159–163. {TN: Translated into English as *Mindfulness*, trans. Parvis Emad and Thomas Kalary (London: Bloomsbury, 2006), 129–136.}

[6] "Die Zeit des Weltbildes, Addendum (8)," *Holzwege*, GA 5, ed. F.-W. von Hermann, (Frankfurt am Main: Vittorio Klostermann, 1997), 102–106. {TN: Translated into English as "The Age of the World Picture, Appendix (8)," *Off the Beaten Track*, ed. and trans. Julian Young and Kenneth Hayes (Cambridge: Cambridge University Press, 2002), 77–80.}

[7] *Schelling: Vom Wesen der menschlichen Freiheit (1809)* [Schelling: On the Essence of Human Freedom], Freiburg Lecture of Summer Semester 1936, GA 42, ed. Ingrid Schüßler (Frankfurt am Main: Vittorio Klostermann, 1998), 282–285.

history itself. The knowledge "of" the *overcoming of metaphysics* (cf. there) is indispensable to this experience.

This *overcoming* stems from beyng itself and takes its inception in the abandonment of beings by being, which intones a fundamental attunement, from which the knower first emerges as the one who inquires after the truth of beyng.

Overcoming is the distinctive essencing of the truth of beyng *in contrast to* the omission of its grounding in the first inception; overcoming lets the essential consequence of this omission become manifest.

Through the *overcoming* as history, metaphysics itself emerges out of its semblance to a mere opinion and doctrine into the decision of the difference between being and beings, a difference which has fallen away from the inceptual essence of being (φύσις).

3. The History of Beyng and the Overcoming of Metaphysics

are not be linked to reason and world-process; they simply cannot be thought "metaphysically."

The uniqueness, rareness, estrangement, momentariness of this history; the temporal course of this history; the long stretches of time during which nothing happens and everything is surrendered to the occurrence of beings.

Time, which takes the essence of beyng – its own truth – into the ground, which is the abyss.

Beyng – in its truth sets the essence of history free – wrests itself from the predominance of beings and thus from the metaphysics, which is grounded upon this predominance and which seems to perpetuate this predominance by itself.

[9] *Beyng* – as the risk of *thought* – of *any* thought and therefore even of the thought that does *not* make representing the guiding thread for the projection of beings upon beingness.

Overcoming – not abolition and putting behind us *–through* "*refutation," for instance*; the irrefutability of any "philosophy."

The winch – in the clearing – the disclosure of the refusal (event).

In contrast to (1) (cf. 5ff.) completely from beyng, *while in (1) from the most comprehensive deterioration – cognition of beings* (positive); (2) (cf. pp. 7–8) neither the one [from beings] nor the other [beyng] and yet at the same time both; (2) what *"is"* metaphysics – the relinquishing of *history* into the abandonment of beings by being; *uniqueness of history*; (1) persistent juncture – and yet still arbitrarily authoritative.

Over-coming – *toward persistence* in the truth of beyng, i.e., toward Da-sein; over-coming through beyng itself. For "our part" only preparation of a preparedness for the event. *Giving oneself over questioningly* as displacing oneself into the fundamental attunement of active hearkening.

4. The Vanishing of Being

How often it seems as though being would never be able to accomplish something against beings and for beings as it vanishes immediately into a mere thought, which becomes completely ineffective when admitted as a means of ordering (categories). If this "seeming" is not a true disclosure, what is beyng even supposed "to accomplish?"

This seeming is not accidental; it springs from the fact that beings are already reckoned to be effective (capable of accomplishing) and the same claim is made of being.

[10] 5. Metaphysics and the Predominance of Beings: The Impotence and the Vanishing of Beyng

Not only the habituation to metaphysics but also what is inceptual in the first inception establishes an unavoidable predominance of beings. Θύσις in withdrawal *releases* "beings" toward presence and thus toward *their own arbitrary authority*. The withdrawal – how and why? To what extent?

The presence and the appreciation of what is at hand. To experience being and know of it only from the standpoint of beings in its orientation *toward* beings (cf. 6. "Overcoming", pp. 14–15), is this not entirely in accordance with the "sense" of *beyng*? – That it is in this way forsaken in its withdrawal!

Has this "from the standpoint of 'beings'" not already forgotten being? Does it not keep to a course of oblivion, so that this course that forgets cannot be reversed anymore, ever since being disclosed itself and placed the human being under interrogation.

Must beings first testify in favor of being for the latter to become worthy of question?

This happens in such a way that it is not the *metaphysical* jointure itself but this jointure in its lack of an inception and an end that holds on to the question-worthiness of beyng in its disavowal. Could we question beyng from a standpoint other than that of beings? Certainly not – yet, what does "from the standpoint of beings" mean here? First and foremost: A being is experienced *as* such by the very fact that we name it. Yet, in an equally decisive way this means: Being is, even if not grasped, pro-jected; and thus, we have the possibility of something that is essentially *unde*cided, that we must not take negatively, but must bring it out in its veiled fullness into a question (the differentiation).

6. "Overcoming"

"To overcome" – to put something behind or to bring something under; either just putting it behind so that it is abolished, or bringing it under, so that what is overcome [11], having been transformed through the overcoming, is at once assimilated in the overcoming other.

The overcoming must grasp itself beforehand and step into the essential. It must at the same time attempt to constitute that which is to be overcome as such. So, in *Being and Time* the metaphysical question of being is "repeated" [*wiederholt*] by means of the question concerning the "sense of being." It is in fact retrieved [*wieder geholt*] and as a more original question, to boot, which is also asked in a completely different way. This question goes back to the ground of the hitherto existing question of being ("fundamental ontology"); this "ontology" and "metaphysics" are thereby overcome, transformed into something else – more clearly, the transition to something else is accomplished in all decisiveness, but at the same time the will to reclaim tradition in its essence for the future, is still alive. Hence the endeavor to designate even the other question with titles that are still prevalent. Firstly, this endeavor does not remain a mere matter of "labeling." But it rather impedes the decisive development into the other question. This is because this question just does not unfold in the manner of an always determinate execution of a plan. Rather, unfolding here means: coming to terms with the unavoidable transformation of this question itself until we come to realize that the active questioning of the truth of being may *simply no longer* be accomplished and interpreted *from any kind* of "perspective" on the hitherto existing question of being; indeed, that this very question already puts philosophy itself into question and must move in an even more essential realm.

Speaking from within the history of beyng, overcoming as the history of beyng; not the planned accomplishment of the human being; the only task that remains for human beings, and that too only when they are wrenched into the transformation of their essence, is to be prepared for the transition into the overcoming. How does the overcoming arise in such a history? Overcoming of the abandonment of beings by *being*; the abandonment by being is however the work *of* beyng and at the same time the most extreme form of metaphysics, whose final upsurge is to be experienced as the history of the unconditional predominance of manipulation. In the instant [12] that *metaphysics is overcome through beyng*, things get serious with philosophy because a decisive moment in the history of beyng arrives; philosophy cannot wish to console itself with its knowledge, cannot wish to seek solace, cannot wish to traffic in such solace.

The course of the first attempt goes like this: To begin with, the first step of overcoming and its preparation (*Being and Time*), then the determination of what is to be overcome (*What is Metaphysics?*)[1] and the (*Kant-book*);[2] that which is to be overcome must now be placed into its essence, which has been veiled so far; it must be elevated to its essentiality; only then does the overcoming itself first receive the essential resistance into itself, to be able thereby to transform into its own essence. Thus, we need not only carry out the overcoming, as if it were from now on the only clear and irrevocable task awaiting fulfillment. It is necessary above all not to resist the essential transformation of the overcoming itself and not to succumb to the danger of restricting the overcoming to the realms and the manner of thinking of that which is to be overcome – metaphysics – only expanding metaphysics, and accordingly applying metaphysics to itself and turning metaphysics on itself – "metaphysics of metaphysics."

Something similar, as Kant's approach evinces, is essential within the realm of metaphysics and leads, where the seriousness and sobriety of Kantian thought reigns, to an abyss; nevertheless, through the predominance of metaphysics itself the essential other way of questioning is not only suppressed, as if it were already there, but also expelled altogether to a place outside the circle of what is possible. Kant's critique of speculative metaphysics is so little an *overcoming* of metaphysics that it rather only now provides metaphysics in its modern essence with its opening credits. Whether in the aftermath of Kant's step, it is absolute logic that defines metaphysics (or, even as a countermeasure, Schelling's

---

[1] "Was ist Metaphysik?" *Wegmarken,* GA 9, ed. F.-W. von Hermann (Frankfurt am Main: Vittorio Klostermann, 1976), 103–122. {TN: Translated into English as "What is Metaphysics?" *Pathmarks,* ed. William McNeil, trans. David Farrell Krell (Cambridge: Cambridge University Press, 1998), 82–96.}

[2] *Kant und das Problem der Metaphysik,* GA 3, ed. F.-W. von Hermann (Vittorio Klostermann: Frankfurt am Main, 1991). {TN: Translated into English as *Kant and the Problem of Metaphysics,* trans. Richard Taft (Bloomington and Indianapolis: Indiana University Press, 1991).}

positive [13] philosophy), or whether, as in the nineteenth and the twentieth century, metaphysics splits itself into an academic ontology and an "inductive" metaphysics that propagates itself on the basis of the sciences and their "results," does not in the least change the predominance of the fundamentally metaphysical character of what remains of "philosophy," which continues to assert itself and whose metaphysical character is no longer questioned.

When rightly seen from the standpoint of the essence of that which happens in the "overcoming" (the active grounding of the truth of beyng – the history of beyng), it is no more an endeavor to attempt thinking, but the history of beyng. That is why everything depends upon accomplishing the leap into this history and to preserve it in its essence: to know "overcoming" in an essentially different way and to join its pathways.

"Overcoming" here does not mean an academic change of opinion and doctrine through the assembly of such opinions and doctrines. It is rather the historical transformation of the essence of beyng out of beyng itself – belongingness to this transformation from the grounds of an essential transformation of the human being. (Clearing *of the history* of beyng).

Because it is about an overcoming of "metaphysics" conceived in this way, this overcoming cannot be thought along the lines of the metaphysical concept of "sublation," which Hegel posited as the law of movement of "history." This is a history of the coming-to-itself of absolute knowledge and of what it knows, from the essence of transcendental subjectivity–objectivity.

Disregarding completely the essential distinctness of historicity, which is determined as the essencing of the truth of being, overcoming is neither a tollere[*], nor an elevare[*], nor a conservare[*], nor is it all of these in their unity; only in negation does there exist a certain overlap with it: overcoming does not merely abolish but just as little is it only the saving of what is past. It is rather the *freeing* of an *essence* (of ἀλήθεια and φύσις) that *cannot be grounded* inceptually, through which what appears to be only a past is elevated into its essence (disclosure of the self-concealing [14] as such) and acquires the character of *what was*, which cannot be sublated in what belongs to the future, but which, to the contrary, departing entirely away from what belongs to the future,

[*] {TN: Latin for that which destroys.}
[*] {TN: Latin for that which elevates.}
[*] {TN: Latin for that which preserves.}

places itself back into itself as the inceptual. (cf. 23. Overcoming, 28. The Overcoming of Metaphysics)

Everything pertaining to Hegel's "sublating" is taking over and *taking* on. Overcoming is (here thought as) *getting over* the pastness of what is overcome – restoring it into the inception of the inception – getting rid of and casting off all historical and inherited strands, which still connect what is overcome to what follows after and which are thus tied up into its essence. (cf. 29. Over-coming is only in the other inception, 31. The End of Metaphysics)

The first inception is not a level, the immediate, that requires mediation to reach its truth. It is rather of a unique essence, encompassing all inceptions – even that one, which as *omission – essential forgetting –* of the first inception is not experienced. This omission (cf. Winter semester lecture 37/38)[3] testifies only to the unfathomable and to the essence of the first inception that is not be recovered again in any subsequent inception.

The decisive aspect of the overcoming lies in a rift that is opened between the beingness of beings and the truth of beyng. This is a rift from which what is separated first comes into its own, without metaphysics perhaps being able to be "sublated" into the thinking responsive to the history of beyng. It is from this point on that the differentiation between beyng and beings is first grounded in an abyss as that which belongs to the history of beyng.

"Overcoming" [*Überwindung*] could be spoken of as a word related to the history of beyng, which thinks the winding [*Windung*] as the winding [*Windung*] of the winch [*Winde*]. The winch lifts high – pressing at the same time into the ground; winding as lifting into another essence (belonging to the history of beyng) and at the same time the active grounding of the ground.

The winding [*Windung*] is a rotating [*Drehung*] and turning [*Wendung*]; insofar as the winch [*Winde*] is embedded in the essence of metaphysics itself – insofar as it emerges from [15] its hidden ground (beyng), metaphysics is elevated into the clearing of beyng and grounded (as *that which was*).

Metaphysics here means the jointure of the opening of beings into the openness of beingness (constancy of presence).

---

[3] *Grundfragen der Philosophie. Ausgewählte "Probleme" der "Logik,"* Freiburg Lecture Winter Semester 1937/38, GA 45, ed. F.-W. von Herrmann (Frankfurt am Main: Vittorio Klostermann, 1984), 142. {TN: Translated into English as *Basic Questions of Philosophy: Selected "Problems" of "Logic,"* trans. Richard Rojcewicz and André Schuwer (Bloomington: Indiana University Press, 1994), 123.}

The over-coming [*Überwindung*] means this winding [*Windung*], which transforms into something that is not metaphysics any more: the winding [*Windung*] as essencing of beyng.

The over-coming *belongs* to the history of beyng, arises from this history as its first clearing, is not an accomplishment in the manner of a modification in the teachings and doctrines of philosophy by other such teachings and doctrines. The overcoming is that history of beyng, which first grants philosophy a possibility to be (the question of being as the question of beyng). The preparation of philosophy as human resolve is only capable here of the preparation for the preparedness for taking history over in a grounded truth. Winding [*Winding*] is the *essential turning* [*Wesenswendung*] *of beingness* into beyng as the disclosure of the refusal (event).

The *winch* – and its *needfulness lies* in the event-character of beyng itself. (cf. below, p.15; 23. Overcoming, p. 31f.)

"Metaphysics" in its consummation becomes a consolidation of the abandonment of beings by being in the predominance of manipulation. (On the essence of manipulation cf. *Mindfulness*[4] and *Ponderings XIII*[5]).

Over-coming the abandonment by being – as the rotation of abandonment toward the *refusal* and its disclosure.

"*Consummation*" of metaphysics – means the fulfillment of its essence; consummation here does not mean perfection in the sense of the exclusion of that which corrupts the essence, but rather the unfolding inclusion of that which corrupts the essence; the *corrupted essence* of metaphysics consists in the fact that in metaphysics – in the question of being supported by it – being simply does not acquire dominance in its *question-worthiness*. [16] Neither being nor beings become questionable, rather everything is salvaged in the unquestionableness of what is feasible through manipulation. "Ontology" is as obvious a task as zoology is research into animals.

In metaphysics, what holds sway is the projection upon beingness *from the standpoint of beings* (cf. 5. Metaphysics and the Predominance of Beings); from this point on, being is misplaced. No "proximity" to

---

[4] *Besinnung* (1938/39), GA 66, 9. *Machenschaft*, 16–25. {TN: *Mindfulness*, 9. Machination (Coercive Force, Power Mastery), 11–19.}

[5] *Überlegungen XII–XV (Schwarze Hefte 1939–1941)*, GA 96, ed. Peter Trawny (Frankfurt am Main: Vittorio Klostermann, 2014), 75–162. {TN: Translated into English as *Ponderings XII–XV* (Black Notebooks 1939–1941), trans. Richard Rojcewicz (Bloomington and Indianapolis: Indiana University Press, 2017), 59–126.}

beings, no such "animated" engagement with beings ever reaches the essencing of beyng.

The overcoming of metaphysics is a distinctive historical moment – distinguished by the fact that the essence of history first emerges in its individuality and becomes decisive for the truth of beyng in this overcoming and as this overcoming. For, *history is* the essencing of the truth of beyng.

The overcoming of metaphysics is the first historical revelation of the essence of history.

To overcome metaphysics is to *ground* its *essence* in such a way that the truth of beyng is experienced and withstood as the *abyss*. The groundlessness of metaphysics is the avoidance of this abyss that remains unfamiliar to metaphysics, an avoidance which is essential to metaphysics and thus continuous with it. There is an avoidance even of the unfamiliar and this is the most disastrous.

Overcoming metaphysics – this might appear like a transcendence of what is the highest in metaphysics – what it soon called θεῖον and thought theo-logically; and then for this reason, we have the introduction of the Christian God, fittingly equipped with reason in order then to conceive of it secularly and emptily as the unconditional and absolute.

Overcoming metaphysics – does this not mean creating "new," different gods? But *who* creates them?

Or indeed going beyond gods – that we no longer need them, in turn to be enslaved more than ever by such a lack of need, to what is past, unfamiliar and historiographically exhausted?

Or is over-coming completely different – not an *elevated-beyond* of a *super*-metaphysics, but an acceptance and recognition of a *lapse* – something very slight and peculiar and [17] simple, whose continued existence makes "demands" on the more essential capacities of the human being than the ascent into the making and despising of gods, both of which belong together, balancing each other out.

Overcoming metaphysics: Overcoming the submissiveness of being toward beings through being itself, insofar as its truth, as that which is proper to its essence, is eventuated *into an urgency*, making it necessary to throw oneself off into this history of overcoming. (cf. above, p. 14).

However, to throw oneself off is to already be thrown by beyng itself. This throwing oneself off is announced in the abandonment of beings by being as self-denial. It is announced everywhere and every time the abandonment by being, reflected in the supremacy of manipulation, disturbs [*entsetzt*] human beings, without their being able to know from where this disturbance arises (from beyng and the essence of its ungrounded truth) and into what it displaces [*versetzt*] them (into the transformation of their essence toward the guardianship of the truth of beyng).

As soon as this disturbance touches human beings, who are mired in historiography, they will be compelled to begin questioning and doubting, which will initially *seem* like a historiographical analysis and determination of their situation. This historiographical dismembering that lusts after situations is so *far* from all reflection that it cannot even be rejected as the opposite and corrupted essence of reflection. However, this dis-turbance affects human beings so essentially that they must become aware of their relationship to being (understanding of being as the ungrounded essence of what is known to date as "reason"), whose essence they bear unbeknown to themselves. If that happens it can awaken the experience of the shattering, initiated by being itself, of the abandonment of beings by being, and, displacing beings as a whole into another unprecedented question-worthiness from the essence of beyng and through this essence. This *dis-turbance* pulls human beings out of the manipulation of beings and displaces them into the ungroundedness of the truth of being, such that they "know" not yet what is "happening" to them and how. In the experience of fading away and of the indifference [18] perhaps still persisting and of the mere "calculability" of all goals, we can recognize and register the mere superficiality of all goal setting and the calculative apparatus of reckoning with just useful "facts." (On as-tonishment and dis-turbance as the fundamental attunements of the first and the other inception cf. lecture winter semester 37/38.)[6]

This experience, which is actively compelled by beyng through disturbing human beings from where they have been so far into something ungrounded, but more essential than everything before, can be prepared by various forms and modes of acceptance, although it can never just be engendered by oneself.

The overcoming of metaphysics is the transfer [*Übereignung*] of the truth of beyng through beyng into the urgency of the grounding, in which transfer the essence of history is eventuated [*ereignet*] and the abandonment of beings by being, the final form of the predominance

---

[6] *Grundfragen der Philosophie. Ausgewählte "Probleme" der "Logik,"* GA 45, 195–201. (*Aus dem ersten Entwurf. Abschnitt I. Grundsätzliches über die Wahrheitsfrage*) {TN: *Basic Questions of Philosophy: Selected "Problems" of "Logic,"* 168–172. (From the First Draft. Section I. Foundational Issues in the Question of the Truth.)}

of beings over being, is taken back into the inceptual nature of the first inception. This happens without disrupting the *inevitability* of the primacy of beings in the ordinary behavior of human beings. This inevitable aspect is based upon beyng's refusal of itself, as a consequence of which it unleashes beings in their forward thrust. This forward thrust appears, within the metaphysically determined history of human beings, as a distinctive predominance of beings themselves over "being."

The *overcoming of metaphysics* does not bring about the disappearance of the metaphysical determinateness of history, which is precisely this primacy [of beings over being], but rather grounds it as something that is no longer. Even after the overcoming, the question of being always *appears* to question from the standpoint of beings and the questioners too experience themselves as beings.

In essential history no "interests" dominate; essential history does not "*depend upon something*," but rather the event [*Er-eignis*] attunes [*stimmt*] beings into the truth of beyng, placing everything back upon the [19] determination [*Be-stimmung*]. In this way we have the possibility of a pure "happening," which inceptually subordinates all intentions and deeds to itself.

The question: Why *are* there beings at all rather than nothing? is considered a fundamental metaphysical question, which is answered metaphysically in such a way that the result is an explanation of beings from a *cause* and a ground. The "are" pertains to the thatness of beings – the thatness of their presence-at-hand, for which an explanation furnishes a justification that takes the form of a reduction to another – something – a being that produces itself.

However, the thinking responsive to the history of beyng implicitly already asks this metaphysical question already differently insofar as it does not place beings under an explanation but thinks beyond the *primacy* of beings, that they keep thrusting forward as such. The answer emerges from the knowledge of the abandonment of beings by being, which itself springs from the essencing of beyng as refusal: Beyng concedes to beings, abandoned by beyng, a predominance and deprives even the *nothing* of the knowledge that it essentially belongs to beyng as *refusal*.

7. On the Formation of the Text

No one who re-flects should be spared the very same routes along which the original thinker has to travel. That is why the versions of the lectures and essays not published so far were reviewed once more and what was often incomprehensible in them due to too succinct a formulation was elaborated.

But the respective stages and the orientation of the questioning have been retained. It has not been later rewritten for the sake of giving the impression of an inauthentic unity. On the contrary: the revision of the texts, on account of the gap in time, allowed for an even sharper formulation of the individual questions in relation to their structure and the field of articulation thereby carved out.

Already all of these attempts move [since the question asked in the introduction to *Being and Time* about the "sense" (that is to say, the truth) [20] of being (not only of beings)] in the wind of the overcoming, without decisively offering it a sail and without unambiguously recognizing that the over-coming descends from beyng itself. (cf. the remarks on the Lecture on Truth 1930)[1]

8. On the Correct Grasp of the Whole

To speak simply, without glancing this way and that, in a rigorous structure coming from essential attunement and yet in a veiled manner.

*

No narration, no invocation, only a transformation in the relationship to beyng through beyng, accomplished in the tranquillity of the essencing of truth.

(Not meant for those who expect a "sensation" and exploit what is said, equally crudely in a "for" and an "against," for furthering the business of philosophy.)

9. The Overcoming of Metaphysics through Beyng

The overcoming brings to light that the abyss essences as the clearing "*of*" beyng.

That as refusal, the beyng of the clearing is an inception of the *other essence of history.*

That refusal (concealment of the concealedness of beyng) is not a

---

[1] "*Vom Wesen der Wahrheit,*" *Wegmarken,* GA 9, 201f. {TN: "On the Essence of Truth," *Pathmarks,* trans. John Sallis, 153–154f.}

limit, a lack and what comes last, but what comes first, the gift and the inception, out of which history arises.

That this arrival actively urges a change in the essence of the *being* of the human because it eventuates [*er-eignet*] Da-sein.

[21] That in this eventuation [*Er-eignung*], thinking thinks from beyng and joins together the in-between related to all beings into the word.

Beyng eventuates [*er-eignet*] the in-between of the abyss and transfers [*übereignet*] to this particular in-between, that which is disclosed from the ground of the abyss as a being.

The event [*Er-eignis*] *"is"* in the inceptual sense; it alone *lets be* [*istet*].

Beyng is never the cause of beings and never immediately a ground.

Beyng knows not power and impotence and needs no domination.

How beings are constantly scheming to lure being away and through such trickery make us *forget* it. Beings grab for themselves historiography and technology as the only structure of their truth and secure for themselves in this way the unconditional capacity to manipulate.

Yet, this age must first fall prey to this double-sided twin violence of historiography and technology before it can give itself up and allow entry into the history of beyng.

10. The Overcoming as the History of Beyng

The active intimation of beyng itself in its underlying abruptness of the clearing *is* the event of the overcoming. This event comes from beyng, as beyng eventuates itself. It is from this event of overcoming (essencing of the truth of beyng) that *history* is first determined. The essence of metaphysics is unveiled out of this history as that which belongs to this history.

Metaphysics – the groundless truth of beings as such taken as a whole; how the everyday historiographical concept of metaphysics first originates from here, even though we became familiar with this concept first. Indeed, it is due to this familiarity that the concept has co-determined the essence of metaphysics and its history. The remarkable history of the genesis of the name is only a reflection of the hidden essence.

[22] What is needed is a first elaboration of metaphysics starting from the concept of its word; but this elaboration immediately loses validity.

Historiographical accounting of history as that of the past.

Historical (persistent) *reflection* upon history as the essencing of the truth of beyng.

1. Provisionally elaborating and indicating the truth of being
2. "Ripe are" . . .
3. The history of beyng (the *abruptness of the uniqueness* of the clearing)
4. What is metaphysics?

11. The Other Inception

Beyng is not a supplement to beings and what is predicated of beings.

Beyng "is" truth as clearing of the event. Here we never reflect back from beings to beyng. Rather, the thinking "of" beyng is the displacement that throws us from beyng into beyng. *But beings happen only* (historically from eventuation) in *the in-between of beyng.*

Beyng displaces into urgency, actively urging, not forcing a change in the essence of the human being; as a result of *this* transformation, the proximity of the human being *to* beyng is first grounded as essential into the distance of the persistent grounding as Da-sein.

12. The Transition

as the manner in which thinking, under the first directive of the *intimation* of the overcoming, is transformed from metaphysical thinking into the thinking responsive to the history of beyng. The transition is nevertheless not the overcoming, but only the entry into the overcoming as history. This is a history, which, as the abandonment by being, turns itself into what is hardly anticipated of a knowledge.

[23] The transition experiences the echo and the interplay. (cf. *Contributions*)[1]

This experience already transforms thinking in its essence even though the existing ways of thinking and speaking still remain in play and must be. This is because the words of metaphysics not only cannot

---

[1] *Beiträge zur Philosophie (Vom Ereignis)*, GA 65, ed. F.-W. von Hermann (Frankfurt am Main: Vittorio Klostermann, 1989), 105ff, 167ff. {TN: Translated into English as *Contributions to Philosophy (From Enowning)*, trans. Parvis Emad and Kenneth Maly (Bloomington and Indianapolis: Indiana University Press, 1999), Echo 75ff., Playing-forth 119ff.; *Contributions to Philosophy (Of the Event)*, trans. Richard Rojcewicz and Daniela Vallega-Neu (Bloomington and Indianapolis: Indiana University Press, 2012), The Resonating 85ff., The Interplay 133ff.}

be abolished through a fiat and a mere counter-movement. They also continue to be needed for a long time in order to point from metaphysics (along the path of the question of possibility) to the realm of the truth of beyng.

13. Metaphysics and the Question of Possibility

(How it has been asked since *Being and Time* and yet it is always at a *turning-point!*) (cf. Lecture on Truth, 1930)[1]

The origin and the insidiousness of the question of possibility; its open and hidden forms.

How (cf. *On the Essence of Ground*)[2] we are always forced into the attempt, to fulfill the overcoming of metaphysics by means of this question. Here the question itself, as a question at all and as the question concerning *possibility*, is in every respect the very jointure of metaphysics. (cf. Lecture on Truth, 1930)

The question of essence – as yearning for the one that is constant and grants constancy – (ground – what lies before); thus: pushed away from essencing as the history of the truth of beyng in the sense of *eventuation*. Essentiality (essentia), essencing (event).

Cf. the concept of "essence" according to Aristotle, Metaphysics Z. (Winter Semester 37/38)[3] (ὑποκείμενον and τὸ τί ἦν εἶναι) the τί ἐστιν.

Commonly τὸ κοινόν – genus – "the *universal*" (*common to all*) [24]; that which is intelligible to all and sundry is made even more common.

What is intelligible to everyone – appears to everyone – familiar to everyone – constant and prior from the standpoint of what comes to presence in this way, thus *emphatically* sighted and yet not grasped and thus more than ever (*in any case*) standing *in view* and face to face – *the visible* in the perfect sense – the ἰδέα – "idea," that which is from the very outset, permanent, in any case and hence what is pre-eminently sighted and visible.

"Ideas" – "ideology" – "*view* of the world" – worldview as the *degenerate and corrupt kind* of metaphysics.

[1] "*Vom Wesen der Wahrheit,*" *Wegmarken*, GA 9, 177–202. {TN: "On the Essence of Truth," *Pathmarks*, 136–154.}

[2] "*Vom Wesen des Grundes,*" *Wegmarken*, loc. cit. 123–175. {TN: "On the Essence of Ground," *Pathmarks*, 123–176.}

[3] *Grundfragen der Philosophie. Ausgewählte "Probleme" der "Logik,"* GA 45, 58ff. {TN: *Basic Questions of Philosophy: Selected "Problems" of "Logic,"* 53ff.}

ἰδέα		perceptum	
κοινόν	"Idea"	objectum	"sense"
ἀγαθόν		object	
οὐσία	"generality"	"concept" (Hegel)	"value"
		value	

14. The Question of Possibility as the Mode of the Question of Essence

as the exploration of the conditions of the *inner possibility* of essence grasped as γένος – κοινόν and *its ground*.

The question of possibility is the only fundamental mode of metaphysical thought; the return to the a priori and the *mis*interpretation of this approach in terms of a causal explanation from the highest causes, both belong to the question of possibility as its forms.[a]

"Possibility" is here conceived as the "enabling" of the essence, as the enabling of the *actuality* of what is *actual*. *Actuality* is however considered to be being in the decisive sense; (to show how ἐνέργεια comes to acquire primacy as originating from φύσις).

[25] Why does this question come down to enabling? Herein hides the question concerning *pro-duction* [*Her-stellung*] in the essential sense, i.e., of making available [*Beistellung*] in the present.

Since being is conceptualized as constant presence[b] and the fundamental relationship to beings remains re-presenting and having-before-oneself, the question *concerning* beings, in order to have them as such, is the question of pro-duction, that is to say, the question of enabling.

The more clearly and the more one-sidedly, representation, by way of subjectivity, is brought to dominance, the more sharply does the question of possibility come to the surface (through the possibilitas of Leibniz to Kant's transcendental question; from here to absolute idealism and its question of the unconditional and in a counterthrust to Nietzsche's *valuative thinking*). In this we see the reign of the transformation of truth's essence; this transformation from the growing withdrawal. Forgottenness *of being*.

---

[a] For what reason?
Being and beingness: (ἀρχή)
πρῶτον ὅθεν
τὸ πρότερον τῇ φύσει

[b] Grasp, grip, take; οὐσία of the ὄν and τέχνη – the "capacity" – "possession" – corresponding to the εἶναι of the ὄν!

The thought of value is the final amendment to the thought of possibility. (Value as *"condition,"* value, validity, validity of judgment, truth of cognition, certainty of objectivity (i.e., of being)).

To what extent can we, having *abandoned* all of *metaphysics* through the question of being, understood in terms of the question *concerning the truth* of *being*, still think along the lines of this question [the question of possibility], when the thoughts of "subjectivity" and "value" have been given up; likewise, "ideas" and φύσις – ἀλήθεια? Inquiring into the ground of inner possibility is only tenable as long as we can actually indicate yet another realm of *questionability*, even if it is completely blocked.

The truth of being – as the transcendental, so to speak, but completely separated from beyng, not affected by its [beyng's] essencing. The kind of questioning in *Being and Time* is either not grasped at all or misinterpreted as transcendental philosophy; aided in this regard by the *Kant-book*, despite its indicating *what is* [26] *properly of the essence*: that Kant arrived at the abyss. One takes this more parenthetically as profound and peripheral instead of as inceptual and clearly simple.

In fact, we can no longer inquire into enabling in the question concerning the truth of beyng – (that through which this truth would be "possible"); thinking is not even true to beyng if it takes beyng as that which enables, even though the event [*Er-eignis*] is the "ground" for the possibility of thinking in terms of enabling.

In keeping with its form, the question of enabling can always still creep into the thinking that is responsive to the history of beyng. Indeed, this question is indispensable for immediate understanding in the still dominant realm of metaphysics.

Yet, the thinking that is responsive to beyng is an active expression of the history of beyng, not "narration," not explanation, not call or invocation ("appeal"), but the simple *transforming word in which the in-between of beyng, as the abyss, bears what is borne out* [*Austrag*]. (cf. *Mindfulness*)[1]

Indeed, the question: Why are there beings at all rather than nothing? still proceeds entirely in the course set by the question of enabling. This results in the following: if the question is answered, we find a reference to the highest cause or to objectivity as the condition of an object being represented, or to both in an unresolved combination. This means: in the course set by the return of *metaphysica generalis* to proper metaphysics, which in turn means: in that which underlies these scholastic

---

[1] *Besinnung* (1938/39), GA 66, IV. *Zum Entwurf des Seyns*, 81–103. {TN: *Mindfulness*, IV. On Projecting-Open Be-ing, 56–86.}

thoughts. This is all pre-configured in the return of the *veritas intellectus* to the *veritas rei* as the *idea summi entis*. (Deus est (qua ens entium) suum esse* and so the following is true: Deus ist esse entium; creatio, conservatio.)*

But what happens if beyng, as the abyss of the ground of the truth of beings, is experienced historically?

[27] Beings *are* "because" the nothing is. And the nothing is, "because" beyng is. But *what* is beyng? What does "because" mean here? The essencing of truth as the history of eventuation [*Er-eignung*]. (Being and truth are the same.) The *why*-question (cf. *Mindfulness*)[2] still thinks in terms of enabling. However, the answer is now no longer concerned by the question, but rejects it. What has happened "in the interim?"

Creative questioning in fact takes its departure from beings, simultaneously taking-off from it into the truth of beyng. Creative questioning no longer thinks back in the direction of beings (which are on the wane) in order to determine a being's essence as inner possibility. Rather the truth of beings attunes [*stimmt*] itself from the event-like experience of the essencing of beyng as something different, determines [*bestimmt*] for itself a different relationship than the one that had established the "differentiation" (which is not experienced).

The "differentiation" itself originates in *its particular formulation* (not difference as such – which is distinct from it) in the question of the essence, following from the manner of the question of enabling. This question of enabling and all the thinking guided by it consolidates the "differentiation," always directing all inquiries into the realm, which is reshaped in the transition along with the differentiation.

The question of enabling thus hinders any de-parture from metaphysics; even Nietzsche's attempt, to abolish at once both the true world and the world of appearance and with them even the difference between the two, is only illusory; the world, seemingly devoid of value, demands a new positing of value. It also demands "values," which by themselves already exhibit the alienation of beingness and truth, becoming precisely now more than ever, the *conditions* conditioned in accordance with power.

The question of enabling is the obstacle that metaphysics itself places before its own overcoming, of which it can never become aware.

---

* {TN: God is (qua being of all beings) his own being.}
* {TN: God is the being of beings; creator; sustainer.}
[2] *Besinnung* (1938/39), loc. cit., XXI. *Die metaphysische Warumfrage*, 265–277. {TN: *Mindfulness*, XXI. The Metaphysical Why-Question, 235–246.}

[28] However, the fact that the first steps that accomplish the entry into the overcoming (*Being and Time*; *What is Metaphysics? On the Essence of Ground*) maintain themselves precisely on the course of such a question, betrays the unavoidable ambivalence confronting the transition from the first inception to the other inception. It would be a pure fantasy for the thinking responsive to the history of beyng to wish to free itself from metaphysics by a mere refusal. For, beyng itself hesitates to essence the truth of beyng for a long time as refusal. How should one then suppose that the thinking, which is only eventuated [*er-eignet*], wants to be forced by means of a violent precipitation, when it tolerates no coercion? How can a habit of thinking, which stretches across two and half thousand years, be extinguished in an instant! If this habit were to be extinguished in such a way (in the foreshadowing of the other inception by individuals), they would still not be in a position to endow the thinking responsive to the history of beyng with a tradition.

Because it is extremely old, the question of enabling also produces this illuminating certainty of its proof even if the "conclusiveness" of this thinking also remains the object of a peculiar suspicion. The grounds for this suspicion lie in the erroneous belief that the inference in this proof supposedly moves in a circle and, for that reason, contradicts itself. For, it does not lead to a ground (principium) that corresponds to a being. Instead, it assumes this ground beforehand and persists in a petitio principii. This is deemed to be the principal flaw of a thinking that is meant to be correct.

Only on the basis of this petitio does a particular argument become a "proof." For, it adheres to the following formula: beings cannot be what they show themselves to be, unless. . . . However, beings can be addressed as those which are enabled in such and such a way only if they are already conceived in the light of what enables, which in turn is invoked once again as the ground.

In fact, this "line of proof" is also not supposed to prove anything. But the question of possibility is the manner in which the already re-presented being of beings [29] is just specifically elevated into a knowledge. It is a manner of thinking being, namely, the manner of metaphysics: ὄν ᾗ ὄν.

What this indicates is the following: The creative questioning of possibility is only the explicit adoption of the already dominant actuality[c] of what is actual. As being, this actuality of the actual is simply not turned into something question-worthy; being is that which is thought on the basis of beings and by referring back to beings. Differences

---

[c] Cf. *Mindfulness* – the *modalities*

develop on the basis of the manner in which the thinking of beingness is understood; on the basis of the perspective to which it adheres,
whether it is visibility (ἰδέα) or representedness as *perceptum*, whether
it is consciousness in the sense of Kant's scientific experience; whether
it is certainty in the sense of the assurance of continued existence in
terms of power.[d] All of this is metaphysics.

The petitio pricipii[e] as the providential advance into "what enables,"
is the true essence of metaphysical thinking; the unique step of philosophy, with which it steps into the unique place and always as metaphysics, says the same, namely, what is loftiest for it.

If we make "empirical thinking" the measure of this "petitio
principii" then we can show the latter to be "flawed."[f] This procedure amounts to persisting in a mode of thinking that is allowed to
assert its superiority in the fact that nothing can dispute it as soon as
a tiny sliver of the essence of philosophy is grasped and available for
reflection.

15. The Truth of Beyng

From where does the essence of truth occur to the human being? Only
from this essence do they have the essence of themselves – and for the
most part, not explicitly *as* the essence but in the form of their works
and accomplishments.

[30] The essence of truth springs from that whose truth it is in its
essence, as truth of *beyng*.

How beyng joins all beings together into the in-between and in so
joining together, it is the junction.

From where does this interpretation of beyng come? Is it an interpretation of beyng or an insertion of the human being into the junction
of the in-between?

The *insertion* comes from the (*event*) – customary practice. *Being
overcomes beings.*

The essencing of the truth of beyng refuses the priority of beings,
that everything is always questioned from the standpoint of beings
and along the lines of the question of possibility and the question of
condition.

---

[d] However, this (cf. above) from the destiny of the essential history of truth.

[e] what is petitio principii – seen from the standpoint of the reign of the *difference*
it is the un-aware.

[f] *explicate*! the *conclusion* – "explain" – ratio – free of contradiction.

The overcoming of metaphysics and the impossibility of the question of possibility.

The transformation into persistence in the *in-between*[a] of Da-sein.

16. "Truth" (Cf. Winter Semester 37/38)[1]

1. means what is "true" in relation to a thing, a behavior . . . and the correctness of a statement about . . .
2. means what is "true" in relation to beings as a whole (on which everything depends).
3. the *essence* of what is true (1 and 2), that is, the universal, what shapes anything true into a truth (κοινόν); here one starts from what is already constituted as "true" and returns to the essence (as supplement).
4. The essencing of truth, which first gifts and eventuates a truth, itself belonging to what the truth as such belongs – the clearing *of* beyng as eventuation [*Er-eignung*] into the openness of the in-between.
5. [31] The essential eventuation [*Er-eignung*] of the human being into the persistence of Dasein; this persistence in the clearing of beyng (event) as the essence of *freedom*. *That is why* freedom is primarily freedom to the "ground" because beyng eventuates [*er-eignet*] beings as such into the in-between.
6. Truth as the clearing of beyng and the beyng of the clearing – clearing "of" beyng is the eventuation [*Er-eignung*] of the in-between in the event – beyng of the clearing is the event of the in-between leading up to the eventuation into Da-*sein*.

17. Truth [Clearing of Beyng (Event) and the Correctness of Representing]

The multiple aspects of the one openness upon which correctness depends:
1. The openness of what can be re-presented (e.g., of the thing)
2. The openness of re-presenting that brings something before itself – of the *approach toward* . . . and the *retreat to* . . .

---

[a] Fourfold

[1] *Grundfragen der Philosophie. Ausgewählte "Probleme" der "Logik,"* GA 45, 19f. {TN: *Basic Problems of Philosophy: Selected "Problems" of "Logic,"* 18–19f.}

3. The openness of the self that makes available to "itself" the re-presented as some one thing.
4. The openness of the self to itself in co-representing and confirming and doubting.

This openness as that which is only visible from the standpoint of correctness, but which is the essence of the *in-between*, already requiring another point of view to grasp it. This essence of the *in-between* is itself the conjuncture [*Fügung*] of the clearing of being as event.

18. The Essence of History

When every support for every single standard within beings has been invalidated and there "is" "only" the abruptness of the clearing of beyng, the singularity of the event, then we have *history*.

There is no calculation of time and no eternity of the in-itself for this history.

[32] *History* – where no something, no this and that happens – but where the that of the essencing of beyng and prior to that beyng is.

"*Being*" –

19. On the Overcoming of Metaphysics

Not a "psychological" – "anthropological" "interpretation" of values, positing of values and devaluations (Nietzsche), but the *persistent knowledge of the truth of beyng that is oriented toward the history of beyng*.

20. Correctness

Abandonment of beings by being – linking openness to a being as that which is manipulable – *existence** into the producing that represents.

---

* {TN: In this entire section, I have translated *Ausständigkeit* as "existence" in keeping with its Latin root, *sistere*- to stand and the suffix *ex*-out, that is, to stand out, a noun used in a dynamic sense by Heidegger, to contrast with *Inständigkeit*, which I translate as "persistence," again in keeping with its Latin root, *sistere* – to stand and the suffix *per* – in, that is, to stand in.}

The exclusive priority of correctness as the criterion of the essence of truth has its ground in the groundless existence of representing, which is salvaged in the subjectum.

Existence means being lost in the re-presenting, a still ungrounded clearing of being emerging from itself. Laid out, that is to say, actually only steeped in the *subjectivity* of the subjectum.

Existence, as the corrupted essence of persistence, is a determination of Dasein in terms of the history of beyng and a disposition of Dasein.

21. The Overcoming of Metaphysics

1. Starting out from *"metaphysics:"* What is it? (a) How does it and how can it conceive of itself; (b) Its history; (c) Inception and end.
2. *The End of Metap*hysics – *Nihilism* and its displacement into the unconditional (as the "transvaluation of all values" – [33] manipulation). Truth of beings – sucked into beings as chaos – anthropomorphism.
3. The End of Metaphysics – as the *abandonment by being* – how and what *eventuates* in the abandonment as abandonment. The *overcoming* – the *essence* of metaphysics first essences as the history of beyng from the overcoming. Beyng overcomes the "truth" of beings – overcoming as the first moment of the clearing of the history of beyng. The essence of history.

22. The Overcoming of "Metaphysics"

Metaphysics is not doctrine and opinion. It is also not just a basic stance of the thinking human, but the *truth of beings*; however, here the essence of truth is ungrounded and transforms in this ungroundedness from ἀλήθεια to the assurance of continued existence. Hence the immediate question: Where and how then "is" this "truth of beings?" Is it an "in-itself" and if not, then is it in "human beings" and how?

Even these possibilities and these questions belong to the ungrounding of the *essence of truth*. This is because ungrounding from early on unfolds a peculiar predominance of beings over being, bringing beings to dominance and even determining the essence of all dominance (justice).

The overcoming of "metaphysics" so understood (in terms of the history of beyng) can therefore not be the proffering of other doctrines and opinions, also not the subsequent grounding of the essence of truth accomplished by human beings; how is that supposed even to happen when everything that has the essence of the human is itself grounded in this truth.

The overcoming of metaphysics is letting its essence come to an end through beyng, in such a way that this coming-to-an-end conceals in it the refusal of being (abandonment by being). Here the essencing of the truth itself, that is, the history of beyng, is everything and the only thing.

[34] The *essencing of the truth* of beyng and the guardianship of the eventuation [*Er-eignung*] of Da-sein is the only thing (cf. 1. The Overcoming of Metaphysics, p. 6f.).

To watch over the tranquil grounding of tranquillity in a long vigil.

The overcoming of metaphysics as overcoming the differentiation as such. Overcoming of metaphysics (as the truth of beings) through beyng – toward the grounding of the truth of beyng as the beyng of truth.

The overcoming as well as the essence of metaphysics and its "history" coming from beyng as (event).

Over-coming as event lets the beings abandoned by beyng fall into the ground-less through the inceptual and active urge to provide a ground for what is inceptually ungrounded.

The first experience of the forgottenness of being: that beyng essences as refusal; in this the clearing of the *abandonment by being*; the *end* of metaphysics; *the complete disruption of the essence of truth.*

ἀλήθεια – ὁμοίωσις – adequatio – certitudo (veritas proprie non nisi in solo intellectu potest) (Descartes, Regulae VIII)*

Overcoming as the history of beyng *–not* "fate" *either*; because even fate is still within the metaphysical realm of *pro-duction – what is sent our way* – which concerns us (τύχη); μοῖρα – fatum; *different in each case.* But? (We still do not have the concept!)

Why the question concerning *truth* becomes urgent *everywhere* through the overcoming of metaphysics (cf. Winter Semester 37/38).[1]

---

* {TN: Heidegger is paraphrasing the following part of a sentence from Regulae VIII: ". . . vidensque veritatem proprie vel falsitatem non nisi in solo intellectu esse posse . . ." [Rene Descartes, *Regulae ad directionem ingenii*, ed. Arthur Buchenau (Leipzig: Verlag der Durr'schen Buchhandlung, 1907), 23, which translates into: "And, seeing that there can be no truth or falsity, in the proper sense, except in the intellect alone . . ." [*Rules for the Direction of the Natural Intelligence*, ed. and trans. George Heffernan (Amsterdam, Alanta, GA: Rodopi, 1998), 117.]

What Heidegger paraphrases reads as follows: There can be no truth in the proper sense except in the intellect alone.}

[1] *Grundfragen der Philosophie. Ausgewählte "Probleme" der "Logik,"* GA 45, 108ff. {TN: *Basic Problems of Philosophy: Selected "Problems" of "Logic,"* 95–96f.}

Since beyng turns to the "grounding" of its truth and this truth of beyng belongs to beyng, determining the essence of all truth.

We do not know *why* beyng turns to the "grounding" of its truth. We only get a hint of this eventuation from afar. We get a hint of this insofar as we bring beyng [35] to knowledge in thought, to the extent that the first inceptual essence of beyng essences as ἀλήθεια.

The question of the truth – therefore does not mean the question of the *"assuring,"* and the certainty and validity of our cognition, does not mean cognition at all, does not even mean the assurance of all human behavior or of human beings; not even this being and definitely not one being. In all cases, the question of the truth, even though it is made explicable in each case on the basis of the realms mentioned, is "grounded" in an essentially different way. *This is because it is eventuated [er-eignet] by beyng itself.* This goes with the unconditional dominance of *power* consisting precisely in forcing the destruction of the essence of the truth (of that which is historical in metaphysics).

23. Overcoming

is to be distinguished from *any* human and modern subjective and above all Hegelian misinterpretation.

How the truth of beyng, which is forgotten, ungrounded, which has indeed not yet been eventuated at all, actively urges the grounding powerlessly and without force.

The tranquillity of the urgency – (The urgency is not the urgency of need, but of making what is not yet appropriate into what is proper (the event that makes appropriate)). (cf. 6. "Overcoming," pp. 13–14, 15–16)

How beyng *un-twists* [ent-windet] itself from the pre-dominance of beings – (winch [Winde] and turn [Wende]).

How beyng *gets over* "metaphysics" [both come from the turning of the winch] in that the winch brings metaphysics back into its essence, first giving back what is inceptual to the inception, allowing only what is inceptual and thus the historical in the history of beyng to essence. The inception essences – the first one, which now means the *ungrounding, forgottenness* of ἀλήθεια.

But never a *sublation* (neither as setting aside nor as preserving nor as enhancing); because the inception [36] (φύσις – ἀλήθεια) is never a preliminary stage and never the immediate, but rather the singularity of the first inception. (cf. 6. "Overcoming," p. 12f.)

"Metaphysics" belongs to the first inception (as the privation of the first inception), insofar as metaphysics *abandoned* by the first inception, has *fallen off* and this fall-off is interpreted as its development (Hegel). The difference between pre-Platonic *thinking* and philosophy, which begins with Plato: ἀλήθεια to ὀρθότης.

With the essencing of the history of beyng, the overcoming opens up the *struggle of the inceptions* (πόλεμος and (event)).

24. "Overcoming" and "the Human"

The human relationship to the "overcoming" as the history of beyng is determined from belonging and *as* the belonging of the human to the truth of beyng. – (Da-sein)

However, this relationship is initially extrinsic – as "metaphysics" is a doctrine, so overcoming becomes a counter-doctrine and an organized activity of human beings – until what is essentially other becomes clear.

To think *from* the overcoming (abandonment by being . . .); that means to be eventuated [*er-eignet*] by the refusal of beyng.

Even this can seem like a mere modification of the question of being.

But this path through "subjectivity" and contemporary opinion is not to be avoided even if the transition can never be permanent. The more widely and broadly the hitherto and its kind are appreciated by way of a preliminary course of action, the more decisive and alienating will the leap become at one point in time.

Overcoming – an "eventuation" of the (event) that is singular, not to be construed in relation to anything familiar, but only in terms of itself – history of beyng.

[37] 25. The Overcoming of Metaphysics

1. The inceptual φύσις; φύσις – ἀλήθεια
    λόγος – ξυνόν
    εἶναι – νοεῖν
2. The φύσις as γένος (Aristotle, *Physics* B, I), cf. *Metaphysics* Γ, 1 among others
3. φύσις – metaphysics/ ἐντελέχεια – φύσις τις, inceptual φύσις
4. φύσις – τέχνη – power – manipulation – τέχνη – ἀλήθεια
5. τέχνη – "technology" – "truth" of beyng
6. technology (modern) and the end (corrupted essence of metaphysics)[a]

---

[a] enframing and event

26. The Overcoming of Metaphysics

1. How all treatises speak in the language of metaphysics and state *the other*: the grounding of the *truth* of beyng and this grounding itself. *At the limits*; cf. "ontology;" nothing of the kind, thus it is right to reject (that *Being and Time* is "ontology"). But what is rejected here? Insistence upon that which in *Being and Time* is already overcome to some extent.
2. To what extent being itself and its truth is never to be creatively thought by means of a stepwise progression of questions of the same kind (a priori), as it sometimes appears.
3. For what reason everything is to be expressed and grasped in terms of the history of beyng. All talk of "concept," of "questioning," "thinking," "fundamental positions" must be thought in terms of the history of beyng. This is to be done *even when* the "discussion" must initially be incorporated into the existing "representations" of philosophy and by philosophy. Such transformed thinking is already a result of being displaced into Da-sein and that means the overcoming of all *subjectivity* and *anthropomorphism*.

[38] 27. The Overcoming of Metaphysics at its End (cf. *The End of Metaphysics and Nietzsche*)

is the overcoming of the "transvaluation of all values," the essence of which lies *specifically* in positing "natural" ("physiological") values anew (*as the standard*) as well as in interpretating existing metaphysics and metaphysics in general as the positing of value (cf. Nietzsche Lecture Summer Semester 39).[1] The positing of value is the most extreme devastation of the essence of truth, whose corrupted essence is already transferred into the consciousness and representations of the objective (certainty and the state of being aware). In this devastation, "truth" is indeed recognized as a necessary value. This recognition is precisely the ultimate annihilation of its essence. It is the establishment of the abandonment of beings by being as that of the

---

[1] *Nietzsches Lehre vom Willen zur Macht als Erkenntnis*, Freiburg Lecture of Summer Semester 1939, GA 47, ed. E. Hanser (Frankfurt am Main: Vittorio Klostermann, 1989), 21–31. {TN: Translated into English as *Nietzsche Vol. III, pt. 1: The Will to Power as Knowledge*, ed. David Farrell Krell, trans. Joan Stambaugh, David Farrell Krell and Frank Capuzzi (San Francisco: HarperSanFrancisco, 1987), 15–21.}

chaos of the unconditional will to power. The "transvaluation," on the basis of which truth is posited anew as value, is the most extreme nihilism.

The overcoming of metaphysics is the overcoming of this abandonment by being, which stems from the ungrounding of truth as unconcealedness. The abandonment by being familiarizes us with the *differentiation* between beingness and beings, which is as such unnoticed and already conceals a danger, in the form of the priority of the "a priori" or rather of its positivist-empirical misinterpretation.

28. The Overcoming of Metaphysics

We realize that in the creative questioning of the truth of beyng, another inception makes its inception and through the reflection upon the beyng of truth, the human being is thrown into persistently inhabiting an abyss of history. With this realization, any sojourn within the history of metaphysics becomes an engagement with the emptiness of [39] what hitherto exists. Any attempt to explain what is present and contemporary through metaphysics becomes a gimmick.

Metaphysics is the *clue-less* (cf. 32. The End of Metaphysics) skipping-over (μετά) of φύσις, which is an inceptual being, to which we certainly can never return, but which in its history as the other inception makes demands upon human history.

Precisely because φύσις is skipped over in the ungrounding of its ἀλήθεια, it remains the fundamental concept of metaphysics in its alteration into a corrupted essence (φύσις as that which is unreflectively skipped over but never to be abolished).

Even "overcoming" is still a word, which in retrospect misleads us, even if understood in terms of the history of beyng and not as an accomplishment.

However, the relation to the first inception is no retrospective glance but a prospective glance into the afflux (arrival) of the unquestioned, which is to be questioned: the truth of beyng (cf. 6. "Overcoming," p. 12f.; 23. Overcoming, p. 31f.).

29. Over-coming is only in the Other Inception

The *over-coming* of metaphysics is existential [*da*-seins*haft*]. It cannot be accomplished by writing a "book" about it. Anything seeming like such a "book" has literally a different essence.

The overcoming is the guardianship of the *transition*. The transition is the history of beyng as (event). Overcoming is *never* a "counter-movement," but rather a *coming-toward* (a going toward the arrival of *what was*) in an essentially historical sense.

The essential knowledge of the inception emerges in the transition.

All "revolutions" (upheavals) are never "revolutionary" enough. They never lead to an inception but renege upon it because they are constantly just *re-turning,* remaining unconditionally entangled in the hitherto, misjudging and forgetting this entanglement.

[40] Everything "revolutionary" is only a counter-play in relation to the "conservative." Both are stuck in the past, which can become a long present.

30. "Worldview" – "Ideology"

To grasp "worldview" more *essentially*. Cf. remarks on the grounding of the modern world-picture.[1]

Already *prior to* the word (name), [worldviews became] available with *modern metaphysics* as the outgrowth into the thinking of the commoner – "free thinkers," whether they be an individual or secret societies, or clubs or associations of comrades or a people.

"Worldview" mostly still coincides by its very nature with what is called "ideology." We only have to note that ideology does not need to be a superstructure or a supplement (the view that economic-material relations constitute what is properly a being, itself only springs from ideology). Ideology is the peculiar shape taken by a metaphysics, which conforms to what is obvious, and which is itself not "proven" – the "ideas," that is to say, goals and values and forms of order, presented, inculcated, preached through the logos in the sense of reason (of what is clear to every individual as "logical"). Thus, an interpretation of beings as a whole is beaten out into something broad in which all the dos and don'ts can be disseminated in such a way that it cares less and less about the "worldview" itself than about the benefits that the advancement of the same yields to the adherents.

The equation of "worldview" and "life view" – "world" as "life" and "life" as "world" – an alteration of the subject–object relationship *into unconditional flattening and leveling – secured in "activism."*

---

[1] "Die Zeit des Weltbildes," *Holzwege*, GA 5, 96–113. {TN: "The Age of the World Picture," *Off the Beaten Track*, 73–85.}

[41] Away from *interpretation* – away from procedure and the philosophy of philosophy – if "meta-physics," then what is meant is "truth."

To what extent is the thought of value already prefigured in ἀγαθόν as the highest "idea" and with it the nihilism of metaphysics decided? ἰδέα as the essence of beings; ἰδέα τοῦ αγαθοῦ – (ἀγαθόν as ἰδέα), nonetheless ἐπέκεινα τῆς οὐσίας*. Beingness moved *under* that which renders useful and this again conceived as ἰδέα. The insufficient interpretation of ἐπέκεινα in *On the Essence of Ground* – in ἀγαθόν the proper destruction of ἀλήθεια.[2]

31. The End of Metaphysics

End here does not mean merely *stopping* or concluding; because only at the end does the redundant self-forgetting continuation begin. End = beginning of the unconditional domination of the corrupted essence over essence; End thus is not = disappearing; to the contrary. From where comes the connection (belongingness) of essence – corrupted essence?

The history of beyng: Event – refusal (cf. 6. "Overcoming," pp. 16–17f.) – abandon.

End is consummation; but consummation is not perfection, in the sense of the fulfillment of the one highest ideal. It is rather the *introduction* (getting over, cf. 6. "Overcoming," pp. 13–14f.) precisely of *the* most radical *corruption* into the essence. With "manipulation," φύσις manages to turn into its corrupted essence; this corrupted essence suppresses the "essence" in the sense of what is inceptual and this suppression and entanglement in the corrupted essence is the consummation of the inception. From φύσις through ἐντελέχεια to actuality as the objectivity of mastery – *will to power* – power –manipulation.

---

* {TN: beyond being.}

[2] *Nietzsche: Der europäische Nihilismus* [*European Nihilism*], Freiburg Lecture of the Second Trimester 1940, GA 48, ed. P. Jaeger, Frankfurt am Main: Vittorio Klostermann 1986), 300–303. {TN: The same text is also published in *Nietzsche II*, GA 6.2, ed. Brigitte Schillbach (Frankfurt Am Main: Vittorio Klostermann, 1997); translated into English as *Nietzsche IV: Nihilism*, trans. Frank. A. Capuzzi, ed. David Farrell Krell (San Francisco: HarperSanFrancisco, 1991).}

[42] **32. The End of Metaphysics**

is to be grasped only from the inception and *the two* from the essence of the truth of beyng (event). This means that we grasp it from the overcoming – as *history* of beyng.

1. End: as the unconditional dominance of the corrupted essence over essence.

Essence: the truth of beings – *being* – logic; consummation in *unconditional subjectivity*. Lack of any question [*Fraglosigkeit*] regarding being – forgottenness, to put it better: *having no clue* (cf. pp. 34–35) of the truth of beyng and its grounding; because the truth of beyng is not in the inception of the ἀλήθεια of φύσις either.

Corrupted essence: the inversion of Platonism and the *unscrewing (deviating) into "chaos" as will to power*. Unconditional subjectivity now as unconditional anthropomorphism; "the worker"

Subjectivity: essentially not at all related to the human being; God and *ontotheology* (cf. Basic words, cf. 1. The Overcoming of Metaphysics, pp. 6–7)

2. End – the domination of the corrupted essence as the abandonment of beings by being (the latter as refusal; clearing of beyng); and as the forgottenness of being; "*Nihilism*" grasped in terms of the history of beyng.

3. End – and the consolidation of the petering-out and which gives the appearance of the opposite; the emergence of what appear to be great "upheavals;" these are however decisive regressions (cf. *Ponderings XIV*);[1] and the history of beyng – the inception/end – the most extremely corrupted essence of the inception: *pure* becoming as the *highest form of permanence*.

[43] 4. End – as *ending* in the sense of the active essence of the end to be thought in a manifold manner (cf. 1. The Overcoming of Metaphysics). This ending in itself comes from the history of beyng and its *moment of the overcoming* of metaphysics.

---

[1] *Überlegungen XII–XV (Schwarze Hefte 1939–1941)*, GA 96, ed. Peter Trawny (Frankfurt am Main: Vittorio Klostermann, 2014), 167–243. {TN: Translated into English as *Ponderings XII–XV* (Black Notebooks 1939–1941), trans. Richard Rojcewicz (Bloomington: Indiana University Press, 2017), 131–191.}

33. The Clearing of Beyng

1. its singularity – not the most universal and the most common.[a]
2. its inceptuality – not supplementarity
3. its being undisclosed – not obviousness
4. its richness – not emptiness
5. its "nearness" (nearer than all that is near) – not far removed – farthest
6. the rarest – not the most familiar, most thumbed through
7. the strangest – not the most commonplace

Inception (beginning) and end of the first inception of philosophy. *The history of metaphysics*. Everything depends upon the ungrounding of ἀλήθεια, which eventuates in the refusal (concealed) of beyng.

This refusal by way of the ungrounding leads to the alteration of ἀλήθεια to ὁμοίωσις, adequatio, certitudo, objectivity, "orderliness" [*Gerechigkeit*][*]. All the ways to φύσις are covered over. The overcoming of metaphysics as the history of the essence of the inceptual truth proceeding toward the untruth of its corrupted essence.

[44] 34. Nietzsche and the End of Western Metaphysics

1. The concept of the end in the sense of the consummation of the unconditional essence in the corrupted essence.
2. Showing this corrupted essence in what Nietzsche's metaphysics asks and says:
   a. Nihilism, transvaluation of all hitherto existing values
   b. Will to power
   c. The eternal recurrence of the same
   d. The superhuman

---

[a] Is this *also* not an inversion? It appears so at first glance. But what is essential is that everything comes from the essencing of beyng. Cf. in this regard: *Die Metaphysik des deutschen Idealismus. Zur erneuten Auslegung von Schelling: Philosophische Untersuchungen über das Wesen der menschlichen Freiheit und der damit zusammenhängenden Gegenstände* [The Metaphysics of German Idealism: Toward a New Interpretation of Schelling: Philosophical Investigations on the Essence of Human Freedom and the Objects Connected to It] (1809), Freiburg Seminar of Summer Semester 1941, GA 49, ed. G. Seubold (Frankfurt am Main: Vittorio Klostermann, 1991), 89.

[*] {TN: *Gerechigkeit*, which is derived from *Gerech* meaning well-ordered, in good condition, upright, just, well-suited, proper, having a proper character.}

e. The procedure: Metaphysics as "psychology" (Truth as certainty); on Nietzsche's "biologism" cf. summer semester 1939;[1] cf. Nietzsche, *Beyond Good and Evil*, no. 23.*

f. Identifying the basic position from the standpoint of the predominance of valuative thought.

3. Obliteration of the essence of truth and the forgottenness of being.

4. The abandonment by being (in terms of the history of beyng) and refusal.

35. The End of Metaphysics as Consummation in the Unconditional Corrupted Essence. (The Metaphysics of Nietzsche)

1. European nihilism as the devaluation of the highest values.

2. This devaluation as the transvaluation of all hitherto existing values.

3. Transvaluation as newly positing the will to power as basic value.

4. Transvaluation as the interpretation of the history of metaphysics as the history of the positing of values; the "moral" interpretation of metaphysics.

5. Transvaluation as *valuation – valuative thought* and the essence of the will to power as positing of value. The values of preservation and [45] enhancement; the assessment of the value of the whole cannot be carried out; hence the *value of the whole* is impossible; "*Highpoints of value*" as the highpoints of *power*. The whole therefore only ever exists as "becoming."

6. The will to power as essence of "becoming" (overpowering); becoming as being in the sense making presence permanent without a goal, without unconditional fixing, presence of the impermanent as such. Will to power as the *eternal recurrence of the same* – the extreme-classical-ecstatic nihilism.

7. The pure chaos of the will to power and the machine-like economy of the world – (dominance over the earth) and its "meaning."

8. The super-human – as unconditional subjectivity.

9. *Subjectivity* and the origin of "valuation" (5); valuation and destruction of truth as unconditional devastation of its essence.

---

[1] *Nietzsches Lehre vom Willen zur Macht als Erkenntnis*, GA 47, 58–93. {TN: *The Will to Power as Knowledge and as Metaphysics*, GA 47, 39–47.}

* {TN: Friedrich Nietzsche, "Beyond Good and Evil," in *Basic Writings of Nietzsche*, ed. and trans. Walter Kaufmann (New York: Modern Library, 2000), 221–222.}

Truth as justice – *necessary value* and hence unconditional nothingness.

10. Nihilism as annihilation of truth; abandonment by being: The nihilistic concept of nihilism; the concept of nihilism in terms of the history of beyng.

11. Nihilism as the highest triumph of the *"spirit,"* because subjectivity becomes unconditional in nihilism; knowledge becomes calculation, which constantly expands; the will becomes the force to command, which does not die out; becoming, as permanence even of the impermanent, becomes the highest value. The interpretation of nihilism as that of the unspiritual and the contra-spiritual is itself the lack of spirit, for which nothing remains but the flight into the earlier, supposedly more genuine "spirit."

12. The flight into "spirit" (the Christian and the ecclesiastical and the pseudo-ecclesiastical) as the most captious and ultimate form of "materialism," which can no longer free itself from what is present at hand and beings. Instead of freeing itself from beings in favor of beyng into the history of the grounding of its truth to come, it avoids this in a [46] "salvation" that is supposedly at hand, engaging with history only in a historiographical and non-serious fashion. That is why it, nevertheless, shouts the loudest about "decision" and "reflection." Nihilism will never be overcome through the "spirit" but only promoted, confirmed, and consolidated.

13. The "spirit" as shelter and refuge of valuative thought; the "lived body" as the field of its unconditional testimony and claim. The "soul" as the way of taking possession of the "lived body" and "spirit" as satisfaction and compensation in "lived experience."

14. The "lived body/spirit/soul" – human being as the human being of metaphysics is the impediment to the truth of beyng. This impediment attains its highest world-friendly power in the "superhuman" and its most tenacious world-hostile impotence in the "divine human" (Christ). However, it is only in the *struggle of the two* against each another that this impediment installs itself unobstructed upon a long avoidance of history, which still belongs to beyng in a concealed manner as the overcoming of metaphysics.

36. The Metaphysics of Nietzsche as the Consummation of Metaphysics (cf. concluding summary summer semester 39)[1]

not because he rejects "metaphysics" and turns *against* it, but because Nietzsche consummates it.

Nietzsche also says (*Will to Power*, n. 1048):[2] "An anti-metaphysical view of the world – yes, but an artistic one." (cf. Winter Semester 36/37)[3]

But still a view of the world, still an interpretation of beings [47] as a whole, but not as "beingness" (truth), but as "life" – "becoming;" that is, will to power.

Art, namely, the highest form of the will to power –, becoming as making the impermanent permanent as such. Cf. *Will to Power*, n. 1046: "One must understand the basic phenomenon of the *artistic*, which is called "life," – the *constructing spirit* . . .;"* therefore always metaphysics and especially so – only: metaphysics of the will; cf. *Beyond Good and Evil*, n. 36.

In addition: an *anti*-metaphysical way of thinking is still always, indeed more than ever, anti-*metaphysical*, so that it consummates metaphysics by inverting it [*umkehren*] and cleaning it out [*auskehren*]. Cf. *Will to Power*, n. 462: "*Fundamental innovation:* . . . In the place of "metaphysics" and religion the *doctrine of the eternal return* (as the means of breeding and selecting)."*

Here metaphysics = Platonism = "religion" = Christian religion, that is, Platonism for the people.

The doctrine of the eternal return – principally t*he permanence of becoming* and its *aim-lessness*.

Aim-lessness not as a lack, but as the advantage of being liberated;

---

[1] *Nietzsches Lehre vom Willen zur Macht als Erkenntnis (Dritter Teil: Die Ewige Wiederkehr des Gleichen und der Wille zur Macht)*, GA 47, 275–295. {TN: *Nietzsche III: The Will to Power as Knowledge and as Metaphysics (Part Two: The Eternal Recurrence of the Same and the Will to Power)*, 161–184.}

[2] Friedrich Nietzsche, "*Wille zur Macht: Drittes und Viertes Book*," *Nietzsches Werke (Großoktavausgabe)*, Vol. XVI (Leipzig: Kröner, 1911), n. 1048, 386. {TN: Translated into English as *Will to Power*, ed. and trans. Walter Kaufmann and R. J. Hollingdale (New York: Vintage Books, 1967), 539.}

[3] *Nietzsche: Der Wille Zur Macht als Kunst*. Freiburg lecture winter semester 1936/37, GA 43, ed. B. Heimbüchel (Frankfurt am Main: Vittorio Klostermann 1985). {TN: Translated into English as *Nietzsche I: The Will to Power as Art*, trans. David Farrell Krell (San Francisco: HarperSanFranciso, 1991).}

* {TN: *Will to Power*, 538, translation modified.}

* {TN: *Will to Power*, 255, translation modified.}

this aim-lessness, however, demands precisely the fixing of "purposes" and what is permanent, namely, "truth."

The essence of "truth" in Nietzsche's sense is only justified through the *eternal recurrence of the same*. This means that it is posited at the same time as "value." Will to power must let itself essence as the eternal recurrence of the same.

However, simultaneously we have as a consequence: "Doctrine" – as *value* (condition of life); its "truth" measured in relation to the will to power – that is in relation to the superhuman – empowering of unconditional power.

[48] 37. The Consummation of Metaphysics: The Positing of Value as Nihilism

1. That and how and for what reason metaphysics consummates in the positing of value (valuative thinking). (*Consummation* as the essential inclusion in its essence of its unfolded corrupted essence.)
2. Metaphysics and the "differentiation" as ground for the positing of value (the modern "subjective" shape of the differentiation).
3. The differentiation and the decision (unexpressed) in favor of the forgottenness of being (in itself forgotten).
4. The forgottenness of being and the awakening of what appears as the opposite through valuative thought (truth as necessary value).
5. The forgottenness of being as the essence of nihilism (nihilism as the ignorant rejection of the nothing that belongs to the essence of being).
6. The transvaluation of all values as classical nihilism.
7. "Transvaluation" is interpreted as positing value "anew." For, transvaluation is, for the first time ever, metaphysics as the positing of value. It is only from its own standpoint that transvaluation interprets all hitherto existing metaphysics as the positing of value, with the latter becoming the old positing of value and the first-time transvaluation becoming the "new" positing of value.
8. Being, conceived as will to power, can henceforth only be represented to thought in its character of power, which determines everything as the means to power and the conditions of power. Even the aims of power, the covert and the alleged, are only a means of empowering power. Everything that is, "is" as a condition of power and that means as a "value." Being as will to power permits *itself* to be thought only if thinking is a valuative thinking. This is a thinking which must posit the conditions of preservation

and that means, at the same time, the enhancement of unconditional power.

9. The proper value of preservation is "truth" in the sense of the assurance of something permanent.

[49] The deposing of the existing highest values (purpose, unity, *truth*) is not a complete abolition, but a depreciation of their status through the alteration of their essence.

The highest value of the "truth in itself" (of the true world of the ὄντος ὄν of ideas) becomes a subordinate but *necessary* value. Meaning must be sought, purpose must be set, what is true must be fixed, but only in the service of the empowering of power; in order that power possess something that can be trampled over as what is ossified and be power; so that power does not, at the same time, waver in this overpowering for its own sake and always has enhancement for its "aim," that is to say, always only the semblance of an aim. An unconditionally fixed aim would indeed again deny becoming in its unconditionality. Truth in itself is not "objectivity" in the sense of "disinterested intuition," but rather the capacity, in accordance with power, to always have control over "for" and "against" and to vary the perspective and the manner of assuring continued existence depending upon the level and the direction of power.

The proper value of enhancement is "art" in the sense of "transfiguration" (provision of an appearance, which opens up new possibilities of empowering power); "Art" as the "art of diplomacy" and "politics." That is why "art" has more *value* than "truth."

10. The statement about art having more value than truth does not only speak about truth, as a necessary value, not being sufficient as the condition of the will to power. It does not only speak about art having to be the sufficient condition for the fundamental nature of power (enhancement as overpowering). The statement says, before anything, that everything must concern the being of value and any kind of thinking can only operate within the acts of positing value. If we see the content of the statement on the basis of this one thing, then it becomes clear that we must and why we must grasp it as the basic statement of the consummation of metaphysics.

[50] 11. If we think rigorously, it can also no longer be said that transvaluation and the new positing of value entangle metaphysics more than ever and decisively in valuative thought. This is because "transvaluation" is indeed only the first interpretation, stemming from the initial positing of value, of its historical relationship to the metaphysics that precedes it, which does not know valuative

thinking. Nevertheless, the preceding metaphysics prepares it in essence. The new positing of value is not the consequence but the ground of transvaluation.

38. The Consummation of Metaphysics Comes to Fruition

in the transvaluation of all hitherto existing values on the basis of the new positing of value. This new positing of value evaluates by taking its departure from the will to power and in the direction of the will to power as the basic value ("principle"). But on account of the unconditional nature of valuative thought, the consummation simply conceals the forgottenness of being and in this way brings the abandonment of beings by being to dominance. The abandonment of beings by being springs from the groundlessness of the truth of beyng. Through the simple unfamiliarity with the truth of beyng, the abandonment by being consolidates the groundlessness into something insurmountable. The most extreme rejection lies in this unfamiliarity.

By positing value, Nietzsche conceives of nihilism as a positing of value. But truly speaking (thought in terms of the history of beyng from the truth of beyng) valuative thought as such is, quite to the contrary, already the final stage and consequence of nihilism, irrespective of what it posits as value and how it understands the nature of the valuable. The essence of nihilism lies in the neglect of the nothing, which comes from nihilism's incapacity to grasp its own essence as the essentially "corrupted essence" of beyng and to experience the inception of the grounding to come, in the abyss of the truth of beyng.

[51] 39. Beyng – (Event)

Event [*Er-eignis*] of the eventuation [*Ereignung*] –*ap*-propriate [*Zu*-eignen] into Da-*sein*; *to one's own* [*Zu-eigen*] = by oneself, that is, self; *appropriateness* – essencing as self, that is to say, as Da-*sein*, that is to say, *in grounding the clearing of beyng. Self-hood* as *ground* of the I and the we – *how!* as *essencing* clearing of the there, namely, *being* there [*Da-sein*].

40. Metaphysics

Even the metaphysics of the "substantial" Hegel is "logic" through and through, that is to say, it satisfies the essence of Western metaphysics right up to its consummation.

There remained only one step more to its unconditionally corrupted essence, which was accomplished by Nietzsche.

About φύσις – τέχνη – technology, the role of Roman culture (actio) and Christendom (creatio).

41. Metaphysics

is the juncture of Western history (the jointure that joins it together) as a history of the abandonment of beings by being which fleshes itself out in forgottenness. History is here the essencing of the truth of beyng – not only and not primarily from the standpoint of the human being. Metaphysics is the concealed disruption of φύσις.

In order to experience this essence of metaphysics (in terms of the history of beyng) and to become persistent and ready for a decision in this essence and thus in the ground of our history, we require the knowledge of fundamental concepts. For, what are fundamental metaphysical concepts?

[52] 42. The Consummation of Modern Metaphysics

Nietzsche's "psychology" as the absolute and total development of the *Meditationes de Prima Philosophia*.

43. Metaphysics as the History of Beyng

is the essential history of beyng as the conjuncture of the truth of beings. (Conjuncture of the truth of beings and the guiding thread of its projection.)

Because the conjuncture simultaneously *inserts* itself into the beings which it reveals (cf., for example, the setting-into-work of truth as artwork) and, because in this insertion, the human being is unleashed into becoming a definite kind of an entity of its own (*animal rationale – Subjectum*), humankind itself becomes historical, in accordance with the conjuncture. It is for this reason that humankind can observe and explain history in a definite way (namely, historiographically) as a passing event. It can thus regard metaphysics historiographically in the form of "views" and doctrines. From this metaphysics, viewed historiographically, there is never a path that leads to its essence as a history of beyng. Rather the inverse is true. The history of beyng is nevertheless only experienced from the creative questioning of the truth of beyng. This creative questioning is eventuated [*er-eignet*] by beyng itself.

44. Metaphysical Errancy

The further the thinking of beingness loses itself in and seemingly flees into what is the most universal, the closer this not yet unfolded thinking of being comes to the nearest, the most singular and purest, the truth of beyng itself, without being able to know it.

But the errancy of metaphysics consists in this: [53] it is familiar with *only one way* out *of* being lost in the emptiest-most universal, which is to flee into the "particular" and the concrete, whether this be the positivity of the sciences or the "praxis" of so-called "life" or the moral "appeal" to individual existence ("*anthropology*").

In this way, metaphysics strays into an errancy that is unique to it – and thereby keeps the opening of beings into beingness open in the jointure.

And yet there lies hidden in this errancy (cf. above) a hidden direction into the question concerning beyng, granted that this question was already eventuated [*er-eignet*] inceptually by beyng itself.

45. Metaphysics and the "Universal"

thinks on the basis of the ἕν and καθόλου; and this means, without coming to know that this is a result of the ungrounding of the truth of beyng, the inceptual self-gathering in the permanence of presence, which for its part is the appearing and, at the same time, the concealing of being as φύσις. The unconcealment of being (in ἕν and καθόλου) still takes its departure from the uniqueness and fullness of the overtly close proximity to being over all beings. Yet, precisely this interpretation of being becomes a misinterpretation of it as beingness, as the emptiest and most general, against which beings in their particularity will acquire primacy and come to be anchored in a first cause.

Metaphysics is sacrificed to the most universal concept that emerges in this way as it seeks to derive its legitimacy as a science from the most universal. The hallmark of this is the decisive role of the "a priori" in philosophy. It makes no difference whether it is interpreted "objectively" or "subjectively." The final echo of this is the doctrine of "values."

[54] 46. Metaphysics (cf. "Basic Words")

Beyng never comes face to face with the human being. This would be the case only if the human being stood someplace outside it as a possible meeting point for being. Such a thing happens only in the relations between one being and another.

If the human being were to come face to face with beyng then beyng would have to become the object and the human being would be reduced to the one who only represents. But is this not in fact the case in all metaphysics? Certainly, here being is only the most extreme iteration of the objective. But metaphysics also never knows of beyng. That is simultaneously its distinction and its ambiguity because it engages with beings after all. Beyng is and is revealed to the extent that it eventuates human beings into Da-sein through a transformation of their essence.

47. Basic concepts (*of Metaphysics*) (Epitomizing Concept see Introduction to the 1st Trimester of 1940)[1]

are alone the metaphysical concepts as ἀρχή – concepts (Inception and disposal) (dominance). They think what is *ground-like as ground*, whereby "ground" itself is thought in accordance with the essence of being (φύσις) in concepts that think back into what grounds as such.

In what way and to what extent are these epitomizing concepts?
(a) as such, each of them thinks beings as a whole;
(b) as *involving* [*einbegriefend*] that which conceptualizes [*Begreifenden*]; the in-volving but *how*? Why can it not become essential? – (Truth of

---

[1] *Leitgedanken zur Entstehung der Metaphysik, der neuzeitlichen Wissenschaft und der modernen Technik* [Guiding Ideas on the Emergence of Metaphysis, Modern Science and Modern Technology], GA 76, ed. Claudius Strube (Frankfurt am Main: Vittorio Klostermann, 2009), 53–77.

beyng not creatively questioned – the in-between of persistence concealed and ungrounded).

In metaphysics only the first attempt and then the appearance of
grounding.

[55] The knowledge of the basic concepts of metaphysics is not a
familiarity with the definitions of universal representations and names,
but rather? (ἀρχή – concepts; ἀρχή: αἴτιον – causa – principium – condition of possibility).

Basic metaphysical concepts – as *epitomizing concepts* – in each a
being as a whole as such is thought, in such a way that the belongingness of the thinker to this being is also kept in mind one way or the
other and the thinker is involved (belonging to being – eventuated as
the expropriated).

Nevertheless, *this* essence of metaphysics in terms of epitomizing
concepts is itself rare or only indirect and partial and this belongs to
the essence of metaphysics.

First and foremost: *epitomizing concepts – each a being as a whole as
such*; and including *the human being* – not as a being among others, but
distinguished; this *distinction* varies [?]:

νοεῖν   – Parmenides
finite reason – Descartes.

48. The Essence of Metaphysics in Terms of the History of Beyng

is "nihilism," which itself must be thought not only metaphysically but
also in terms of the history of beyng.

Metaphysics is (cf. to the already mentioned ἀγαθόν as ἐπέκεινα τῆς
οὐσίας) the destruction of ἀλήθεια; but thus, it is the obliteration of the
differentiation between being and beings in its capacity to be grounded;
and herein lies the abandonment of beings by being and the forgottenness of being. Obliteration of the "differentiation" whereby this in itself
is already the ambiguous beginning of the possibility of the question of
being and the grounding of ἀλήθεια (obliteration for the sake of beings).

If a highpoint and grounding had been specifically reached within
the history of metaphysics as the history of the truth of beings –
experienced from beyng and its truth, what would have become evident,
however, is still the unfamiliar fact that the history of beyng has not
at all been reached yet in the course of the history of metaphysics.
[56] This may be the reason why transitions in this course are brought
about by the great, namely colossal, incidents in the struggle for
power, and instead of essential history, technology (metaphysical) and

historiography impose themselves, and then everything is entrenched in an unknowable blindness..

49. Metaphysics and "Physics"

Because history as the overcoming of metaphysics is upon us [*bevorsteht*] – it stands before us [*steht bevor*] because we "stand" in it as thrown; thrown into the abandonment by being – the knowledge of the essence of "physics" as the definitely ordered truth about φύσις is a necessity for us. The acuteness of this necessity is essentially superior to all the exigency of "what is important for life."

50. The History of Being (The Overcoming of Metaphysics) – *Being and Time* (The Question of Being)

*Meta*physics is meta-*physics*, thus "physics" – and indeed in the sense of Aristotle; not just "also" and indirectly, but essentially and only.

The creative thinking of the *essence* of φύσις as the οὐσία of the φύσει ὄντα – indeed the ὄντα ἦ ὄντα, insofar as οὐσία – οὐσία τις is in the *original*, not just in the supplementary sense.

Why, to what extent and for what reason is this physics *meta*-physics? Because it treats physics in a *still more essential sense*. But this sense is no longer dominant, *but only an echo*. Hence meta – after and yet toward it! – away from and back toward – (unclear, because not moving away from φύσει ὄντα, but back toward φύσις).

The inceptual thinking of φύσις. In what way does the inception close itself off, getting unleashed instead of being dominant.

The ungrounding of ἀλήθεια.

ἀλήθεια and φύσις/The question concerning the "*truth.*"

[57] 51. Metaphysics
Cf. the Why-question (Leibniz, *The Rational Principles of Nature and Grace*)

τί τὸ ὄν – What is *a being*? "as a whole," "as such."

A being – essentially (in keeping with the differentiation and preserved without being grounded in it and therefore springing from it) doubled, but this doubling is not grasped and is always arbitrarily one-sided or mixed up.

A being – that which *exists individually* [*ein Seiendes*], that is, "determined" by being, without thinking of being – a being of the *overlooked* being. Hence
1. a being of the being that is not looked at
2. a being of the being that is considered – a being as one such
3. a being *with regard to* its being – the latter itself – determined from the standpoint of a being – "categories" and "causes" and principles
4. but in all of this *never* being itself in its truth; here we have to question in a completely different way.[a]

52. "The Metaphysical"

νοητόν – non-sensual and super-sensual; ἰδέα
intelligibile
commune (κοινόν)
abstractum
ὄντος ὄν   τὸ θεῖον
ἐντελέχεια
The eternal – "which keeps standing" – the divine
The rational –
The ought – the ideal – (God is dead)
Nietzsche's *moral interpretation of the "metaphysical"*
"*Meta*" – supra – post

[58] 53. The Role of "Science" and Philosophy as Metaphysics

Modern *science* (cf. "Guiding statements," 1940):[1]
1. mathesis – the basic form (indeterminate) of knowledge and certainty – reason – enlightenment
2. so much in proximity to the realm of self-certainty – of the person – of the spirit
3. thus the way to world conquest – *"technology"* and *"historiography"*
4. "Science" and unconditional knowledge

---

[a] in this regard "*the pathways*" [of questioning]: from where and how?

[1] *Leitgedanken zur Entstehung der Metaphysik, der neuzeitlichen Wissenschaft und der modernen Technik* [Guiding Ideas on the Emergence of Metaphysics, Modern Science and Modern Technology], GA 76, ed. Claudius Strube (Frankfurt am Main: Vittorio Klostermann, 2009), 117–125.

5. "Positivism"
"Science" –   (A) "metaphysical" – knowledge – truth
               νοεῖν – λόγος – ἀλήθεια – φύσις
               (B) operational – cultural
               (C) vacillating between the two, in keeping with the
               indeterminacy of metaphysics.

Because and insofar as philosophy is metaphysics (νοεῖν – λόγος – τέχνη – ἐπιστήμη), there is a peculiar role for "science." Because the fundamental relation to a being as a being finally consolidates itself as *νοεῖν, διανοεῖσθαι*, the cognitive acquisition of this relation itself becomes the pre-eminently authoritative "knowledge." Since then, metaphysics has been constantly inclined toward defining itself as *"the"* science. We find two possibilities here according to the kind of "truth" and kind of authority of the mode of knowledge (re-presentation; ratio): Philosophy *passes* itself off as the authoritative science or takes the standard for its form of knowledge from the existing sciences (i.e., from a metaphysics that no longer knows itself).

Thus, we have within the history of metaphysics a constant disruption of philosophy by "science" and correspondingly by the role "of the sciences," ἐπιστήμη, scientia, in the history of the West.

[59] In the *overcoming of metaphysics*, this relationship must also be brought into the open and "science" must be decisively rejected. However, this requires "science" to play the role of a vanguard precisely in the transition, not for its own sake but the for the sake of knowledge. (cf. *What is Metaphysics?*,[2] Lecture on Truth,[3] "The Grounding of the Modern World-Picture,"[4] at the same time by contrast: *Truth* and the Work of Art; *On the Origin of the Work of Art*).[5]

54. On *What is Metaphysics?*

1. The directions to the position from which alone one first speaks about "science" (cf. 53. The Role of "Science" and the Philosophy as Metaphysics).

[2] "Was ist Metaphysik?" *Wegmarken*. GA 9, 103–122. {TN: "What is Metaphysics?" *Pathmarks*, 82–96.}
[3] "Vom Wesen der Wahrheit," *Wegmarken*, loc. cit. 177–202. {TN: "On the Essence of Truth," *Pathmarks*, 136–154.}
[4] "Zeit des Weltbildes," *Holzwege*, GA 5, 75–113. {TN: "The Age of the World-Picture," *Off the Beaten Track*, 57–85.}
[5] "Der Ursprung des Kunstwerkes," *Holzwege*, loc. cit. 1–74. {TN: "The Origin of the Work of Art," *Off the Beaten Track*, 1–53.}

(a) Science as the relationship to beings – modern science.

(b) This relationship is what grounds in the relation to being.

(c) This relation – *persistence* in the truth of beyng.

(d) This persistence as "eventuation" by beyng – or, however, the abandonment of beings by being as in modern metaphysics; hence the peculiar predominance.

2. The *"nothing"* – the most monstrous in the *essence* of beyng.

"Heidegger makes the nothing into a proper object of metaphysics" – indeed! But *not* in the way meant here! But rather because it is the most monstrous element of beyng and specifically not an "object," but the most question-worthy.

The "night" – (the twilight) – *ab-senting* – the "light – φάος – φύσις"

3. Anxiety *–disturbance* [*Entsetzen*] as experience of the abandonment of beings by being; the first [60] proximity to being as such that originates from metaphysics, not a "feeling" that could be moralistically devalued as "*unheroic*."

4. Logic – (cf. Summer Semester 35)[1]

5. Simultaneous with "On the Essence of Ground"[2]

In the foreword to the Japanese translation of *What is Metaphysics?* (June 1930)[3] the following is set as a task: "Fleshing out more originally the inherited guiding question of Western metaphysics: 'What is a being?' into the basic question, which supports and leads it: 'What is being?' Thus, what is asked at the same time is this: 'In what is the inner possibility of the manifestation of being grounded?'"

"Not the description of human consciousness, but the comprehending *awakening of the Da-sein* in human beings, is the path on which we will once again recover the small number of simple but hard questions of philosophy."

---

[1] *Einführung in die Metaphysik*, Freiburg Lecture of Summer Semester 1935, GA 40, ed. P. Jaeger (Frankfurt am Main: Vittorio Klostermann, 1983), 127–131. {TN: *Introduction to Metaphysics*, trans. Richard Polt and Gregory Fried (New Haven, CT: Yale University Press, 2000), 176–183.}

[2] "Vom Wesen des Grundes," *Wegmarken*, GA 9, 123–175. {TN: "On the Essence of Ground," *Pathmarks*, 97–135.}

[3] *Reden und andere Zeugnisse eines Lebensweges 1910–1976* [*Discourses and other Testimonies of a Course of Life 1910–1976*], GA 16, ed. Hermann Heidegger (Frankfurt am Main: Vittorio Klostermann, 2000), 66.

55. On *What is Metaphysics?* The Nothing

The misinterpretation by *What is Metaphysics? – the nothing.*
1. for itself – in place of a being – therefore the passage and essencing of beyng
2. the singular – instead of only *a* passage – from the standpoint of the sciences
3. the highest and the final word of philosophy in general – against which only the point of entry
4. as "nihilism" – instead of as the metaphysical step toward the overcoming of nihilism, which itself equals an overcoming of *metaphysics.*

[61] Accordingly – "anxiety" – singular fundamental attunement, accordingly – "logic" – simply against the *irrational* – without insight into logic's provenance in "metaphysics."

On the whole, a realm not circumscribed in its essence, "*science.*" This is because it is placed under a standard and simultaneously used as a business operation and under and overestimated with a happy medium not found. That is why it is at once a strange step.

The anxiety about anxiety – the misconception of the nothing (not grasped as beyng); *one prefers to wallow in disgust about destruction and nihilation* – and to extensively count on the *accounts of one's own history; the Christian world* and *political heroism.*

56. *On the Essence of Ground:* Ground – Freedom – Truth – Beyng

Why the question concerning the essence of *ground*? Because we are seeking the "ground," not some particular ground for some particular being, but the ground for beings as such, that is, for *beingness*, that is, for *being*, the ground that being as such "demands" or rather "has" and "is" – *its truth.*

The *truth of beyng* is *creatively* questioned and nothing else. But it is still always questioned within its provenance in metaphysics and incessantly with the intention of making a still more original *question* about questioning, worthy of metaphysical thinking.

And this is done unavoidably from the standpoint of human beings: *Human being* and being. But the human being is not the "I" despite "being in every instance mine." But the human being is not the "subject" (because it is not certainty and objectivity and value).

But the human being is not anthropological (person – spirit – soul – body; animal rationale). But the human being is not *anthropomorphic* – unconditional subjectivity, rather *Da-sein*, but entangled in a metaphysical undergrowth.

*

[62] *The freedom to ground* essences from *thrownness* into the abyss. This *thrownness* is the *transfer* into the in-between. This being transferred is the *eventuating* of the clearing "of" beyng. Eventuating is (*event*); event is beyng.

Freedom is neither only freedom from, nor only freedom to, nor both at once. For, in this way freedom itself is not yet grasped in its essencing – in terms of something other than what it itself is capable of being.

Freedom essences from beyng. Beyng eventuates the essencing. From freedom comes the directive to *regulatory order* [*Richte*].

The manifestness of the comportment toward beings "is" persistence in the clearing of beyng. Persistence is the continued existence of the thrownness into the abyss as the inception. Continued existence essences as the attunement [*Stimmung*] of what is in tune [*Gestimmtheit*], the one attuning being the voice [*Stimme*] (word) of beyng. Persistence comes from being transferred into the in-between of the abyss. Only *because of this* is a ground urgent. *Hence*, the *why* and any question, which belongs to what is question-worthy. This is because that which is worthy of question is beyng itself. How is beyng what is worthy of questioning so that questioning is here the highest appreciation (not valuation) and has no trace of intrusiveness and lust for power but is rather belongingness to the (event)?

57. "Ground" and "Truth"

The forking into the ontic – ontological – the differentiation; question concerning the "inner possibility" of this "forking" of "truth" as *unconcealment.* "*Ontological truth*" – the concept is unclear; compare this to the concept of "ontic truth."

Truth about beings as such is ontological truth. Here we are not concerned with the truth *of* beyng, but only with how the unveiling of beingness unfolds through categories. Beingness itself is already a definite clearing of beyng.

[63] The distinction between ontic and ontological is obsolete, founded upon the difference that indeed levels out everything into "two

worlds" and "differentiates" neither of the two adequately – neither beings as such nor being as such. It is also already implied that the differentiation between ontic and ontological is plurivocal.

Remaining stuck in "transcendence" is a lapse into *metaphysics* despite the more original interpretation from the standpoint of Dasein.

Transcendence as *being-in-the-world*; more precisely as its *enabling* ("world").

The blind alley of the question concerning inner possibility (cf. *Kant-book*)[1] – what is already established in it and where at all have we gained ground, and what is reachable?

The "factical" as the guiding thread! But there is indeed no fact.

Inner possibility of the forking of truth is restored to the transcendence *of Dasein* – ("differentiation" as "transcendence") – and *Da-sein*?

Here we do not yet have the decisive rotation [*Drehung*] in beyng and the truth of beyng, because we are stuck in the question of possibility and then *gradually advancing* toward what lies further below. This rotation [*Drehung*] is no mere reversal, but a completely different inception, which must take leave of everything hitherto existing, that is metaphysics as such.

Freedom as transcendence – *but freedom more essentially emerges from the essencing of beyng as (event) – freedom as having being eventuated in the event.* The truth of beyng – clearing of its essencing happens only where it is eventuated [*er-eignet*] from the event into freedom and its essence. Only where there is "freedom" there the truth of beyng is capable of being grounded. Only where there is the abyss, there we have the urgency of the grounding. However, here all "metaphysics" and the "differentiation" is abandoned.

[64] 58. Projection and Eventuation [*Er-eignung*]

Only from thrownness and in thrownness does the *throwing* essence. *Throwing* – throwing oneself (who?) away into the essencing of the truth of beyng – "oneself" – *the historical human being who is defined* by metaphysics. Pro-jection and *freedom – freedom and beyng.*

---

[1] *Kant und das Problem der Metaphysik*, GA 3, 116f. {TN: *Kant and the Problem of Metaphysics*, 82f.}

59. "Ground"

What is "ground" and from where does "ground" come? *grande principium* – the pre-eminent *fundamental* principle of sufficient reason? Ground – where there are beings, where there is being, where there is truth – for what reason? Of what nature is beyng (truth of beyng and beyng of truth), that *grounding* belongs to it? What is understood here under grounding? Assuming the relinquishing of ground and grounding?, of the why?, of ἀρχή – departure and domination. ὑποκείμενον – ratio – reor – estimation – showing something as something and determining it *on that basis* and *through it* – placing it into presence in its what.

60. "Grund"

φύσις – λόγος – and *"ground"* – ὑποκείμενον – ἀρχή – αἴτιον, cf. Aristotle, Physics, B. 1.

Ground – because it is an abyssal ground – clearing – as the essence of beyng (event)

Abyss as the essential refusal (eventuation [*Er-eignung*]) of the fundamental – non-ground – the *groundless* – where the ground is supposed to be – semblance of a ground – appearing in such a way as.

Ground[1]

[65] 61. On the Essence of Ground

The truth about beings as such – the truth about the beingness of beings (overcoming of modern metaphysics, "beings").

Ontic-ontological truth – a being of the being that is not looked at (overlooked), a being of the being *that is of concern.*

But not *the truth of beyng* – this truth is what is meant and, on its basis, all further steps; but this is still meant in the sense of a superelevation of the a priori and of transcendence.

Instead: The active grounding of the abyss from the experience of being itself – *the extreme nearness to the refusal* (the nearness itself as what is nearest).

---

[1] Etymologically cf. *Zeitschrift für vergleichende Sprachwissenschaften* [*The Journal for Comparative Linguistics*] 51(1923): 18.

The role of attunement – *being in tune* – as being (persistently) placed into the truth of beyng.

Cf. *On the Essence of Ground*:[1] the *differentiation* as *unity* of being and beings, i.e. beings as such, thus *truth* – which one?

Step toward transcendence inadequate/by contrast![2]

Intention: The essence of ground from the essence of *transcendence* – the latter? *metaphysical* – *understanding of being*, although not the subject (understanding of being and event).

What is the reason for the *question* concerning what is "ground-like?" How the abyss? In what sense? Firstly, the un-grounding of the truth of beings as such, hence the truth of *beyng* is the abyss. Beyng – *is that which essences* – but is not to be founded upon beings. For beyng (from the standpoint of beings!) *what is essential is* the *abyss*, it is itself the *abyss* – only from the standpoint of beings or in itself? Primarily the latter, because it *urges into the grounding* (Event). Abyss – not *lack*.

"Ground" as *"clearing"* (but not "transcendence" – the latter *metaphysical*, i.e., based on the standpoint of beings, even if not "subjective," but based on *Da-sein*).

[66] Event – propriation – to its own (by itself) *self* – selfhood and Da-sein.

"Fact" of Da-sein; *eventuated* [*Er-eignet*] – as thrownness.

Da-sein as essence of the "will" [*Wille*], i.e., being a *self*; and therefore first "for-the sake-of" [*umwillen*]. Da-sein ex-sists for the sake of [*um-willen*] itself, *insofar as it* is the grounding of the truth of beyng, i.e., eventuated [*er-eignet*].

The interpretation of ἀγαθόν is inadequate to the extent that the essential destruction of ἀλήθεια happens in it.

Freedom as the *ground* of possibility – this ground as *abyss*. This means: We can no longer think in terms of the sequence of steps of the *usual* question of essence (condition of possibility, cf. above 14. The Question of Possibility as the Mode of the Question of Essence, pp. 21–22ff.), but we must begin differently. From where – from the *truth of beyng* (*refusal* – one that essences – secret. The human being *as Da-sein*)

Freedom as ek-sistent – and ek-sistent, because of *thrownness*. (cf. the appendix to *On the Essence of Ground*).[3]

The letting-be as the persistent support of the grounding of the clearing of beyng to which we are transferred.

[1] "Vom Wesen des Grundes," *Wegmarken*, GA 9, 133f. {TN: "On the Essence of Ground," *Pathmarks*, 105f.}

[2] Ibid., 156f. {TN: Ibid., 121f.}

[3] Ibid., 162. {TN: Ibid., 125}

62. The Differentiation

"The Difference" –
1. falsely as the *justification* for the interpretation of truth as forked
2. falsely as the *point of departure* for questioning back to the ground of its *possibility* – transcendence
3. Truth – not from the Leibnizian standpoint and thus also not in this manner "connection" with the "ground"

[67] 63. Metaphysics and the Differentiation

The differentiation, taken for itself and left groundless without abyss, is already the destruction of the truth of beyng, so little is it ever specifically grounded.

The history of the differentiation is the history of the *un-grounding* of truth and its essence as the truth of beyng.[a]

The talk of the differentiation first needing to be grounded is ambiguous; it could mean that metaphysics ultimately only consolidates itself. Yet, what it means is that beyng, which is already misunderstood in the differentiation, is to be grounded in its truth. This implies that *we just give up on the differentiation*, which is to give up on the groundless ground of metaphysics, from the insight that the differentiation coincides with the thought of the guiding thread of the question of enabling (cf. there).

The differentiation first comes from the *parting* (departure).

64. Metaphysics

as the abuse of the differentiation, as the abuse of what is ungrounded, to the point of being consumed by the futile flight from it through its complete inversion (abolition of the true *and* the apparent world as the unleashing of pure power).

The differentiation as such is already metaphysical and its inner παραδείγματα – character is *being* – as παράδειγμα, as ground, as condition, as the *true* – "norm" – "law."

This is already an *essential suspension* of the still inceptual ἀλήθεια-*character* – beginning of the destruction of the hardly essencing ἀλήθεια.

---

[a] Staying away of beyng itself

The differentiation as the ungrounded and unconceptualized *clearing* which is irremediably out of joint and therefore *the overcoming of the differentiation – thus* determines the proper overcoming of metaphysics belonging to the history of beyng.

[68] That *the differentiation* between beings and being is already the source of the unsettling and destruction of ἀλήθεια, i.e., the manner in which the differentiation is grasped (a priori) and skipped over.

The path to its *grounding* (the essence of the ground) is not yet inceptual enough, but in danger of regressing into a *metaphysics of metaphysics*! (cf. above 22. The Overcoming of "Metaphysics," *Kant-book*,[1] *On the Essence of Ground*).[2]

A grounding of the *differentiation* recognizes this and consolidates the questioning in the direction of the basic position of metaphysics.

The paradigmatic character (ἰδέα) of being and the origin of the differentiation in the sense of the leveling into two "*worlds*."

And *On the Essence of Ground*:[3] The essence of truth is determined as forked on the basis of the difference as a fixed mark – instead we do the reverse and overcome the "differentiation" as such (into the *difference*) through the essencing of the truth of beyng.

---

[1] *Kant und das Problem der Metaphysik.* GA 3, 230f. {TN: *Kant and the Problem of Metaphysics*, 162f.}

[2] "Vom Wesen des Grundes." Wegmarken, GA 9, 133f. {TN: "On the Essence of Ground, *Pathmarks*, 105f.}

[3] Ibid., 134. {TN: Ibid., 106.}

The Overcoming of Metaphysics

I. Sequel

I. THE DIFFERENTIATION

(cf. Summer Semester 1935[1], II. Trimester 1940[2])

[73] **65. The Differentiation[1]**
The Differentiation and the Origin of its Formulations in the Question
of Essence (Question of Enabling)

The word taken plainly, especially to begin with, means: the differentiation between beings and being. However, it merely indicates that differentiation, which is employed thoughtlessly, unnoticed and ungrounded, prior to anything in the realm of the thought that is metaphysical in nature and grounded in metaphysics, but left in darkness with regard to its birth. If metaphysical thought does not invent anything, but only discovers, what this attests is that in the differentiation the difference is of the "essence." Wherever a being itself is "experienced," and this means always already, even if in various modes of explicitness, *as such and such a being* and stands in the open, it is always projected upon being (illuminated). What remains hidden in all this is that being is thrown. It is itself the throw that opens. The differentiatedness (of beings and being) is already eventuated in all metaphysics, even though the difference is neither elaborated as a topic nor grounded nor capable of being grounded. Otherwise, the aspect according to which what is differentiated is differentiated would have to be named, if not also grounded. In this differentiation, which is unelaborated, only put to use and abandoned to its hardly noticed obscurity, being is meant as beingness (κοινόν, γένος). Beingness

---

[1] *Einführung in die Metaphysik*, GA 40, 33ff. {TN: *Introduction to Metaphysics*, 45ff.}
[2] *Nietzsche: Der europäische Nihilismus*, GA 48, 279ff. {TN: See footnote 2 to section 30.}
[1] The Overcoming of Metaphysics. II. Sequel, cf. below, 117ff.]

is however meant as the enabling of beings: cause. In fact, being is represented as ὄντως ὄν – once again a being. This happens with the elevation of being to what is properly a being and the simultaneous demotion of beings to what are not properly a being and yet meant to be taken as a being (μὴ ὄν). Why is this so at the beginning of metaphysics? Being is a supplement and a generality and finally only a mist and appearance; even if it is also initially inflated into the being that is fullest in being.

[74] The differentiation is grasped as "the" differentiation for the first time in *Being and Time* and communicated as "ontological difference." In *On the Essence of Ground* it is introduced and in fact taken as the basis for a completely different question that is alien to any kind of metaphysics. This question creatively questions the "sense of being," i.e., the essencing of the truth of beyng, which is the truth belonging to beyng itself. But in this way, the "differentiation" still remains decisive and can thus manifest into a hesitation about overcoming metaphysics.

Our attempt to think the differentiation and that means, to first represent what is differentiated, beings and being, results in a dilemma and a disaster. The *dilemma* consists in the fact that being remains unrepresentable, if by representation we mean forming an image and having something effectively before ourselves as a being. Being is then to be encountered as some kind of thing that is available. From one side, this differentiation caves, so to speak, into emptiness. Only the side of beings remains, namely, some specifically intended being: this mountain, that tree, this human being.

The disaster consists in the fact that right from the outset, already from the intention to re-present, being is put on the same level as beings. So, before it is carried out and in carrying it out, the differentiation is already given up. What is evident here to a dogged reflection is only this: The differentiation is simply not possible if a representation of that which is differentiated dominates the differentiation through and through. Is this because the act of differentiating is in accord with the nature of representing or is it because of that which is supposed to be captured here in a difference? It is due to both because both belong together. That the differentiatedness of beings from being becomes the foundation despite this, certainly without any reflection or questioning, and is granted validity as something that is decided in advance, is the nature of all metaphysics.

But if we reflect, without flinching, upon the dilemma and disaster which confront us here, they become the impetus for an essential question: Is being, [75] which is distinguished by contrast to beings, to be grasped in itself at all and if so, how? If yes, what results from this for the differentiation? *Being* – now was it just a stream of words, yet, always something more, even something unique, incomparable?

Naming – explicating and simultaneously the revocation of the differentiation in the sense of a reification of a difference; essentially here we have the unrepresentability of being; the collapse, the transformation into the in-between and from this the persistence of Da-sein; *Da-sein itself* as that which is eventuated [*er-eignetes*]. To pre-pare to name the differentiation through words from the first inception. (In *On the Essence of Ground*, the *transcendence* of Da-sein is shown to be the root of the differentiation.)

But the question: 1. Whether differentiation is at all a possible approach and not already a misinterpretation and also the entrenchment that follows from it.

2. Whether reflection must not rather endeavor to name the "differentiation" but also instantly *concede* to its insidiousness (cf. II. Sequel), and that means to put metaphysics into question as the truth-structure [*Wahrheitsgefüge*] of beings as such taken as a whole.

66. The Differentiation
(and the Question concerning the Nothing)

is inevitable and yet inadequate because it does not allow beings and beyng to come into their own.

Can those which are so separated, which were also never ever separable, because they were never one, ever be brought into the closest of relationships, even if it is only to tie together those which are so unconnected?

In what aspect would they remain united then and could it ever be creatively thought? And yet, we are able to handle the difference. Or is this all a semblance? Are we only aided by the pretence that even beyng is actually only a kind of being?

[76] The differentiation still demands a com-parision – and from what standpoint does one accomplish the equation and how does one equalize? In such a way that we turn being into a being and indeed even validate this procedure by explaining all beings on the basis of the highest being – the ultimate cause.

The nothing is, in terms of scholastic ontology, not only the other of a species; the indicator of another species within the realm of beings, but also generally remains differentiated in relation to *beings*.

67. The Differentiation
(Beyng is the Nothing) (cf. "Guiding Words")

Beyng and nothing are as little to be arrived at through a diminution of beings. Re-presenting and calculating are always only sufficient for beings, which remain the same in relation to being, whether they are endlessly large or endlessly small.

But this is also true when differentiating something "infinite" (namely, beings) from the finite. One may very well speak of an infinite difference (Pascal) here. One still remains with the same – namely with beings – and is still not able to arrive at "being."

Already the talk of the difference and the differentiation wears too thin and wrenches even being into the realm of beings.

And everything becomes tangled and obfuscated once more when we consider that beyng alone *is* and a being only arises and ceases to exist within being.

68. Being and Beings
Metaphysics – the Differentiation

A simple piece of evidence from the classics for being and beings being thrown together in the discourse of metaphysics: "Monas est un mot [77] Grec, qui signifie l'Unité, ou ce qui est un."[1] "Monad is a Greek word that signifies unity or that which is one."

But monad is the Leibnizian name for "substance" in the sense of a simple substance. But even this name means: Beingness (substantiality) and one that is in each case a being. Leibniz, speaking simply of "ou" – "or," points to the fact that the differentiation between being and beings is indeed fully accomplished but is of no consequence *because*: Being is always beingness *of* beings, is a being in general, where "in

---

[1] G. W. Leibniz, "Principes de la Nature et de la Grace, fondés en raison" in *Die philosophische Schriften von G. W. Leibniz*, Vol. VI, ed. C. I. Gerhardt (Berlin: Weidmannsche Buchhandung, 1890), 598, n. 1. {TN: Translated into English as "Principles of Nature and Grace, Based on Reason," in *G. W. Leibniz: Philosophical Essays*, ed. and trans. Roger Ariew and Daniel Garber (Indianapolis and Cambridge: Hackett Publishing Company, 1989), 207.}

general" is clear and belongs to beings.

69. Differentiation and Event

In the differentiation, i.e., in all metaphysics, being stands to *one* side and in this way already turns into what is dependent and finally a supplement to beings.

But, as the event (of the difference), beyng first lets beings separate out from one another and so "move into" the clearing; but what is borne out in this way is what is borne out [*Aus-trag*] into being *as* God and man, as world and earth.

And what is borne out in this way is not how something human originating from the μεχανή might appear, namely, as πόλεμος. It is rather the event [*Er-eignis*] and "only" this. But the "only" here does not mean a restriction, but the preservation of the innermost dignity of essence.

[78] 70. Differentiating Being from Beings and the Distinctness of the Two

One may say that they are infinitely distinct – distinguished by an abyss – separated from each other by an abyss, which is beyng itself.

And yet: the being *of* beings: beings *in* their being.

71. The Differentiation and What is Borne Out

From what we (inadequately) call the differentiation, metaphysics projects the beingness of beings without grounding it. From this beingness the essence of being is determined metaphysically – the a priori, the supplement, the precedence of beings and all of this is still the essencing of what is corrupted in the essence of beyng. (Corrupted essence here is the essencing of beyng while withholding its truth.)

So being stands differentiated in some manner (Idea – Idealism) from beings ("ideas," "values," "order").

Different in the other inception: What is borne out is itself the abyss of the in-between as the essencing of beyng.

Indeed, even here one can yet again completely distinguish beings from being due to being habituated into metaphysics. Yet, this is possible only by virtue of the alienation of all experience into the dominance of beings, in contrast to which being is always just leftover waste.

72. Metaphysics
("Being" – an Empty Word)

We escape what supposedly exists or what really exists in all metaphysics, namely, the emptiness of being, through the flight into the fullness and [79] manifoldness of "categorial" relations, stages, levels, and regions.

But the *essence* of beyng is not determined in this way. Rather the emptiness is presupposed and replenished with that which is not creatively questioned from the essence of being but calculated with the aid of the beingness already decided.

73. The Differentiation

proceeds from the most preliminary and far-reaching indefiniteness. To creatively and questioningly experience what is meant by the "differentiation" originally, properly and inceptually, in terms of something else.

By thinking it from the standpoint of metaphysics and in its juncture, we take the "differentiation" to the footbridge that should take us the quickest to the other shore.

But we must move away from the river altogether and seek land completely elsewhere.

Thus, the footbridge is a seduction and yet a final sign of a turn around and turn away from the differentiation in general and what is differentiated.

How is it then with the question of being?

*

Being from the standpoint of beings –
Differentiation
according to the "truth" of beings and
the "truth" – from beyng
being and truth/human being – measure/
The *same* –
The differentiation.

[80] 74. Being and Beyng

Being as beingness – here being is re-presented; is it so?

Yes, one actually means ab-stracted; taken out, detached from beings, namely as the most general. But how do we get to it if something that remains the same does not exist here, and what "is" this?

Beings keep claiming to be the standard for being and its determination. In the end, this goes to such an extreme, that beings tolerate being only as the most dilute dilution and evaporation of themselves.

*

The differentiation as what is borne out
what is borne out as the in-between
the in-between as the abyss
the abyss and the inception.

The "differentiation," what is thus named and meant, shatters.

*

Of what event-like essence is *being*? – what appeared at the time as differentiatedness, sameness and so forth and would come to be called the "most general" and the "*most formal.*"

How is it the case that in the apparent "emptiness" – the fullness and gathering of the establishment of the abyss.

"Difference." (The event of differentiation and its being borne out)

75. The Differentiation – What is Borne Out

First of all, what is the basis of what is borne out in this way between being and beings, who or what bears them apart?

[81] As beyng, being is what is borne out [*Aus-trag*], the clearing, from whose openness there arises a solemn bearing [*Getragenheit*] toward beings and a bearing [*Tragen*] of beings. Beyng brings beings to bear [*Tragen*] and bears [*trägt*] them forth into their "essencing."

What is borne out [*Aus-trag*] *is* ambiguous: 1. Superficially, in the sense of the differentiation (διαφέρειν), this is however not "logical" and not to be taken as an act.
2. from the essence of beyng as event)
3. as *the* appropriate [*ge-eignete*] persistent relation to beyng.

76. The Differentiation

and the "as such"   τὸ τί/   essentia (possibility)
the as a whole   τὸ ὅτι/   existentia
  Being *infinitely varied* (difference, Inter (in-between)/parting) from beings.

*

The *differentiation* of being from beings
what is borne out
persistence in it ————————— Being
attuned through voice ⟋
neither "rational" nor "irrational"
truth of being
belongs to *being* itself
Differentiation is not an "act," but the happening of a history and this history is "of" beyng itself (Da-sein – Being). "Metaphysics" is grounded on *what is borne out in this ungrounded manner*, without any cognition of it; *projection of being* – thrown – practice from persistence (Da-sein).

*

[82] *From where* does the differentiation come? When φύσις – ἀλήθεια become *ἰδέα*.
  Grounded in what?
  Which truth?
  The ungrounded ground itself of metaphysics–
  Whether *metaphysics* can *itself* be commensurate to its essence! And not rather the proper beginning of the destruction of the truth of beyng.
  Being from beings and going back to beings – being – the general – the supplement and for this reason *a priori*.
  Difference – as *the consolidation of the realm* of the question of enabling. The futile flight from it! Nietzsche!
  This question as the question concerning letting-appear –
  to differentiate εἶδος and thus the "good" from the one who is endowed with goods.
  But for the launch of the question concerning enabling, beings as such are already placed into truth –
  how and for what reason – φύσις – ἀλήθεια

Yet the *differentiation* as such must first intermittently be called out along with the fact that it veils what is the most question-worthy.

To begin with, blindly – thoughtlessly, indeterminately what against what? From where – whereto? Into which realm?

[83] II. ON THE CONCEPT OF METAPHYSICS

(differentiated from the thinking responsive to the history of beyng)

"A priori" – "Art" – "Theology"

[85] 77. Metaphysics and the Thinking Responsive to
the History of Beyng

It is one thing to metaphysically mislay being, as beingness, into a being fullest in being (τιμιώτατον ὄν). It is another thing to experience beyng from the essencing of its truth as "the fullest in being" *in the* sense that it is simply not "a" being and also neither the highest nor "the" absolute.

Going from one to the other is not a "transition" of the kind where the metaphysical question could *itself* unfold into another. However, the thinking that is responsive to the history of beyng also does not constitute itself as an opinion of a particular kind. It arises from the history of beyng and more particularly from the epoch of the abandonment of beings by being.

78. The Overcoming of "Metaphysics"

is only possible when it proceeds from metaphysics and from reflecting upon it in its ground in the history of its essence, and to begin with, under the name "metaphysics."

The necessity of the overcoming arises from the history of beyng. It arises from the completely hidden urgency of the abandonment of beings by being brought on by the truth of beyng. This hidden urgency announces itself as the human being's forgottenness of being at the end of the age of metaphysics and it can be made familiar to us for the first time only through the necessity of an original question of being (concerning the "sense of being").

Neither a "betterment" of "philosophy" nor a "satisfaction" of emotional needs is what is definitive [*Be-stimmend*] here, but only the hardly audible voice [*Stimme*] of being.

The overcoming of metaphysics and the liberation of the first inception into its inceptual nature. The tranquillity of the long decision.

About the *"concept" of metaphysics* and the *inner unity* of the [86] five-fold essence of metaphysics (cf. *Nietzsche's Metaphysics, the Final Presentation*)[1]

79. The Transition of Metaphysics within the History of Beyng into the Other Inception of the Truth of Beyng

In a completely superficial way, this transition can be shown from a still unclarified and ambiguous relation of current humanity to being.

The *relation to the possible* as the relation to what is to come and thus the veiled relation within history to the history (of beyng) itself.

The "sense" for the possible can be:

1. *The anticipation of a possible actuality*, consequently the planning and ordering of beings in the direction along which it will only be pushed further by the being (manipulation) that has been long decided and thrust into the unconditional.

2. *The active fore-boding of the actual possibility*, consequently the reservedness in being attuned by the arriving that essences, which is what beyng itself is in its original truth.

The two are separated by an abyss and the transition [from one to the other] is the leaping-over this abyss. The ambiguity of the transitional age itself becomes unconditional. That is the reason why there is no agreement and no understanding here, but also no "antagonism" anymore. Antagonism is mislaid to the level, pushed entirely to the fringes, of some kind of competition amongst "world-views" and could very well be decided there.

The thinking responsive to the history of beyng is no "world-view" and for that reason and it can also never turn into one by entering into an antagonism. At no point is it is possible to be "indifferent" to this

---

[1] *Nietzsches Metaphysik*. GA 50 {TN: Published as 1. *Nietzsches Metaphysik* 2. *Einleitung in die Metaphysik: Denken und Dichten*, GA 50 ed. Petra Jaeger (Frankfurt am Main: Vittorio Klostermann, 1990), 3–82, the text of *Nietzsches Metaphysik* in GA 50 is similar for the most part, with minor differences, to GA 6.2 part VI, *Nietzsches Metaphysik*, 257–333. Translated into English as "Nietzsche's Metaphysics," in *Nietzsche III*, trans Joan Stambaugh, Frank Capuzzi, and David Farrell Krell, ed. David Farrell Krell (San Francisco: HarperOne, 1991), 185–255.}

thinking. Rather the urgency of the abandonment of beings by being "only" urges us into its abyssal other.

[87] Inversely, for the world-view of the modernity that is consummating itself, the thinking that is responsive to the history of beyng and any sort of reflection related to it must remain a nullity, something that is at most still in the service of annihilation.

80. The A priori

We arrive at the interpretation of being (οὐσία) as a priori because φύσις has become ἰδέα, because being has become presence and because the latter has likewise become the *soul* from *having been perceived* through perceiving.

Indeed the a priori character shows that being is no more and will henceforth never at all be interrogated in all of metaphysics, that is to say, will never at all be creatively questioned from itself and back into itself. – The a priori denies being its own essencing back into itself. A priori and the *mathematical* and – μάθημα and ψυχή. The a priori – essentially related to soul, spirit, reason, consciousness.

81. Metaphysics and the A priori

Cf. the development of οὐσία as πρῶτον – διανοούμενον (Theaetetus 185a8–9),* τοῦτο γὰρ μάλιστα ἐπὶ πάντων παρέπεται (ibid., 186a2–3)*

The *a priori* is the determination of *being* as such, of its essencing.

Being is that which *properly comes to presence*, because it is *presence* (and as presence it is disclosure), i.e., φύσις.

The meaning of the a priori changes, however, in accordance with the interpretation of being in each case.

Already decided by the interpretation of being as ἰδέα, the a priori is at once related to *enabling*. It is then related to the enabling of what is certain, of what is assured [*Sichergestellt*], of what is re-presented [*Vorgestellt*] and objective, *in this manner [it is] what is re-presented and*

---

* {TN: in the first place – object of thought.}
* {TN: That, above all, is something that accompanies everything; *Plato, Complete Works*, ed. John Cooper (Indianapolis: Hackett Publishing Company, 1997), 205.}

what is to be represented from the very outset, but in this way everywhere already πρὸς ἡμᾶς.*

[88] To what extent ("is") being (not perhaps "in itself"), but what is prior as such? and indeed prior to all beings as such? Not just in the region of representing.

(The differentiation into "*objective*" and "subjective" a priori is completely misleading because even the "objective," and precisely the "objective," is "subjective.")

82. The "A priori" – Character of "Being" (cf. Basic Words)

A priori – the very first, in that regard only the nothing – but that which belongs to beingness – where is the limit? If so, is not the all-determining "a priori," in the broad sense of the always antecedent, always preceding, something provisional?

Certainly – equivalently even the "differentiation" and the difference between "ontic" and "ontological" and what is boosted with it, the "*pre-ontological.*"

With the "a priori" – cf., for example, the authoritative exposition in Plato's *Theaetetus* 184ff. – being itself is οὐσία on the way toward ὄντως οὖσα – but in the sense of οὐσία as *presence*, what *first* comes into presence (even with this: *Being* is – but in some particular truth).

A priori as the veiling of the essence of being.

83. Metaphysics and the Differentiation

How the whole is divided or just differentiated into the supersensible and the sensible world; to what extent the sensible becomes the leading criterion for the differentiation: the sensible as the physical; the "physical" and the "meta-physical?"

Howsoever much the differentiation into being and beings appears to coincide with the above differentiation, truly speaking however, it does not coincide. This is because in the ambiguity of the ὄντως ὄν νοητόν (ἀγαθόν), of the ens entium, [89] Deus as summum bonum and spiritus; as ens rationis and category and idea, ungrounded being turns into a being, but more precisely into the supersensible.

---

* {TN: relative to us.}

Thus, the differentiation correctly grasped, which thinks from the truth of beyng, relegates the supersensible and the sensible, as particular formulations, entirely to the status of beings and is simply not to be compared to the metaphysical differentiation.

84. Metaphysics

begins with Socrates insofar as we mean metaphysics in the narrow sense as the establishment of the truth about beings and not as a phase in the history of beyng.

With the evolved "doctrine of ideas," Plato created the instrument for all metaphysics; the real creator, however, is Socrates.

We indeed believe that Socrates brought philosophy from heaven to earth and turned it against metaphysics in order to "care" for the human being alone.

This opinion is erroneous on two counts.

For one, there was still no metaphysics before Socrates; the thought of Heraclitus and Parmenides is "physics" in the sense of a creative thinking of the essence of φύσις as that of the being of beings. But this "physics" is neither what we have today nor the ontology of the φύσει ὄντα in the sense of Aristotle, nor in any way "the philosophy of nature" because there is no "philosophy" and no "nature."

Secondly, the turn toward the human being is, however, precisely the precondition for all metaphysics. Prior to this, the human being, as in any inceptual (i.e., non-metaphysical) philosophy, was inessential and not more essential than the gods, who remained out of consideration. Socrates makes it his business to strive after the good and with this metaphysics is first posited; (Nietzsche's interpretation of the essence of metaphysics strikes us as decisive and yet it is not of the essence on account of the valuative thought that is at play there).

Now all "anthropology" and "existential philosophy" has a free [90] hand and Christianity can usurp philosophy (Pascal) and simultaneously bring it to its doom. One can, with the possession of the eternal truth, now play with everything. One day, everyone will see that *Being and Time* aims at abolishing the human being and its priority in philosophy and appreciating beyng alone in its essencing. Everyone will see that not only subjectivity but also that the role of the human being is shaken up with *Da-sein*. How else should the abolition of the human being be brought to fruition than by traversing through its essence. However, in so doing, the essence is from the very first step determined from the relation to being (understanding of being).

All "faith" is grounded in the knowledge of being. "Faith" as the root of blindness. How "faith" occasionally chooses "reason" as its pseudo-adversary without ever being able and wanting to reflect on the essence and the provenance of this essence of reason (ratio – λόγος – νοῦς).

85. "Metaphysics"

The ambiguity in the determination of the being of beings extends across all of metaphysics, since Plato's ἰδέα τοῦ αγαθοῦ; being is δύναμις in the sense of what enables something to appear and in the sense of what causes beings to emerge.

The same recurs in Aristotle: ὄν ᾗ ὄν as καθόλου ὑπάρχοντα and as τιμιώτατον ὄν – θεῖον.

All questioning concerning the being of beings is a questioning concerning the κοινότατον and the θεῖον, that is to say, *theory of categories and theology* – both are respectively misconstrued – even in Nietzsche. The ground for this "essence" of metaphysics lies in its essential beginning itself; the truth of being and the interpretation of being and the essence of truth as that which grounds in being remains unquestioned. That is the reason why "beings" must one day race away beyond being.

"Metaphysics" – the thought "natural" to it: all beings must [91] emerge from an exalted and most elevated being. In what does the "naturalness" of this thought have its ground? Beings are what come to presence and, in this way, they *emerge* and emerge *from*.

The most intimate engagement with beings is familiar with the production of such beings. Thus, emergence is misrepresented as a first pro-duction (δημιουργός).

The "naturalness" of this thought is grounded:
1. in the unquestioned interpretation of being as presence,
2. in the uninterrogated invocation of production (τέχνη as knowing one's way around in it) as the mode of making plain, unveiling, and ex-plaining beings.

In both, the interpretation and the invocation, there reigns the groundlessness of the already befallen decision about being; being is skipped over in this formidable but groundless and hence natural invocation. The predominance and the power of beings, as that which is available, is already conceded at the dawn of metaphysics.

86. Being Conscious and Being
(Modern Metaphysics)

From the standpoint of German Idealism, we can say: Being [*Sein*] is being conscious [*Bewußtsein*]. In *being* conscious [Bewußt-*sein*] alone "being" [*Sein*] is already claimed, despite all reference to consciousness and knowledge (i.e., re-presentedness in the sense of "thinking" – representing something as something). For this reason, there also remains no possibility of inverting this proposition (*being conscious* is the essence of being), and to say, being is the essence of being-conscious and the latter is only a "mode" of being that is still ungrounded. For, in this way, everything dissipates into the same groundlessness and lack of questioning [*Fraglosigkeit*] in relation to being. Not to mention the fact that "inversions" simply never free us from anything.

In the concept of "being"-conscious we find the [92] interpretation hitherto of being as ἰδέα, i.e., presence, which has never been reflected upon. Being-conscious: having-before itself as that which comes to presence and so the having-before-itself as itself that which comes to presence, that is to say, it is "confirmed" as that which is co-present – before the claim to presence.

87. Metaphysics and "Theology"

All metaphysics is "theological" (that is to say, it derives beings from a highest being as the first cause). For this reason, the transcendental idea has to play an extraordinary role in coupling the transcendental analytic and dialectic in Kant's *Critique of Pure Reason*.

All metaphysics is theological in the way that it gives itself over to the God of calculation and explanation. For this reason, metaphysics is never capable of even just *facing up to* a decision about God, to say nothing of coming to a decision.

The attempt to make place for "faith" (Kant) is only the ultimate entanglement in metaphysics and its groundlessness.

88. The Relation to Being within the History supported by Metaphysics

The relation to being and being itself are not known. Only beings are and even the "are" and "being" are skipped over.

Being is known as the most universal (beingness). But the "relation" is not heeded.

Being and the relation to it are acknowledged, that is to say, asserted as such and thus already interpreted – ("e.g.," Plato grasps it as ἰδέα and calls it ψυχή). Everything about metaphysics is thus decided.

Being and the relation to it are interrogated as such on the basis of the ground of their essence. It is thereby shown that the truth about [93] beings is not adequate even simply to pose this question. Rather, this truth leaves us with only one possibility: that of interrogating the relation to being by analogy with the relation to beings on the basis of the conditions by which beings are enabled.

Being is not determined on the basis of the human being's relation to it, just as though "the human being" and "the human" were *already* decided without this relation or even by it. Being becomes worthy of question when it remains a question as to whether the talk of relation could ever come close to its essence. Could it not be the case that the nature of this relation along with the essence of the human being has been decided on the basis of being and in such a way that this decision and its realm belong to the essence of being?

With this, the claim made by being and its essence is no longer misrepresented by the distortion of beyng into a "relation to the human being," as if this relation were such that it could be understood on its own or were produced by the human being insofar as it possesses a "consciousness."

89. "Metaphysics" and the Thinking of Beyng

In the age of the consummation of metaphysics, being is unleashed into the corrupted essence of manipulation. The corrupted essence calls itself the will to power. This will is the essence of power, which finds it "urgent" to veil the essence.

Being, in the veiling of its essence by power, which pretends to be the salvation and the welfare of all, maintains and reinforces the opinion that the only relation to being (by which is meant "a being" as that which is actual) is "property" – having and the management of the

having, i.e., the organization of the unconditional usurping of everything for everyone in the same way.

How should even a foreboding dawn here that it is not just not-having,
indeed not just renouncing but only a return to the abandonment that
will become commensurate to the distance of beyng as refusal, that is to
say, *keep its distance* from the refusal? The distance to beyng.

[94] 90. Metaphysics as Theology

θεός, θεῖον – the name for the highest being; A being, however, means
that which comes to presence, that which is produced; θεῖον, the "first"
being – the primordial being [*Ur-Seiende*], the cause [*Ur-sache*], a being
which conditions all beings in their being.

How it is that the Christian thought of creation inserts itself into
the interpretation of beings in terms of the trained and the demiurgic
(manually producing – εἶδος – ὕλη) and this is then transferred to beingness as subjectivity.

How this subjectivity appears as unconditional subjectivity in the
sense of the *absolute* and thus constitutes the *primordial* and *all-encompassing actuality*. (cf. the Schelling lecture,[1] *Mindfulness*[2])

91. Metaphysics and Modern Humanity

Beings as such – in their objectification, "technology" in the essential
sense.

Beings as a whole – in their dominance, in the sense *of the mastery
founded on power*.

Being (that reigns here) is manipulation as the consummation of the
essence of power.

The human being in the midst of beings is the perpetuation of the
unconditional forgetting of being.

Aim-lessness as the fundamental condition of the changing and
the continual positing of "aims" and their disconnectedness from the
matter at hand.

---

[1] Schelling, *Vom Wesen der menschlichen Freiheit* [Schelling, On the Essence of
Human Freedom], GA 42, 87f.
[2] *Besinnung*, GA 66, 108. Metaphysik, 372–375. {TN: *Mindfulness*, 108.
Metaphysics, 330–333.}

The deification of "dynamism" is only the consequence of this humanity, which appears to dominate and yet must recognize what it can never know.

[95] *Descartes to Picot* (Opp. ed. Ad. et Ta.) IX, 14.

"Ainsi toute la Philosophie est comme un arbre, dont les racines sont la Métaphysique, le tronc est la Physique, et les branches qui sortent de ce tronc sont toutes les autres sciences . . ."[1]

92. Metaphysics and "Theology"

Only within the realm of metaphysics and the transformations of its essence is the relation to "God" a "religious" one – a religio, a binding back to the first cause and control. The concept of religio is metaphysical, i.e., it takes its departure from a being that is bound back and connected to a highest being – the "fullest in being" because it is what causes. This "highest being" was called being and is called so even now in "existential philosophy."

This confusion begins with Plato and Aristotle the moment the question concerning beingness is explicitly posed in terms of the question concerning εἶδος and κοινόν and at the same time ἀγαθόν and δημιουργός and τὸ πρῶτον κινοῦν ἀκίνητον are posited. Since then, we have the intertwining of ὄν ᾗ ὄν and θεῖον – "ontology" and "theology" (cf. *Mindfulness*,[1] section on metaphysics and cf. *Contributions*[2]).

The temporarily used title "Ontochrony" (Interpretation of Hegel's *Phenomenology of Spirit* 1930/31)[3] is not simply put in the place of λόγος and θεός – χρόνος, rather *we have a completely different question*, shown by the name "time."

---

[1] R. Descartes, *Oeuvres de Descartes: Meditations et Principes: Principes de la Philosophie*, ed. Charles Adam and Paul Tannery, 1897 ff. Tome IX (Paris: Leopold Cerf, 1904), 14. {TN: Translated into English as "Principles of Philosophy, Preface to French Edition," in *The Philosophical Writings of Descartes, Vol. I*, trans. John Cottingham, Robert Stoothoff and Dugald Murdoch (Cambridge: Cambridge University Press, 1985), 186: Thus, the whole of philosophy is like a tree. The roots are metaphysics, the trunk is physics and the branches emerging from the trunk are all the other sciences . . ."}

[1] *Besinnung*, GA 66, 108. Metaphysik. [*Mindfulness*, 108. Metaphysics.]

[2] *Beiträge zur Philosophie (Vom Ereignis)*, GA 65. [*Contributions to Philosophy (From Enowning)* and *Contributions to Philosophy (Of the Event)*].

[3] *Hegels Phänomenologie des Geistes*, Freiburg Lecture Winter Semester 1903/31, GA 32, ed. I. Görland (Frankfurt am Main: Vittorio Klostermann, 1980), 144. {TN: Translated into English as *Hegel's Phenomenology of Spirit*, trans. Parvis Emad and Kenneth Maly (Bloomington: Indiana University Press, 1988), 99–100.}

[96] The inception of "philosophy" as the *thinking of being* is more original than the beginning of metaphysics.

This beginning is the first ending of the first inception and as ending the preparation for the consummation. The consummation is but the beginning of the end that lasts over and beyond the other inception.

Philosophy is the history of the truth of beyng, which essences forthwith only as the truth of beings.

93. Nietzsche and Heraclitus ("Metaphysics" and the First Inception of Philosophy)

to be juxtaposed in a different way in contradistinction to what even Nietzsche himself made popular, according to which both are supposed to teach that "being" is "becoming." Setting aside the fact that πάντα ῥεῖ is doubtful as a term of Heraclitus, the common idea of "flowing" and "becoming" in this sense does not in any way fit the Greek interpretation of being and thus not even that of γένεσις.

In the "Twilight of the Idols" (1888, VIII)[1] Nietzsche calls being "the last whiff of an evaporating reality."

In Fragment 7, Heraclitus says: εἰ πάντα τὰ ἔοντα καπνὸς γένοιτο, ῥῖνες ἂν διαγνοῖεν. If all beings were to become smoke (and were to have their being in this), it would be the noses that would quintessentially bring being to our attention.[*]

Is it or is it not the nose with which we arrive at the essence of beings? If not – if not with any "sense organ" – what is the status of being and the "reality" of the real?

How "would" it be if noses had to "decide?"

*

[1] F. Nietzsche, "Götzendämmerung," *Nietzsche Werke (Großoktavausgabe)*, Vol. VIII, (Leipzig: Kröner, 1919), 78. {TN: Translated into English as "Twilight of the Idols," in *The Portable Nietzsche*, ed. and trans. Walter Kaufmann (London: Penguin Books, 1982), 481; *Twilight of the Idols*, trans. Richard Polt (Indianapolis/ Cambridge: Hackett Publishing Company), 19; *Nietzsche: The Anti-Christ, Ecce Homo, Twilight of the Idols and Other Writings*, ed. Aaron Ridley, Judith Norman, trans. Judith Norman (Cambridge: Cambridge University Press, 2005), 168, translation modified.}

[*] {TN: The more conventional translation of the Greek is as follows: If all things turned to smoke, the nostrils would sort them out; *The Art and the Thought of Heraclitus*, trans. Charles H. Kahn (Cambridge: Cambridge University Press, 1979), CXII, 79.}

[97] The beginning of the consummation of modernity announces itself in the fact that now for the first time, world history will *be made*.

"Self-consciousness," which is essential to modernity, as the founding moment of being, now reaches fulfillment as the unconditional. This happens as soon as self-consciousness brings to attention this making of world history and this making in its execution, that too with its means (of technology), recording it as an *essential moment of being*.

94. The History of Beyng
"Overcoming"

The overcoming of metaphysics is to be borne by us historically as the preparation for the other inception, i.e., for the creative questioning of the truth of being.

But this preparation consists not in the anticipatory planning of the other inception and thus in what is already "achieved" bit by bit. If that were the case, there would be no pre-paration and no inception; rather we would only ever have a beginning which was of *our own* making and an ob-struction of the essentially abyssal nature out of which alone the other inception is capable of essencing as the other. Pre-paration here means: to completely uncover that which cannot be preliminarily glimpsed in its historical conjuncture, what is only to be suffered in the urgency of its essence – the question-*worthiness* of the truth of beyng.

The singularity of the *overcoming*; the constant danger of being misled by "historiographical" calculation and by bringing oneself into play "historiographically."

95. Kant and Metaphysics

Kant as "pulverizer of metaphysics;" however, he only shattered a pseudo- and scholastic figment in order first [98] to erect metaphysics properly in the modern sense of "subjective" idealism and to create the grounds for the first consummation of metaphysics at the hands of German Idealism.

*

What is elevated to "value" (as "truth" and being are), sinks into the deepest nothingness; it is the most value-less, if value signifies dignity of the truth of beyng as essencing beyng.

96. "Metaphysics"
("Subjectivity" and Substantiality)

Hegel's proposition (that in modern metaphysics substance becomes subject), takes the "subject" already in the "subjective" sense of rationality as the essence of beingness.

The proposition indeed conceals the fact that in this transformation the *subject*, i.e., *subjectivity* is transformed, *subjectivity* signifying the beingness of the subjectum, ὑποκείμενον.

Only when this transformation is recognized does what reigns pervasively come to light and with it what is decisive, namely, that in modern metaphysics *nothing* essential is decided: now more than ever the essence and the truth of being (of beingness) is concealed and given over to forgetfulness. This concealment and forgetfulness, however, proceed from the "naturally" appropriate opinion (of "subjectivity" as representing). This opinion states that in subjectivity, being is conscious of itself, and this means that being is unconditionally unquestionable. This usual and traditional opinion that being is that which is most obvious now becomes metaphysical and unconditionally justified.

[99] 97. The Overcoming of Metaphysics

has to be experienced in the historical moment at which the end of metaphysics achieves the resurrection most peculiar to it in the form of "worldview."

*

In *Being and Time* up to *On the Essence of Ground,* the entire history of metaphysics is seen from too *close,* is still too indecisively released and placed back into its own inceptual essence. There is still too much effort put into finding in metaphysics an aid and pointer to the other questioning, diluting the incomparable nature of this other questioning itself and thereby misinterpreting it. (cf. II. Trimester, *On the A priori*).[1]

---

[1] *Nietzsche, Der europäische Nihilismus*, GA 48, 148–152. {TN: See section 30, footnote 2.}

98. The Essence of Metaphysics and its Overcoming

Metaphysics, as the truth "of" beings as such taken as a whole, is the truth "of" beyng that is refused. This refusal is by beyng and is beyng itself. It is at its most extreme when beings are unleashed into the truth of manipulation. Manipulation does not even require knowledge of the essential ground of truth (manipulation and event) anymore.

This most extreme manifestation of refusal is the proximity to a decision.

The *retraction of refusal.*

The *echo* of beyng as event:

The history of beyng.

In terms of the history of beyng, the essence of the overcoming of metaphysics, that is to say, of the priority of the truth of *beings* as such taken as a whole, by beyng, is the *retraction of refusal.*

The overcoming as the pre-resonance of the other inception.

[100] 99. The Consummation of Metaphysics

(φύσις)

how and why φύσις becomes ιδέα

ιδέα
ουσία
ὑποκείμενον
ἐνέργεια
actus
substantia – subjectum

subjectivity:
conditional
unconditional
inverted – first consummated in this way.
will to power (production that represents and wills itself)
(manipulation)
event

100. The Overcoming of Metaphysics

What is thought in terms of the history of beyng and that is to say, undertaken questioningly and historically, is everywhere grasped from the "consummation," with the consummation of metaphysics experienced *within the history of beyng*.

This consummation (Hegel is only the preliminary stage still ungrasped and still stopping short of the inversion) is not mere conclusion. Rather as the *end*, it is the advance to the edge of the abyss. It is the preparation *to be at this edge*.

Consummation, thought historically, *is futural*. The historical emerges so essentially that *metaphysics* is *disturbed* out of its history-bearing essence with something other (truth of beyng) *re-placing* it as its abyssal ground.

Hence the title: The Consummation of Metaphysics, – the necessary plurivocity becomes greater and more essential. [101] What is insidious in the talk of the "over-coming" [*Überwindung*](let us do it!) disappears. Effort; (not well pressed down by the winch [*Winde*]!)

*

The "*Kant-book*" grew out of the attempt to make the question asked in *Being and Time* more accessible by means of a historical memory.

The attempt is in itself erroneous. But it does not put the essential nature of the Kant-interpretation in question.

The attempt necessarily drags the question posed by *Being and Time* into a region that was in fact already abandoned by *Being and Time* and can never ever be referred to as a fundamental position. How then is the *Kant-book* supposed to become an "introduction" to *Being and Time*? It becomes a deception. This is so even if, in the realm of the schematism, certain echoes can be detected that point to the relationship of being to "time."

*

Kant "Metaphysics:" For Kant, the fundamental metaphysical concepts of substance, causality never become questionable as the determinations of beings as such. He only puts the kind and the limits of metaphysics into question, never metaphysics itself.

101. The Consummation of Metaphysics

φύσις (of the inception)	and Nietzsche's "nature" as will to power
Plato's ἀγαθόν	and Nietzsche's "value"
The Platonic–Aristotelian	
οὐσία, ἐνέργεια	and permanence as the eternal recurrence of the same
[102] ἀλήθεια as ὁμοίωσις	and truth as justice
ζῷον λόγον ἔχον	And the realized animal as the superhuman

All of this is comprehensively ungreek; *the philosophy of the anti-philosophical Latin world.*

*

The supplement and
the pre-calculated zenith;
the same – "Platonism."
The enforced nature of the consummation.

*

Subjectivity (unconditional)
and
"Automatism"
and
"Economy"

*

Toward the confrontation between the thinking that is responsive to the history of beyng and that of metaphysics (cf. the fresh interpretation of Schelling's Freedom Essay 1940/41).[1]

*

The human being
The essence of the human being is determined from the essencing of the truth of beyng by beyng itself.

---

[1] *Die Metaphysik des deutschen Idealismus. Zur erneuten Auslegung von Schelling* [The Metaphysics of German Idealism: Toward a New Interpretation of Schelling], GA 49, 187–191.

[103] 102. Metaphysics – Consummation
(Inversion into the most Extreme)

ἰδέα — will to power
οὐσία — eternal recurrence of the same
(φύσις) — "nature" – innocence of becoming
animal rationale — super-human – the realized animal – "body"
ἀλήθεια – ὁμοίωσις – justice
nihilism
revaluation
valuing
abandonment by being
groundlessness
truth

103. The Interpretation of the Cogito

as self-assurance and laying the ground for the subiectum in terms of *a* will *to* power and especially "stability" – "being" / only one "side." *This interpretation* – "psychological," that is to say, *even* the will to power / "values" and *accordingly, toward* the *inner presupposition: Subjectivity* and now especially human essence. How *subjectivity* is misinterpreted more and more as the being of the human and this later becomes the will to power; "producer and owner"

In contrast to this, we have Pascal: "Ne cherchons donc point d'assurance et de fermeté."[1] – (namely) not as something that we could assert ourselves. But the "seeking" and *being in the act of seeking* indeed the only proper subjectivity.

---

[1] B. Pascal, "Pensées." *Oeuvres. XII*, ed. Leon Brunschvicg (Paris: Librarie Hachette, 1904–14) 86, n. 72. {TN: So, let us not seek certainty and stability, translation slightly modified; Translated into English as *Pensées and Other Writings*, ed. Anthony Levi, trans. Honor Levi (Oxford: Oxford University Press, 1995), 70.}

III. ART AND METAPHYSICS

(on the Lectures on the *Origin of the Work of Art* 1935 f.)[1]

[107] **104. In the Lectures on the *Origin of the Work of Art***

the definition of "art" within the realm of metaphysics (τέχνη, form-content, beauty) and the interpretation of the essence of "poetry" [*Dichtung*] in the inceptual sense in terms of the history of beyng (not as "poesy" [*Poesie*]), are intertwined. Thus, the illusion continues to be sustained that the essence of metaphysical art, which alone may be called "art," is to be thought more originally and properly in terms of the history of beyng. Whereas, in fact, what looms here is an abyss and what must be decided is the end of art, unconditionally and from the essence of metaphysics in general, not only in Hegel's sense.

That is the reason why the attempt to salvage art afresh, by means of a more original interpretation of the work of art, is misleading. But the ambivalence of these lectures should remain. For, it corresponds to the attempt to also grasp the question of beyng yet again as a "metaphysics of Dasein," as we see in *Being and Time*, which grasps metaphysics as it is being overcome. This mislaying of the other inception back into the history of the first, the merely "more original" grasping, are unavoidable entanglements in transitional thinking. They cannot be artificially expunged.

Yet, a clear distinction is necessary overall and a renewed reflection is sure to grant us knowledge of the inner tension between the following:

The end of art (Beauty as a truth of beings; καλόν – ἀγαθόν – ἰδέα)

---

[1] "Der Ursprung des Kunstwerkes," *Holzwege*. GA 5, 1–74. {TN: Translated into English as "The Origin of the Work of Art," *Off the Beaten Track*, 1–56; as well as "Vom Ursprung des Kunstwerkes." [Of the Origin of the Work of Art] *Heidegger Studies* 5 (1989): 5–22.}

and the consummation of metaphysics (cf. Nietzsche's interpretation of art as "the stimulus of life").

The experience of the truth of beyng in terms of the history of beyng and "poetry" and the establishment of "art" as manipulation into the devastation of beings.

[108] 105. "Art"

We must treat what still counts as art now, whether it be "good" or "bad," in the way we do wilted leaves, which without life and cut off from the force of the root, let themselves be whirled around by a wind and by means of this, exhibit a "movement," which impersonates life.

This "art" – taken into the protection of conscious control and support – will last a long time, longer perhaps than its predecessor has, whose corrupted essence it brings to its consummation.

Art, as something that was, however, conceals itself back in the inception and thus belongs to the future in a sense that is still hidden from us, even though its essence does not recur anymore.

Metaphysics   and   technology

τέχνη   –   "*art*"

"Art" in every form is only within and with metaphysics. That is why in "worldview," we have *the politics of art* and the continuation of "art," but everywhere without "*poetry*."

Poetry as grounding – the *founding of beyng*. From here on, we need to clarify more precisely, what it is that is asked in the lectures on the work of art.

Poetry – no more as art; when metaphysics ends, so does "art" – τέχνη. It becomes slowly clear, what is asked by means of the lecture *On the Origin of the Work of Art*; truth of beyng, that which is the hidden poeticizing essence in art.

106. When Metaphysics Ends, so too does Art

This end of "art," that a work itself can ground truth, is no loss. If we assess it this way, we think on the basis of what has proceeded so far and do not know of the increasing indeterminateness of the essence of truth and the [109] lack of a decision with regard to its grounding that intensifies with this end. Still less do we sense the guarantee of what has long since been decided– of beyng, from which alone will stem other groundings.

(The place of the lectures on the origin of the work of art within the overcoming of metaphysics.)

*

Art and Metaphysics (cf. the Frankfurt lectures)[1]

*

"Symbol" and Metaphysics und τέχνη

Since beings have been rendered empty and stripped of being, *beings* must *receive* and *exhibit* a sense or must be interpreted on the basis of such a sense.
How can that be, however, if everything related to beings *already essences* in beyng?

"Representation" [Repräsentation]

A being as that which is present [*praesentes*] represents [*repraesentiert*] being; the *re* – as *deterioration* –; the sign points to an unmastered inception!

"Art"

Thinking and *art-less* poetry (Hölderlin's Draft on Columbus "By a few minor things" IV, 395).[2] When he is quite at the limits, Hölderlin comes close to this realm; how are the lectures on the work of art aimed at this realm?

[1] "Der Ursprung des Kunstwerkes," *Holzwege*, GA. 5 {TN: See footnote 1 on p. 91 above.}
[2] F. Hölderlin, "Bruchstück n. 30 zu Kolomb," *Hölderlin, Sämtliche Werke*, Vol. IV, ed. N. v. Hellingrath, 2nd edn. (Berlin: Propyläen Verlag, 1923), 395.]

IV. METAPHYSICS AND "WORLDVIEW"

(cf. the Grounding of the Modern World-Picture,[1] *Mindfulness*[2] among others)

[113] 107. Metaphysics and Worldview

The transition of metaphysics into its corrupted essence.
"Worldview" as the necessary corrupted essence of metaphysics.
In keeping with the long history of metaphysics, the corrupted essence of metaphysics will more than ever inaugurate an extended age of the corrupted essence of history.
The *transition* into the corrupted essence of metaphysics is the longest delay in the inceptual decision.
The dominance of worldview as the corrupted essence of the groundless truth in the sense of "certainty" (faith) develops into the unconditional nature of the average. (The uncanny), cf. the saying.
The transition of metaphysics into worldview is its reduction into the unconditional mixture of everything existing hitherto, by means of which we brew the latest.

108. Worldview is the Perishing of Metaphysics

The perishing makes the "end" that springs from the consummation (Nietzsche) enduring and reinforces it to such an extent that a reflection or even just the urgency of a reflection could never again arise from it.
The perishing is the essential outcome of the consummation.
Today, we stand in the unfolding of the consummation and thus at

---

[1] "Die Zeit des Weltbildes," *Holzwege*, GA 5, 75–113. {TN: "The Age of the World Picture," *Off the Beaten Track*, 57–85.}
[2] *Besinnung*, GA 66, 131. Metaphysik und "Weltanschauung," 402f. {TN: *Mindfulness*, 131. Metaphysics and "World-View," 355f.}

the beginning of the perishing. This appears historically–technically as the new order of the "world" and "dominance" over the earth.

*

The positions arrived at today within the consummated metaphysics, without being able to match up to its essence anymore:
1. the political "worldview." "Worldview" as deterioration [114]; the will to power vulgarly as "vitality" and "biological".
2. the adventures in the elemental and the return to the indestructible. (E. Jünger)
3. the transformation into the "inner" (inner-worldly space) and the recognition of the "earth." (R. M. Rilke)

Setting anxiety aside

the heroic realism

mere overcoming of anxiety

The anxiety that is still *not experienced* in its essence; (as the disturbance [*Ent-setzung*] into the abandonment of beings in the midst of the "proximity to the actuality" of all life and the "proximity to the life" of all human deeds).

Everywhere we have incomplete and extreme nihilism and Christian reconciliation. Merely rambling aimlessly in a metaphysics that is always flat and essentially impassable.

109. The Consummation of Metaphysics (Nietzsche) (cf. 107. Metaphysics and Worldview)

The consummation of metaphysics by Nietzsche is already similar to how German Idealism is in *its* own way the beginning of the alteration of metaphysics into "worldview."

Nietzsche, above all, always moves on the path of the transition; the indeterminateness of his conceptual construction, the manner of his presentation, the language itself bears everywhere the stamp of "worldview." Among his contemporaries he is the one who urges most loudly in this "direction."

Any interpretation of Nietzsche that attempts beforehand, to think him through on the basis of metaphysics and indeed from the history of its essence, grants him more metaphysical heft than he can really possess. Any interpretation of this kind also [115] lends his basic concepts a determinateness that is not "historiographically" commensurate with the vagueness and the tone of Nietzschean philosophy. Any such interpretation must overestimate Nietzsche. And yet, it is necessary to do so in order first to bring out the corrupted essence and thereby also the complete essence of metaphysics.

110. "Worldview"

The essence of *world-view* springs from metaphysics *as* its corrupted essence when the history of metaphysics arrives at its essential consummation. That is the reason why the essence of "worldview" (cf. *On the Essence of Ground*, 1930)[1] cannot be viewed from the perspective of a "worldview" that is current these days and that calls itself so. For, we still have to ask to what extent we can speak of "worldview" here and the reason why, what claimed to be so, satisfies the essence of a worldview.

However, where a worldview is rightfully a worldview, there also belongs to it a necessity, which comes from the history of its essence. All attempts to "contra-dict" specific "contents" and "propositions" fall through. This is not just because there is no space for "contradictions." It is rather because the "contents" and "goals" are not what is essential. This is due to the fact that the essence of truth is now structured in terms of "worldview" and in accordance with the worldview's lack of content – which is its strength and not its shortcoming – nothing "that" could be held to be "lasting" remains at our disposal. What is supposed to "last" is *the faith in faith*, i.e., holding-something-for-true (certain), which is unconditionally sustained for its own sake and predetermines all "positions."

Faith must be "blind" because *that which* as binding, could still in each case demand something of its own accord cannot essentially exist anymore.

[116] The holding-onto-itself in the holding-something-for-true of that which holds something for true points to the corrupted essence of unconditional subjectivity that has exhausted all of the possibilities of subjectivity and has attempted the abolition of truth and being without knowing them and without being able to know them.

World-views are without "content." This means that no "being" can as such still make a claim to being, which is its own foundation. It cannot do so for the reason that being itself has abandoned all beings

---

[1] "Vom Wesen des Grundes," *Wegmarken*, GA 9, 155. {TN: Translated into English as "On the Essence of Ground," *Pathmarks*, 120–121.}

and has left them with the appearance that interacts with us in the form of "actuality" and "life."

What is the reason for the question concerning the "content" and "goal" of "worldview" to lapse?

The "world" is posited as "picture." A "picture" of the human being is validated in the same way. But "picture" here means that which has a long lineage beginning with Plato's ἰδέα and that is re-presented by calculation and counting. In the case of the picture, it all comes down only to ensuring the effective capacity of power, whose essence (manipulation) thoroughly dominates everything.

The overpowering of power, which is considered the essence of power, only thinks of how to establish itself and thus to assure its effectiveness.

The effective as effective satisfies the essence of *actuality* and the latter stands for being. Positing a "picture" is thus everywhere the empowering of effectiveness in the service of manipulation. "What" is thereby actual is only valid insofar as it assures the effectiveness of what is already planned. Thus, we also have the primacy of "value" and eventually "the dynamic" in itself as the proper "value."

111. "Worldview" and "Philosophy"

"Worldview" is the corrupted essence of metaphysics. It *is* metaphysics in its consolidation as baselessness and lack of reflection. It thinks in "ideas" and according to "values," oriented toward the "positing of goals." [117] All of this is however only a means in the service of manipulation, whose essence it can never penetrate.

With the consummation of metaphysics, its corrupted essence begins its domination.

The consummation of meta-physics is the end of philo-sophy.

The thinking that is responsive to the history of beyng remains outside any comparison to "philosophy."

Philo-sophy as the way of thinking the being of beings and interrogating them from the standpoint of being, has existed only since Plato.

112. *"World-view"*
("Life")

turns the world into a "picture" for human beings who are living through their experiences.

"Lived experience" as the confirmation of the "living."

The living sought in "life."

"Life" is confusingly taken as the general mixture of "nature" and "history." Hence the predominance of "biology" and "psychology" and their being stirred in the brew of "anthropology," which comes to correspond to "universal life."

One seeks the living in "life" and cannot know and cannot ever ask what the "living" is. One substantiates its "essence" with all that is wished and desirable in one's own "time," to exist according to what is considered as proximity to "life."

"Life," however, receives its hidden interpretation from the hardly reflected upon animality, which is deepened eventually in the direction of the "mental," due to which even the "mental" sinks into the "animalistic."

But what is it that is unknowingly yearned for in the search for the "living?" Beyng; but this is unveiled only in the essence of truth. And "life" would have to be experienced as the endurance [*Beständnis*] of beyng and would then have to shatter the silence of beyng with the "vitality" it has arrogated.

[118] 113. Metaphysics – Worldview
The True, the Good, the Beautiful

The essential consequence of the ἰδέα is the designation of ἀληθῶς ὄν, καλόν and ἀγαθόν; the beingness of beings as the true, the beautiful and the good.

The triad, to which even "the sacred" will belong later, redescribes the goal of "culture," i.e., the conception of history, which begins with the Italian renaissance and introduces modernity.

Finally, the three become values and cultural values, to which one assigns knowledge (science), aesthetic art and ethics (politics). How one determines the true, the good and the beautiful, whether in terms of German Idealism or according to a kind of positivism or in the footsteps of Nietzsche or in the terms of a fourth or fifth humanism that invokes Heraclitus and Hölderlin, is in all respects the same – ungrasped metaphysics on the way to "worldview."

114. Metaphysics and Worldview and the Thinking Responsive to the History of Beyng.

As worldview, metaphysics explicitly becomes one of the ingredients of "life" needed by the praxis of life. It is seemingly only justified in this way and metaphysics in the true sense (not as some kind of "doctrine") thereby falls through. Where reflection is still sought, it can at most be taken for "metaphysics." The question of beyng that responds to the history of beyng is thus necessarily subject to a double and simultaneously, seen from the standpoint of what is enduring, even an all-round misinterpretation: that this question is simply "distant from life" in relation to "worldview" and that this question, in referring to metaphysics, gets equated with metaphysics. This daily seduction grows to simply advocate both sides [metaphysics and worldview] and [119] become dependent on both, with the result that the inceptual is always given up. This is because the urgency of saying brings with it the necessity of making itself understood. Essential thinking thus already admits that it accepts a deterioration of what is most essential to it. But thinking does not have to make *itself* understood. It must rather forcibly turn what is agreed upon toward questioning, through the un-coercive nature of what is simply said – into what is unheard in the spoken word.

*

Elementarism as symbolism, cf. *To Junger*
metaphysics – worldview
the a priori
"mathema"
worldview – heroic
values – ideas, "symbolism" and the *elemental.*
    The flight into the elemental and the picture as the powerlessness to cognize the "sense," and that means, to overcome it through the knowledge of its essence as truth. The flight into the elemental – the ultimate helplessness of Platonism and theology.

*

μάθημα – not *through the invocation of a being, thus* remains only ψυχή; for what reason: for the reason that beings and being are not grounded in a truth that is distinguishable and because being as beingness is itself ὄντως ὄν, but certainly an *extraordinary* relation of the soul to ὄντως ὄν.
    By contrast, *in the other inception: beyng* and its essencing *neither* ψυχή *nor* ὄντα.

To what extent for Plato is τὰ μαθήματα, in the narrow sense between εἴδωλα and εἶδος, ὄντα and ὄντως ὄν?

*

[120] The necessity of the *a priori* from the ungrounding of ἀλήθεια and finally the necessity of mislaying it into representing (consciousness – will to power).

115. Metaphysics and Worldview
(cf. "Grounding the Modern World Picture through
Metaphysics," 1938)[1]

Worldview is only possible, but then also necessary, when we have the occurrence of the metaphysics of unconditional subjectivity, but which at the same time cannot be halted by humanity. Human beings, although standing in this metaphysics, dispose of *the whole* of beings *wholly by themselves*, as that which is re-presented. Human beings are yet no longer equal to the truth of beings as such as a whole, as they can no longer know the essence of this truth at all. But the "ideas" (and then the values) remain preserved. Indeed, they only now become the means for the determination of the world picture. No knowledge anymore, that "idea" is being itself and "value" is to be likewise grasped as the condition for the possibility of beings.

Worldview necessarily stands *within* metaphysics but misconceives it and supplants it due to its incapacity to endure metaphysical truth. *Thus,* we have the emergence of the flight into the sciences. Even human beings understand and explain themselves "psychologically." Morality becomes "politics" and sociology and biology.

Worldview consolidates itself and forces metaphysics into *anthropology.*

"Anthropology" and "geography" become the fundamental sciences; perhaps still underpinned by a general "biology."

Initially at the beginning of the nineteenth century, under the cover and [121] the guidance of the metaphysics of German idealism, "worldviews" still undeveloped, are restricted to individuals or transferred into political parties or claimed by confessions. Only where metaphysics itself in the last step becomes the metaphysics of consummated

---

[1] "Die Zeit des Weltbildes," *Holzwege*, GA 5, 75–113. {TN: "The Age of the World Picture," *Off the Beaten Track*, 57–85.}

subjectivity, must *worldview* decidedly aim at unconditionality and become "total." It then corresponds to the complete subjugation of all the "sciences." What is called philosophy is merely the "scholasticism" of worldview. Scholasticism prepares the truth of worldview and "grounds" that which does not require any grounding and only tolerates such "groundings" as ornaments of "cultural" prestige. Worldview cannot for an instant take seriously this scholastic pseudo-philosophy so long as it understands itself.

The inner unfolding of the essence of "worldview" is the fundamental process from which we can illuminate the *metaphysical* history of the truly enigmatic nineteenth century and the transition into the twentieth century. The role of Schopenhauer finds its metaphysical place here.

116. Metaphysics and Worldview

The essential difference between the two can be exhibited through the reference to the "biological" interpretation; to put it better, the half-baked biological understanding of the will to power.

The will to power as the essence of being is neither "spiritual" nor "bodily" (vital). But it is situationally most appropriate for the subjectivity of the human being as "lived body." Over and above this, Nietzsche claims the "body" as the guiding thread for the interpretation of the world. This does not mean that everything should be thought "biologically." Rather, the "biological" should be grasped as will to power and this implies that beings as a whole must be experienced as the eternal recurrence of the same and taken over. One avoids doing this and interprets the doctrine over and beyond Nietzsche by making the doctrine of the will to power a [122] prescription for a political worldview. Moreover, the affirmation of the "body" is otherwise, too, a very pleasant "worldview." Binge drinking and fornication have received their metaphysical validation. Eventually, we have the arrival of the "swamp"-"philosophy" of Mr. Klages.

V. BEING AND TIME

IN THE HISTORY OF BEYNG INSOFAR AS THIS HISTORY IS EXPERIENCED AS THE OVERCOMING OF METAPHYSICS

(cf. a summary of this: Interpretation of Schelling: Treatise on Freedom, 1941)[1]

[125] 117. *Being and Time* and Metaphysics

At first it appears as if *Being and Time* only strives toward a kind of "epistemology" of "ontology" (How is ontology possible at all?) If it were so, *Being and Time* would be a mere supplement to metaphysics.

However, it is *being* that is in question, not "ontology." Is *Being and Time* then perhaps a more original metaphysics, but still just a metaphysics? No.

Truly speaking, what we have here is an entirely other inception from the essencing of beyng itself.

However, precisely for this reason we even have a more inceptual relationship to the first inception; "destruction" is quintessentially a return to the inceptual. It is thus entirely a historical reflection; hence the questioning is also occasionally called "metaphysics;" cf. the *Kant-book*, metaphysics "of" Dasein; *What is Metaphysics?*

Being and Time does not in fact correspond to anything that one rightly expects from a regular metaphysics, namely, that it only ooze with the forgottenness of being.

---

[1] *Die Metaphysik des deutschen Idealismus. Zur erneuten Auslegung von Schelling,* [*The Metaphysics of German Idealism: Toward a New Interpretation of Schelling*] GA 49, 26–76.

118. Time and Eternity

How the essence of eternity is to be determined from the more inceptual essence of time differently from in metaphysics (ἀεί – nunc stans).

The eternal is *the erstwhile* and, in fact, in the essentially unified dual sense of the *previous* inception *that was* and of *that which is to come at one time*. Not the boredom* of an all-round endless present that is quietly laid out.

[126] 119. On the History of the Concept of Time

In Aristotle's *Physics* Δ 10–14, χρόνος must be understood in correspondence to τόπος: the "time, in which," "at the time when," "during the time, there," "in the time of 1 day," i.e., as "dated," i.e., first of all, in the immediately present and perceived time.

For, even "location" (space of a house, place) is a proper *being* – space – because it is immediately present (οὐσία); in the same way "time;" the latter as ἀριθμός is εἶδος, not the modern "number."

By contrast the dimensional is indeed recognized, but as that which only serves as the ground of determinability.

Different from the above, for modern thinking (in the sense of the calculating – preplanning projection), the dimensional – the pure form of order – the emptiness of sequence is what comes first and what determines the essence; cf. Leibniz – ordo; cf. Kant, who only gives a transcendental turn to the primacy of the dimensional. Any particular space (and correspondingly time) is *limitation*. By contrast, for the Greeks the "particular" is properly speaking first a being for itself, which then loses itself in a μέγεθος (outside one another).

The difference between the ancient and the modern concept of time does not consist in the fact that in the former the "present" and in the latter the future (the Faustian) stands in the foreground. In each case the whole of time is experienced. However, in one case it is experienced as dated and present and in the other case as the pre-given dimension (parameter) of an unconditional calculability and planning.

---

* {TN: The German for boredom is *Langeweile*, which literally translates to a "long while."}

120. The Essence of Time

As long as calculated time is experienced and thought (be it as ἀριθμός; be it as parameter), in each case the sequence, the flow of a series of nows is experienced. And here we then have the possibility of a difference in direction and its varying primacy.

[127] Soon time is only the pure passing-away and self-consumption (Hegel), soon it is the rolling out and arriving (future – eschatologically or in terms of progress), soon everything is thought cyclically as a becoming that is looped back upon itself.

All the above cases remain within the essential determination of time, wherein one comes across it as something present at hand. Nowhere is the ecstatic essence and the essencing cognized as temporalization.

But the temporalization of time has to bring into existence the in-between – the time-play-space, the openness of the abyss of the truth of beyng. This means that, to begin with and for a long time after, during the dominance of the calculable essence of time, it has to conceal this in-between. This goes hand in hand with the self-concealing of being and the surrender of beingness to the primacy of beings.

121. Time and Being

Why is time grasped inceptually as οὐσία τις, definitive for the West since Aristotle?

Because the question of being is only asked metaphysically as the question concerning the being of beings, a being of any kind is projected in accordance with "being" (as οὐσία).

Since the question of being becomes metaphysical at its inception and has remained so since, time is grasped on the basis of being which is interrogated no further.

And time that is grasped in such a way again prevents us from ever inquiring into the temporal essence of being (as presence and permanence), because beingness is indeed outside of time and *not* like beings inside time. Beings alone could trigger the impossible question here concerning the temporal essence of being.

Thus, it is the time that has concealed itself (as the clearing of being, even of οὐσία) that basically prevents the manifestation of itself in its essence. This means: it veils itself. But, to the extent that time is the essencing of being and thus being itself, it means that beyng refuses itself in the first inception.

[128] 122. Being and Time

Looking at the title, if one should juxtapose what is mentioned in it to what is prior to it (metaphysics) (what will unavoidably be a deceptive equivalence) then "one" must say with all reservation: *Being and Thinking*. But it is precisely here that all the undecidedness would lie veiled. "Being" as beingness of beings and thinking as representation – gathering bringing-before-oneself of the one – as the universal and the highest.

Thus, it is better to say: *Thinking and Beings.*

Thus, the placement already shows that "thinking" simply places beingness *in relation to itself* (ἰδέα) and "thinks" from the standpoint of beings and back to beings (explaining and grasping them). By contrast *Being and Time* – being itself is the inceptual and time – the first name of its "essence" as the in-between of the abyssal eventuation [*Er-eignung*].

Time is the *first* name for the ungrounded and hence that which is to be creatively questioned first. As the ungrounded and ungroundable (among beings) it is the first name for the essencing of the truth of beyng which is to be creatively thought only as the beyng of truth.

Hence, time is still ambiguous because the first name is simultaneously still turned toward metaphysical thinking and yet has already abandoned metaphysical thinking in the anticipatory thinking of being.
Thus:
1. "Time" *as the horizon of the projection of being* as such – not of beings as being. "Horizon" and "projection" still in terms of conditions of possibility – thus seemingly "tran-scendental;" indeed the word itself is used and yet:
2. Time as the intimation into the essencing of the event [*Er-eignis*] – *of the in-between.*

[129] 123. *Being and Time*

In essential decisions, which indeed perhaps stem from the essence of history itself, because this essence of history grounds in the truth of beyng (so that beyng always essences in this and not in any other way), we can never skip a step. Specifically, that which must reach consummation beforehand, shall be borne out and shall be first dealt with by starting with the ways of the transition.

That is why it is not intentional but as if from the urgency of history itself that *Being and Time*, still in a certain way, questions "transcendentally," that is to say, it questions simply in terms of meta-physics, for which all being as beingness remains the enabling condition of beings.

Indeed, the question of enabling seems to have been simply placed over enabling once again in the way the question is posed: How is beingness itself possible? Indeed, it seems as if the motivation here is precisely to ask questions of this kind and repeat it ad infinitum. How would things look if this were the case? They would look like this: what is essentially necessary as the advance into metaphysical truth would be reduced to a vain gimmick and used as a means to invent "prob-lems." Whoever would like to seek this motive behind *Being and Time* may do it. But the discussion of this treatise remains stuck so much in the superficiality of anthropology, that we never ever go beyond every "moralizing" and "psychologizing," to consider the questioning impulse mentioned above.

Certainly, what is asked is this: How is beingness possible? It is asked in the following manner: what is the "sense" (namely, the essencing realm of projection, namely, the unconcealed element, namely, the truth) of being? But *why* is it asked in this manner? Only in order to climb to the immediately higher level of the question of possibility? No, but it is asked from the fundamental experience of being itself (nothingness, history, the truth itself, Da-sein). Projection and the question of projection comes from being thrown into the truth of being. Thrownness has thrown the questioners [130] into Da-*sein* so that they know Da-*sein* as such and take the first name of essencing being itself: time.

Time is not only and not primarily a backdrop, which can once again be shoved behind being so that being itself can again have a ques-tionable background. Time is the name for the way being essences as unconcealedness itself. But how, in the face of the steadily continuing pressure exerted by metaphysics, should one question for the first time, if not through the ways in which metaphysics is practiced? We thus come to the "transcendence of Dasein," which stands in a peculiarly ambiguous manner between "subjectivity," which is comprehensively and substantially overcome, and the Da-sein that underlies it. This is because nowhere [in *Being and Time*] does one think in terms of the subject. History is thought as the historicality of Dasein and Dasein is thought as that which is essentially determined through the under-standing of being. However, under-standing as projection, which in persisting is thrown into its open and should never, so to speak, attrib-ute the projected to itself as its accomplishment.

124. Being and Time

We need to grasp what the "retrieval" [*Wiederholung*] of the question of being means. Not undertaking once again the same question that has been taken up historiographically, but rather to fetch the question again in its unquestioned aspect, i.e., to make the question essentially question-worthy. The necessity of the other inception, and that is to say, the experience beforehand of the overcoming of metaphysics, is implied in this.

Thus, where we can indicate the relationship of "being" to "time," there we must each time first question how being and time are meant and how their relationship is thought. We can point out that *Being and Time* isolates the temporal character of οὐσία (παρουσία). But we can thereby only illustrate that this Greek thinking prepares a completely different way and does *not* question in the direction of being and time – which is only made clear afterwards.

Despite this, it gradually becomes commonplace to point to [131] Plato's *Theaetetus* 186a10–b1, where it speaks of ψυχή: ἀναλογιζομένη ἐν ἑαυτῇ τὰ γεγονότα καὶ τὰ παρόντα πρὸς τὰ μέλλοντα – that the "soul" – within itself – brings together the past (what has become) and what is present into correspondence with the future on the basis of itself.* What is meant here is the simple reckoning with beings. What is prefigured here is rather the calculative aspect of λόγος and of the later ratio. Here in no way is the temporal essence of being indicated but rather that beings are within time. In addition to this, this "temporal" character of beings is mentioned *alongside* several other determinations of beings. But in no way is that which is said of the determinations of ὄν (sameness, difference, ἀγαθόν ἢ καλόν etc.) grasped from the essence of "*time*;" if at all creatively questioned in the terms of a suggestive question. To actively think the essence of time, lies completely outside the task not only of this dialogue but also of the whole of Greek and Western philosophy.

Leading ἀγαθόν-καλόν back to "time" obviously does not mean tracing some kind of temporal character in accordance with the customary concept of "time." It rather means recognizing the character of the "in-between" by way of the ecstatic essence of time, which is to be actively thought first, and in this way to penetrate into the essence of

---

* {TN: A more conventional translation is as follows: [The soul] seems to be making a calculation within itself of past and present in relation to the future. *Plato: Complete Works*, ed. John Cooper, trans. M. J. Levett, rev. Myles Burnyeat (Indianapolis: Hackett Publishing Company, 1997), 206.}

the "clearing" of the there and thereby into the openness, recognizing "time" as the *first* name for the *essence of the truth of being*.

For this reason, Part 1, Division 3 of *Being and Time* (cf. pp. 34–35) was to have been about "Time and Being." This means: the temporality that is exhibited from the standpoint of "Da-sein," which is also to be thought completely differently first, was to have been thought back to the essencing of ecstatic "time," that is to say, to the time-space as in-between. Being itself should become originally question-worthy for the first time from this essence of the *truth* of being.

[132] 125. "The Sense of Being"

1. *Not* the sense of the being *of the human being* – as subject (as in Nietzsche: Zarathustra, Preface),
2. But the sense of being as such.
3. Being as "truth" of the essencing of being and not truth of beings.
4. Truth as clearing and its grounding – essencing from beyng itself as (event).
5. The abyss in opposition to Nietzsche and – the whole of metaphysics as such.
6. But we get stuck on the wording and the word-equivalents, sparing ourselves any original reflection, which must abstract from our own prejudices in the same breath, out of which we open ourselves to those who critically know better.

126. Being and Time

One says that there is no real "description" here, but a devaluation. "Dasein" is evaluated from a definitively one-sided perspective and an "attunement" is privileged, which in addition drags one down and is not at all uplifting: Anxiety.

But the "hermeneutics" [of *Being and Time*] is indeed not supposed to describe something present at hand, but *project*. The deficiency does not lie in the fact that the descriptive stance is not satisfied. But to the contrary, the projection and its decisive character is *not* developed *decisively enough*. Instead, what emerges through "phenomenology" is the semblance that it should concern description (Analysis). But "analysis" is not "analytic" in the sense projected.

Thus, the task is to avoid any semblance of an intention to "describe" and to truly and exclusively think, namely, *beyng*.

This is also why the contrived and extensive going astray into [133] apparently "concrete" discussions of particular "phenomena" is of no help – what is needed is simply the "abstract" knowledge of beyng.

127. *Being and Time*

In *Being and Time* any "contact" with "being" is left behind, if, by means of the thoughtless equivocation that we have indulged for long, we take "being" to mean "a being" and "interpret" the latter as the "actual" and "effective" and the most effective in the sense of the "elementary." For, in *this* "contact" with "being," which is now more clearly expressed as "proximity to life," we never experience something of beyng itself; indeed, those who are "touched" and "move" in such a way (who thoughtlessly and helplessly agitate the concocted brew of the metaphysical tradition) are so because of their proximity to actuality and their contemporaneity (E. Junger, for example). They are excluded from ever getting an intimation of a trace in relation to beyng. Those who are agitated in confusion must appear as though they were the closest to so-called "life." The one who does the agitating is the accomplice of metaphysics in its reduction to *worldview*.

Everyone who thinks, needs to immediately renounce the contact with being perpetuated by those who agitate.

The overcoming of metaphysics is never a metaphysics of metaphysics or simply an accompanying "methodology" of philosophical thinking.

In fact, all of metaphysics and its derivatives can only understand the thinking responsive to the history of beyng metaphysically, at most as methodology and therefore lie permanently outside that which is to be creatively questioned and primarily experienced.

[134] 128. Being, the Understanding of Being and Beyng

Being, by virtue of the *interpretation* by human beings, if not simply of human making – value.

The metaphysics of *subjectivity* still speaks in favor of the *human being* determining truth and being (anthropomorphism).

Certainly – *dominance over beings*, but an illusory dominance over being; later, subjectivity from unleashing beings into manipulation because of which the human being forgets being and because of which beings are abandoned by being.

Truly speaking, however, the understanding of being as *projection* and projection is what is thrown.

What essences in thrownness and throwing is being itself.

But a *being* present closest to one's hand [*Vor-hand*] as the *present at hand* [*Vorhandene*]!

129. Da-sein and "Care" – "Attunement"

Care and attunement in relation to Da-sein and *only* so; but Da-sein in relation to the truth of beyng.

Προμηθεύς the one who cares – προμηθέομαι – if so, then not much needs to be said about the "heroic" in this instance.

"Care" has nothing to do with grief and melancholy – but everything to do with the truth of beyng. Audacity and knowledge – inner sedateness and foreboding – distinguishes this "everything" from the "adventurousness" of the clueless and "those who flee" only into the elementary.

"*Attunement*" – not fleeting feeling and the easy state of being lightly affected in contradistinction to πάθος and rage, but something that is beyond all this – *being-attuned* through the attuning voice of silence as the origin of the word.

[135] 130. Being and Time

The historical dialogue with the essential thinkers about what is for them the simplest, gives rise, ever more decisively, to the foreboding that they have never said what is most essential to them. This is because, what is in each case their most immediately felicitous word indeed still resists the most hidden attunedness, which comes through what is to be said.

Heraclitus's λόγος, Plato's ἰδέα, Aristotle's ἐνέργεια, Leibniz's monad, Kant's "I think" and "freedom," Schelling's "identity" and "lack of ground," Hegel's "concept" and Nietzsche's "will to power" as "eternal recurrence" say the same thing: the being of beings.

They do not make "propositions" about it as though it were an object that has been put away. Being itself is said. As something said it is elevated into a word, which word is here not an arbitrary linguistic expression, but beyng itself, which has become the truth (clearing), which is raised into the clearing of what is cleared. What the thinker says does not speak in "images" and "signs" and "ciphers," does not dabble in oblique circumlocutions that must be equally incoherent to everyone. What is said is being itself. But this is certainly also not for the ears of a reasonableness emerging by accident, which would like everything explained; what essential thinkers never say is always simpler than what they say. That is why being, from time to time, is constantly demanding that thinking go back to the inception. But being commences with this demand only when the creative thinking of being has in each case become more inceptual and, as something completely other, still has the power to remain the same and as the other inception *re*-trieves the first insurmountable inception.

The other inception of thinking creatively questions the truth of beyng. The thinking responsive to the history of beyng creatively thinks the truth (opening of the clearing) of being first as time-space, as this ground of the unity of "time" and "space." It lets them emerge in their belonging together as the channels and expanses of the rapturous pull exerted by the clearing of the abyss. [136] "Time" first reveals the unity of the rapturous pull more pressingly than "space," which is not any less, but exerts a rapturous pull of a different kind. To that extent the attempt to think the truth of beyng (the "sense of being") must begin with "time." At the same time, however, we must prepare the projection of time-space by exhibiting the *spatiality of Da-sein* (cf. *Being and Time*). It is for this reason that the next unfolding of the question of being in its re-inception, stands under the title "Being and Time."

Here "time" names a being that cannot be explained by merely discussing the earlier and the current concepts of time. It is rather predetermined in an incomparably different way only by the question of the truth of being itself. All "treatments" of the "concept of time" can only have the limited task of making clear that which has sprung from original time. This original time does not have even little in common with *durée*, for example. This task can conversely serve to circumscribe this completely different time without indeed ever permitting a transition to it. This time which is specified in the thinking responsive to the history of beyng already holds sway as the horizon, and indeed the unquestionable horizon for "presence" and "permanence" (οὐσία), for that which is gathered together (λόγος) and perceived (νοῦς), for the visible clarity of the look (ἰδέα) and for the re-presentedness (perceptum der perceptio) of objectivity. However, this horizon is the very one that suggests itself to "thinking" (νοεῖν, λέγειν) first by itself out of itself, in such a way that thinking is settled in this horizon and is supported by it, never needs to remember it. Rather, thinking establishes itself as the guiding thread of the determination of beingness and its constitution. In correspondence to the interpretation of the one that thinks (animal rationale), it unfolds into the "I think" and absolute thinking. As a consequence, all the determinations of beingness are branded as categories following the guiding thread of the fundamental form of thinking – the judging statement (κατηγορεῖν).

Thinking – first as per-ception (that which makes present) – active beholding, the view of what is clearly visible – re-presenting – (a) oneself before that – [137] to let oneself be placed and stand before that which presents itself as one such; (b) *inversely: as bringing-before-oneself.*

However, within the history of metaphysics, the thinking of being never recognizes (despite the knowledge of the πρότερον, of the a priori, of the transcendental) the horizon that has designated it as cognition. (*From where* does this horizon come at all? What does it signify?) Rather philosophical thinking takes itself to be sufficiently grounded by the distinguishing feature that philosophy thinks being (beingness – categories); whereas the sciences and common opinion represent beings and explain them. Indeed, this distinguishing feature itself is not decisively clear in all respects. In the place where it attains the highest clarity within the history of metaphysics, in Kant, this thinking of being is soon falsified into a "theory of knowledge." The inner ground for this process lies in the fact that Kant grasps beingness as objectivity, limiting objects to their amenability to experience – to the mathematical cognition of nature – and in connection with this *limitation* he must provide something like a theory of cognition. Philosophy as the creative questioning of being is *thinking* at all times.

What does this mean? Representation of *something as something* (νοεῖν – λόγος); (the "as" does not necessarily need a "universal" to be posited as such); *Re-presenting* as standing within the "truth" (manifestation of something); not necessarily a mere ogling, this is only *one* possible form. Re-presenting as having in consciousness; cogito me cogitare: setting it toward oneself, in the permanence of the as *what.*

However, just for this reason, this thinking must determine itself as original from that which it creatively thinks: from being. Thus, if for the sake of being formulaic and titular, *Being and Time* is required hereafter instead of *Being and Thinking*, then this does not mean any dismissal of thinking in favor of an "irrationalism" and a "mood," but completely the opposite: creative thinking is now for the first time forced into the acuteness of the abyssal nature of its horizon, that is the original truth of beyng, which up until now *has not received consideration.* An essential [138] *thoughtlessness*, which is necessary for the task and the continued existence of metaphysics and which therefore dominates its entire history, is only now overcome, and the thinking of philosophy becomes something *essentially more thoughtful*. It is only now that creative thinking acquires its freedom in so decisive a manner that the naming of "time" can only be the next clue to what is question-worthy. Inceptual thinking knows itself to be "on the way" to it. *Being and Thinking*, taken as the title for the manner in which the *metaphysical* question of being is posed, does not mean what is commonplace: that "thinking" is precisely the form of the operation and activity of philosophy. Rather this title is already thought in response to the history of beyng from the standpoint of being and time. In this way it means: metaphysical thinking does not yet reflect upon what is most proper to it: presentness (time) as the horizon of the interpretation of the beingness that is proper to it. Rather the thinking of metaphysics takes itself unreflectively for all intents and purposes to be the sufficiently definitive court of appeal for all the essential boundaries of being.

What does this *unreflectiveness* mean? The retreat to the λόγος as statement, representative determination of something as something. Why this? Because being is taken as ἰδέα? And what is the reason for this? The ἕν-κοινόν is taken as the *presencing-permanent itself*.

Metaphysical thinking is unreflective in relation to the veiling of its own complete essence, which is consolidating itself more and more. In metaphysics, this peculiar domination of the thinking that is obvious to itself is indeed the ground for all the "irrationalisms" emerging again and again within its history, which are distinguished only by a still cruder rationalism, if by this word we should mean the priority of calculative thinking in all the determinations of beings and being. The reflection of thought in the sense of the persistently creative interrogation of the clearing in which all creative thinking of being moves, is certainly no "reflection," which may be designated by the formula "thinking of thinking." This is because the history of metaphysics indeed accomplished this reflection in grand style in the age of German Idealism, so [139] decisively, that even reflection in the form of the philosophy of reflection was once again mirrored back and absorbed back into the absolute concept of unconditional knowledge. This happened in such a way that henceforth the reflection upon the horizon of thinking became even more impossible because it became even more unneeded. For, absolute knowledge as the truth of beings as a whole knows itself and thus excludes any questionability. From this, we can see in historical reflection that metaphysics, as soon as it becomes the thinking of thinking, distances itself, if anything, from reflecting on the truth of being, which is to be creatively thought and thus distances itself from the truth of thinking itself. As the question concerning the realm of the projection of the creative thinking of being, its opening and its grounding, the question of the sense of being is thus never a matter of "reflecting" upon thinking and the "I think." Rather the more inceptual question of being demands a leap from the human being as "subject" and that means, at the same time, from the relationship to the "object" and even from the latter itself. "Subjectivism" will not only not be overcome by a turn to the "object," but will be left all the more unperturbed and all the more unshakeable.

(Whether the overcoming of "subjectivism" and "objectivism" is at all an essential necessity of the thinking responsive to the history of beyng will preferably remain undiscussed here. For, this overcoming could indeed one day be exposed as a superfluous pseudo-battle that is only staged with unfailing enthusiasm so that the metaphysical thinking of the gaze can fancy itself to be relieved of its own questionable nature.)

The Overcoming of Metaphysics

II. Sequel

I. THE CONSUMMATION OF METAPHYSICS

THE ABANDONMENT BY BEING AND DEVASTATION

[145] 131. Metaphysics and "Science"

We can grasp beyng from beings even less than we can learn about mountain forests from the Steppe plains. Yet, the insidiousness persists; if being is to be extracted from anywhere, it would still have to be extracted from beings.

Yet, the requirement held by "science" for such an extraction, which of itself is not original, strengthens this insidiousness and elevates taking the actual as the point of departure into a law. "Science" as the support of metaphysics, created by metaphysics itself (of the kind of questioning that takes beings as its point of departure and is turned toward beings).

132. At the End of Metaphysics

which is simultaneously the end of the first inception, the *capacity to brutalize* becomes the characteristic feature of the actuality of anything actual, already after which actuality, for its part, has laid claim to beingness and the consummation of the essence of beingness.

133. Inception and Metaphysics

Metaphysics, and particularly its beginning, which already contains everything, is the advance from the first inception and the relinquishment of that inception.

Thus, *at one point in time* at the end of metaphysics and as that end, the abandonment of beings by being.

134. The Essence of the Consummation of Metaphysics in terms of the History of Beyng

The essencing of beyng as concealment in the form of the unleashing of beings into unconditional *abandonment by being*.

[146] Being in the essence of the corrupted essence as manipulation.

Manipulation as the consummation of beingness in the sense of the "*will*" (subjectness).

The will to love (Schelling) and to know (Hegel) as *taking leave* – into being unleashed as the will to power.

135. The Consummation of "Modernity" within the History of Beyng

is actualized in the handover of metaphysics (Nietzsche), which has developed unconditionally into an unconditionally corrupted essence, to the "worldview" that is appropriate to it. It is in this way that we first arrive at the realm of devastation, that is to say, that history, in which the permanence of the unconditional denial of any inception finds itself completely established. In this realm, the abandonment of beings by being will be definitively, that is to say, absolutely incapable of being experienced. For, abandonment has become the ground of all "beings." This consummation of modernity can only be Western, that is to say, can only be accomplished with the will and knowledge of *Europe*. It can thus be only accomplished there, where the essence of power is not only unleashed [*losgelassen*] but also *dispatched* [*losgeschickt*] and thrust into the unconditional. "Bolshevism" can never achieve this.

136. The Nothing and Devastation

The wasteland: The permanence of the denial of the inception. Devastation as assuring the ability to prolong a comprehensive uprooting of everything in such way that everything hitherto existing still remains preserved; that one strives toward a "politics of culture" for the sake of de-vastation.

[147] 137. Abandonment by Being

The pain, which must first be experienced and wrestled with, is the insight and the knowledge that the lack of urgency is the highest and the most hidden urgency, which urges from the farthest farness.

The lack of urgency consists supposedly in one having a grip on the *actual* and actuality and in knowing what is true without needing to know what truth is.

138. Abandonment by Being

The abandonment by being is the essence of nihilism in terms of the history of beyng, if what is eventuated in abandonment is the unleashing of beyng into manipulation. This unleashing puts human beings into an unconditional servitude. It is in no way a fall and a "negative" in any sense of the term.

It is also for this reason that no random humanity is fit to historically actualize unconditional nihilism. It is for this reason that a struggle is indeed needed over the decision as to which humanity is capable of bringing nihilism to an unconditional consummation. Bolshevism is only capable of destruction, but lacks the power of devastation, for which the highest spirituality continues to be needed.

139. The Abandonment of Beings by Being

The power of beings as the power of everything that is *actual* (success, operating, what is driven; the actual needs to be veiled by what is reported) is *so* decided that beings can renounce the claim to reflect upon being. It appears that there "are" only beings, facts and reports oriented toward facts [*Tatsachen-be-richte*], that is to say, such facts and factual provisions which correct [*be-richtigen*] facts, [148] setting it up [*einrichten*] for manipulation without ever being able to recognize manipulation itself as such.

Beings – as the real, factual and thus lived are left to themselves, being has withdrawn.

Beings, "existing" in this way, perpetuate the forgetting of being.

The signs and consolidation of the forgetting of being:
1. The authoritative role of *lived experience*; it decides what is actual and not actual. This happens such that "lived experience" itself

remains without reflecting upon and without any need for reflecting upon "life" ("life" and the organic, i.e., "organized").

2. The uniqueness of *"technology."*
3. *Historicism;* "the analysis;" "the description" "of the twentieth century;" ("facts" instead of cognition); flight into the past and random "memories;" misconstruing the future by deriving it from provenance.
4. The devastation leading to the lack of history (without the possibility for the decision about the essence of truth).
5. Finally and superficially in "philosophy:" the *business of ontology,* as the sign of the cluelessness about beyng.

140. Manipulation – Technology – Beyng

That manipulation as the abandonment of beings by being must perpetuate the forgetting of being and so at its most extreme must leave behind even what it itself is.

The self-destruction of the truth of manipulation – the unconditional aspect of the destruction is the devastation leading to the abandonment by being; this in the guise of the nihilating nothing, against everything "actual" that has come into its own, because it is actual and requires "analysis" with the intent to maintain the unconditional nature of calculation and technology.

The unconditional nature of "technology," which indeed comes to power in the place where it is guaranteed to dominate, is the mask [149] of the impotence of manipulation against its own essence. Impotence is the mode of complete *devastation,* which surpasses all destruction even more essentially because it once again invokes (in the impotent) the permanence of presence (that is to say, of what has fizzled out) and thus invokes beingness.

Technology will only be controlled if it is also given space in what is seemingly non-technological (i.e., here machine-related); the power of "organization" is in servitude to technology and "controls" it just as slaves through their complete subjugation bind their masters to themselves.

141. "Technology"[1]

The essence of technology is grasped as that which gives modern machine-technology its inner truth and necessity; thus, not according to a concept (general representation) of the immediately available "fact," which we call "technology." It is also not that which thinks this "technology" in a similar direction, as the appearance of "culture." For, "culture" itself grasped metaphysically belongs to the essence of a "technology." Technology is the truth of *subjectivity*, subjectivity grasped as beingness of beings (Nietzsche lecture).

The consequence of this "technology" taken in its essence, is the mathematical aspect of the sciences, the "system," the "dialectic."

"The technological" (merely limited to apparatuses and operations) is also not to be sought out in the sciences, art, politics as though these were in addition and essentially still something other. What is other and what is proper *is* precisely the metaphysical, indeed the "technological," understood in terms of the history of beyng. "Technology" grasped in this way stands in relation to τέχνη, which springs from φύσις, presupposing and perpetuating its occlusion.

"Technology" and abandonment by being.

[150] 142. Manipulation

is the unconditional consummation of being as will to power. But, as the essence of being, manipulation itself still has a corrupted essence.

The corrupted essence of manipulation demands a humanity that does not perhaps devastate all tradition, but that rather perpetuates a devastated, essentially rootless tradition of metaphysics (and that is to say, of Western history) over and beyond devastation, that is to say, into its corrupted essence. This establishment of the corrupted essence of manipulation is reserved for Americanism.

More gruesome than any Asiatic wildness is this morality that is uprooted and developed into an unconditional mendacity.

Here the abandonment by being first reaches the most extreme condition of a permanence.

Whether we sufficiently recognize that everything gruesome lies in Americanism and not *at all* in the Russian world?

---

[1] Cf. *Überlegungen XII–XV* (*Schwarze Hefte 1939–1941*), GA 96, 256f. {TN: *Ponderings XII–XV* (Black Notebooks 1939–1941), 203.}

II. THE ORIGIN OF METAPHYSICS IN THE HISTORY OF BEYNG

(cf. the final confrontation with Nietzsche's Metaphysics: "A priori" – [cf. Overcoming, Mindfulness])

THE ORIGIN OF METAPHYSICS AND THE ESSENCE OF TRUTH IN THE FIRST INCEPTION

(cf. The Inception
Anaximander
Heraclitus
Parmenides
The Advance of the First Inception
into the Beginning of Metaphysics)

[153] 143. Overcoming

The overcoming of metaphysics is *history* and is thus inceptuality and indeed as transition.

What essences [*west*] in transition is the gathering of that which was [*Gewesenen*] as it is coming to an end *and* of that which is to come as it is being prepared.

The end as the unconditionally corrupted un-inceptuality of the inception; with the inception unleashing itself into the corrupted essence.

The variations of *beingness* in the history of beyng – for which reason being has this name: οὐσία

1. as κοινόν – the most universal; καθόλου
2. as αἴτιον – the *fullest in being*; which is the *primordial* being.
3. Re-presentedness in certainty (subjectness)
4. Re-presentedness as *represented representing of oneself*; the doubled repraesentatio of Leibniz

5. The objectivity of Kant in the transcendentally clarified sense
6. The transcendentally clarified, unconditional re-presentedness of the putting-to-itself of the re-presenting itself developed into systematicity. Unconditional knowledge as will.
7. *Beingness as will* to power; the unconditional corrupted essence of absolute subjectness.

The historical essentiality of Kant for the preparation of the consummation of metaphysics:
1. The transcendental as the decisive clarification of subjectness; only by means of which Platonic–Aristotelian metaphysics becomes capable of a transformation.
2. The notion of *construction* from concepts.
3. The non-sensible *intuition*.
4. *Freedom* as the selfhood of reason; freedom and beingness.

[154] 144. One of the Characteristic Features of Metaphysics

is the discussion of the relationship between "nature" and "spirit" and of what has primacy between the two and the mediations that hereby arise between them by way of "life," which is, above all, taken to be "spiritual" and "natural."

The opposition of "nature" and "spirit" is then immediately folded into that of the "sensible" and the "supersensible" and the latter distinction again stands for the distinction between the "real" and the "ideal."

Above all, under the repercussions of Nietzsche's metaphysics adopted superficially, of which little has been grasped, the discussions and positions on the naturalness of the spirit and the spiritual essence of nature fall into the mixing bowl of the all-encompassing corrupted concept of "life," without having rigorously inquired into and grasped its essence as the "will to power" within the history of the truth of beings.

These discussions, which free themselves from designating the supersensible, seem then to be almost free of all metaphysics. They are this way also due to having given up on the unambiguous character of the metaphysics that is understood to be Christian. But on the contrary, they are completely entangled in the fundamental essence of metaphysics, as they engage less than ever with the question of the beingness of beings. Rather they undertake only pre-established areas of inquiry in order to fall within the decisions of these areas.

145. The Age of "Theologies"

That in the age of the end of all metaphysics, metaphysics itself emerges in its most palpable essence should not astonish us. "Theologies" demand primacy and, in fact, require no "God" or a decision about gods at all.

[155] These theologies are those of "providence" and "adventure," both of which exist for the reason that "technology" (planning and production and the uncertainty within that which is calculable) constitutes the truth of beings, which characterizes metaphysics at the end.

Theology becomes *diabology*, which certainly does not limit itself to the harmlessness of the "devil" as a fallen angel. It rather only admits and then unleashes the unconditional corrupted essence of God into the truth of beings. The explicit development of *diabologies* is imminent.

146. The Essence of Metaphysics
Theology and Mathematics

The dual role of a guiding thread played by "theology" and "mathematics," belongs to the development of the essence of metaphysics. At all times, theology and mathematics are themselves co-conditioned by the essence of the truth of beings.

In Plato the transformation of ἀλήθεια to ὁμοίωσις in connection with the interpretation of οὐσία as ἰδέα becomes the ground for designating ἀγαθόν as the authentic αἴτιον. With this, the *theological* character of metaphysics is decided because now and only now – the explicit determination of being (οὐσία as such) through ἐπέκεινα – being and the fullest in being taken as the divine are merged together. What does it mean to say that all metaphysics is "theological?" To what extent do we find the grounds here for the possibility of a fusion of Christian faith into metaphysics and a consolidation of this from the side of Christianity?

"Theology" in the essential development of modern metaphysics from Descartes to *Nietzsche*.

"Mathematics" becomes decisive for metaphysics only with the transformation of veritas to certitudo. But mathematics is thus not only a model for the "most rigorous" cognition. Rather, mathematics [156] – the being-certain – characterizes the fundamental mode of being as re-presentedness.

However, this role of mathematics must fail as soon as being-certain as subjectness becomes clearer, and self-consciousness, especially as the unconditional, proves to be a realm whose dimensionality can in essence never be reached by the "mathematical." Mathematics remains in the region of "quantity," and that means of immediate consciousness and its *calculation*.

147. "Truth" and Metaphysics
(Grades of the True)

Metaphysics does not at all think the essence of truth. It rather takes truth, as the essence of the "true," to be unquestionable and does not know of the realm of the decision, within which "truth" can seemingly consolidate itself into the unquestionable. (Truth as ὁμοίωσις, adequatio, correctness, certainty, validity, value). Metaphysics, when it arises, arrives at the grades of the *true*. But these grades are what they are within the historical essence of truth as *certainty*, which is rather one-off and singular and by no means "eternal." And these grades are also only apparent grades. For, none of these grades decides an essence of truth by itself and none of them even touches upon it.

In the event that one lumps together the thinking of the essence of truth that is responsive to the history of beyng with the opinion that truth is the unquestionable essence of the true, or that one is simply unable to work one's way out of this metaphysical belief, everything is lost; one can then be disturbed about the "relativity" of "truth" without even thinking truth.

Metaphysics is also unable to come upon the question as to why this zealous reduction of truth to a kind of essence of truth, namely, adaequatio, has consolidated itself so decisively, when this kind of essence is itself still hardly grounded. For what reason should [157] "truth" be one and the same throughout. Who demands this here and on what grounds?

The assurance of salvation as bonum and the assurance of the granting of salvation and the orientation toward the summum bonum would have had necessarily to arrive at the fabricated notion that the "true" (the correct, the sure) must be "eternal." With this step one immediately equates the truth itself with a historically necessary kind of truth without grasping the question concerning essence.

From the thought of "eternal truth," one has then reinterpreted the Greek ἀεὶ ὄν, which is of a different origin from aeternitas, but comes really close to it.

In this way, Plato becomes the first "Christian thinker." A bogus concept lurks behind this title. One accepts Plato and would like to reject Nietzsche, when both are the same.

148. On the Essential Determination of Modern Metaphysics in its Consummation

1. Being as the re-presentedness of the placing-before-oneself, is prefigured in the essential transformation of truth as veritas to certitudo. The essence of subjectness develops within being as re-presentedness. The simplest name for the determination of the beingness of beings that looms here is the "will;" Will *as willing oneself.*

   The fullness of the essence of "willing" cannot however be grasped from the perspective of "willing" as a "faculty of the soul." In fact, the will must be brought into an essential unity with appearing: ἰδέα – re-praesentatio – becoming manifest – pre-senting-*oneself* and so reaching-*oneself* and exceeding-*oneself* and so "having" – oneself and *so* "being."

2. In the essential existence of "willing" so grasped, lies the necessity of the "system" as the constitution of subjectness, i.e., of being itself as the beingness of beings.

3. [158] "System" is "system" only as "absolute" system. (On the concept of the "absolute" cf. the new interpretation of Schelling's Freedom Lecture.)[1]

4. Hence the two characteristic features of the essence of the consummation of modern metaphysics: (a) the manner in which the concept of philosophy is determined from the standpoint of absolute system, (b) the way in which system is placed into the corrupted essence in the most extreme consummation of metaphysics (Nietzsche) and appears to be negated.

   (a) Philosophy should abandon the name: "love of" "wisdom." Since knowledge itself is found to be essentially unconditional as certainty, "striving for," the middle position between having and not-having has become alien to it. This striking out of φιλία shows the consummation of "philosophy," that is to say, of the Platonic thinking about beings. Ἰδέα becomes "absolute idea," that is to say,

---

[1] *Die Metaphysik des deutschen Idealismus. Zur erneuten Auslegung von Schelling* [The Metaphysics of German Idealism: Toward a New Interpretation of Schelling], GA 49, 139f.

the spirit's unconditional appearing-to-itself in all its essential forms and structures. This appearing-to-itself is the coming-together and the assembling-together (σύστασις) of absolute knowledge in the unity of unconditionally developed certainty: "System."

(b) As soon as being manifests itself as will in the mode of the will to power, the selfhood of the subjectness, in which the will wills *itself*, is the constant empowerment toward the possibility, always assured, of being able to command, which is the decisive way of wanting to go beyond oneself (the overpowering). This unconditional self-assurance of the unconditional ability to command must renounce any "system." But this is only for the sake of being entirely in command of an organization of beings as a whole at all times and to forcibly assimilate this whole within itself. If Nietzsche's metaphysics *cannot* be grasped as a system of "being" and the thought of "system" [159] is rejected then there are hidden grounds for this, which were not clear to Nietzsche himself. These grounds lie in the systematicity of being inverting itself into the unconditional capacity of being to command as will to power, which is system-less and assured a fortiori. This unconditional capacity to command is oriented toward the total organization of beings, which is indeed always needed and although needed, often directly opposed.

The un-systematic aspect of the essence of power only generates a counter "systematicity" (i.e., essential concentration) of the corrupted essence of unconditional subjectness.

The relentlessness of organization, its essential emptiness and its unavoidable groundlessness, are no defects for the empowering of power. Additionally, organization also serves to dissimulate a "system" of power and this dissimulation is appropriate for concealing the essence of power in its most proper aspect, its lack of a system, within which it always exudes "power" *over all*. This deception is an essential moment of the assurance of power itself.

149. If Being is "Will" . . .

We can present the essence of modern metaphysics by a complete explication of this if-statement.

150. Metaphysics and "System"

1. System, as that which coherently comes together, is only possible when being in general becomes the objectivity of re-presenting; the inner relation of re-presenting as the self-assuring putting-to-oneself of the re-presented and assembling together as the re-presenting unity constitutes the essence of subjectness. (cf. "*Nietzsche III*")[1]

[160] 2. Thus, if the guiding concept of system can be located in the *mathesis* universalis and in the "mathematical" generally, then this can only be adequately accomplished if mathesis is shown to essentially originate from the certitudo of the ego cogito me cogitare.

3. Corresponding to the primacy of re-presenting and unifying in the sense of a certain having-put-to-oneself, the notion of the universe gains a completely different essence and weight. Just like mathesis even the universe must be determined in terms of the subjectness of the subjectum. The "universe" is thus to be thought differently from ordo and again differently from κόσμος.

4. With the transformation of representing commensurate with subjectness, the essence of ratio is also transformed. Following 1 and 2, it becomes clear that the inner relationship of reason to system is prepared and reason must in itself be "systematic."

5. At the same time, it is decided that reason as knowledge (representing putting-to-oneself) is "teleological" and thus the will.

6. This does not rule out the fact that what is essential to system is sought, above all, in understanding and in reason, where these are not taken as the capacities of the intellect, but are grasped as capacities for unification (cf. in Schelling: the understanding as "*universal will*").

7. The question propels us into the decision as to whether the will is to be the will of the spirit or the will of love; whether the "spirit" could be said to be the highest.

But even the interpretation of being as will of love remains within the metaphysics of subjectness.

---

[1] *Nietzsches Metaphysik*, GA 50, 40ff. {TN: See footnote 1 of section 78, translated into English as *Nietzsche III*, 216ff.}

[161] **151. The A priori
(cf. on Kant, Prolegomena Summer Semester 1941;[1]
cf. on Schelling, Treatise on Freedom, New Interpretation)[2]**

The essential connection between the emergence of the a priori and the transformation of ἀλήθεια; already the relation of εἶναι and νοεῖν to ταὐτόν.

Disclosedness – manifestness (presence)

How that which precedes visible clarity becomes *supplementary*:

1. through its dependence on the ἰδέα τελευταία.
2. through mislaying it into the fullest in being – ens entium, intellectus divinus.
3. thus mislaying it *generally into the intellectus* – ἰδέα to idea as "perceptio."
4. subsequently mislaying it into the intellectus humanus as egoity and self-consciousness, certainty.
5. yet again but finally the ἰδέα turns into Hegel's "absolute idea," into the unconditional self-appearing of beings as a whole in their essence in absolute knowledge.
6. *Schelling's* history of "revelation."

152. The First Inception and the Origin of Metaphysics

Being comes undone as beings are revealed as beings.

The being of beings is that which is to be perceived – what is needed is to think being from and in this inceptuality.

However, if being is determined as ἰδέα, the thinking of being (σοφία) becomes φιλο-σοφία. More precisely: From the ἀγαθόν taken as ἰδέα, φιλοσοφία is now interpreted as the thinking of the κοινόν and the οὐσία that grasps the idea.

[162] The thinking of being that has now become "philosophy" is in its essence metaphysics.

And therefore, the thinking of being is strangulated from its inception and can never again reach this inception *as* metaphysics, i.e., attain an appropriate inceptuality that faces up to the first inception.

---

[1] Intended for publication in: Seminare: *Kant-Leibniz-Schiller* [Seminars: Kant-Leibniz-Schiller], GA 84.2.

[2] *Die Metaphysik des deutschen Idealismus. Zur erneuten Auslegung von Schelling* [The Metaphysics of German Idealism: Toward a New Interpretation of Schelling], GA 49, 117.

The talk of the "collapse" of ἀλήθεια (cf. *Contributions*)[1] is a misunderstanding and in fact also inconsistent, because ἀλήθεια itself is never completely grounded. Rather, it is perhaps already from the inception assigned to the ὄν, which is opposed to νοεῖν. But that ἀλήθεια still concerns the two and consequently the ὄν on the whole more originally than φύσις, is what moves Parmenides and Heraclitus.

153. Being as ἰδέα and the Collapse of ἀλήθεια

still grasps unconcealedness. But at the same time, we find in the ἰδέα the emphasis on and thus the primacy of the relation to ἰδεῖν and νοεῖν, i.e., to the ψυχή (by which we neither mean the subject yet nor that the "idea" becomes "subjective"). However, something other, which is by far the more essential, is already in preparation. The later transformation of the ἰδέα to perceptio is only an essential consequence of this.

Unconcealedness comes under the rule of the ἰδέα. This ἰδέα, which in essence is only an appearing of ἀληθές, becomes the cause of ἀλήθεια. The idea proper – the good – guarantees ἀλήθεια and makes it available. Ἀλήθεια itself transforms into that which, commensurate with the ἰδέα, *is calibrated to the* ἰδέα, is *right* for the idea and is thus correct.

And with this, the essencing of the unconcealedness disappears and cedes its place to correctness. Henceforth, correctness must be explained in a different way, given the forgetting of ἀλήθεια: Unconcealedness is something unknown, ungraspable, self-evident, and unworthy of consideration. And any hint that it belongs together with being is already completely quashed with regard to its very possibility.

[163] 154. ἡ τοῦ αγαθοῦ ἰδέα*
The Beginning of Metaphysics
and the Crash and Collapse of the Ungrounded ἀλήθεια

The visible clarity of the good, the good as *the* visible clarity is τὸ ὄν τὸ φανότατον (Republic VII, 518c9), a being – that which is the most apparent.

---

[1] *Beiträge zur Philosophie (Vom Ereignis)*, GA 65, 334f, 339f.
{TN: *Contributions to Philosophy (Of the Event)*, 264–265f., 268–269f.; *Contributions to Philosophy (From Enowning)*, 234f, 237–238f.}
* {TN: *Republic*, Book 6, 505a2: the idea of the good.}

This pure appearing that enables everything goes beyond any being and its beingness, ἐπέκεινα τῆς οὐσίας, because it determines the essence of beingness. (cf. the interpretation of the Allegory of the Cave)[1]

The appearing of what is most apparent is once again forgotten and the "good" is understood as cause in the sense of a merely "productive" effectuation and preservation and only as this.

However, after the collapse of the Christian illumination of the world this cause as ground is appreciated as ratio – reason. What is appreciated and that on which it depends becomes "value."

τὸ ἀγαθόν – as τελευταία ἰδέα* is αὐτὴ κυρία . . . παρασχομένη ἀλήθειαν καὶ νοῦν.** Unconcealedness of beings and the perception of an unconcealed being. Here we have the decisive reversal: The idea becomes the ground of the unconcealedness of beings instead of unconcealedness being the ground of the ἰδέα.

The pushing forward of the ἰδέα within ἀλήθεια and ahead of it and thus the pushing away of ἀλήθεια and the burial of the completely unseized possibility of its inceptual grounding, all of this springs from the essencing of beyng. It occludes itself and leaves the just disclosed beings to themselves and to what the human being, who is placed in this way among beings as such, is capable of doing with them.

Beings in their consolidated disclosedness are installed in this truth and have their history in it. This truth is the essence of what is then later [164] called "metaphysics." This can only be ἐπιστήμη and σοφία as φιλοσοφία because of this truth of beings and as long as it essences and happens.

Metaphysics is thus the history of the truth of beings as such as a whole.

155. How Metaphysics Begins and Peters Out

Designating ἀγαθόν as the τελευταία ἰδέα over ἀλήθεια and ἀληθές as γιγνωσκόμενον is the first and that is to say, the truly most far-reaching step toward the serialized production of long-range fighter jets and the invention of the radio-technological essence of newscast, with whose help the former can be employed in the service of what has likewise

---

[1] "Platons Lehre von der Wahrheit," Wegmarken, GA 9, 203–238. {TN: "Plato's Doctrine of Truth," Pathmarks, 155–182.}

* {TN: ultimate idea.}

** {TN: Republic 517c2–3, Plato: Complete Works: that which controls and provides truth and understanding.}

been pre-figured by this step – the unconditional mechanization of the globe and its human beings.

Whether this "spirit" is grasped biologically or spiritually, whether "mentally" or "materially," whether one finds "materialism" here or whether it is refuted and rejected, is the most *inconsequential* of what is inconsequential within the unconditional unleashing of power into its essence: *pure manipulation*.

156. "Watching" and "Thinking"
(The End of Metaphysics)

Reflecting on metaphysics as the history of the unsettling of the essence of truth, consummating in the extreme abandonment of beings by being, which happens as the succeeding phases of modernity proceed and peter out, could appear as if one were only watching a drama of inevitabilities, which is allowed to reach its conclusion.

But this supposed "watching" always arises from knowing the ground and inception of this history. And this knowledge is the persistence in the essence of truth and its [165] more inceptual grounding. Such persistence is the patience of mildness that has dared the greatest tranquillity and demands a courage, which must leave heroism behind.

Is such a reflection as the active silence of the more inceptual words of beyng, a "watching" and "letting-pass?"

157. The History of Being and Metaphysics

Since metaphysics is the history of the truth "of" beings as such as a whole, it belongs in the history of beyng, and given the essencing of the truth of beyng, it belongs to beyng itself. The history of the truth of beings arises in every one of its stages, every time there is an unleashing of being into explicable beings and thus into a veiling of the essence of truth as unconcealedness. To that extent, the alteration to truth as certainty signifies a characteristic feature of this unleashing.

The history of beyng is not to be thought rationally, not to be deduced according to a plan and a sequence of steps (in Hegel's sense, for instance); it is essentially inceptuality and its concealment. Here, everything remains in the unforeseeable. Even "comprehensive accounts" of a historical process are unable to provide any clarification here. For, the leap into the truth of beyng is to be prepared more inceptually every time and the readiness to be claimed must be awakened.

158. "Worldview" and "Metaphysics"

The *apparently* essential question as to whether the spirit supports and determines the body or whether the spirit is only an emanation ("expression") of the body-mind, all of this has already fallen completely outside the true thinking of being and plays out within the realm of anthropologism.

[166] Nothing will be decided by the back and forth of these possibilities because all of this remains outside the question of being. This back and forth becomes the last *glint* of a "thinking" that is lost in frenzy, a frenzy that cannot be escaped any longer by any kind of school-masterly "ontology" of philosophical savants. In this way, a new "late-scholasticism" arises that is in keeping with the time of the contemporary present, which is a conceptually selective, retrospective presentation and systematization of the theoretical content of a "belief," indeed of an unconditional belief, as long as what it believes to be the highest is belief itself. One believes in one's belief (extreme nihilism).

159. Animal rationale – absolutum (causa)

During and after the *overcoming of metaphysics*, we will neither inquire into the human being (psychologically – morally – politically, in short anthropologically) nor into the absolute, highest being (theistically, atheistically, in short theologically).

Both no more because beings (pre-determined as human – divine) will no longer be investigated on the basis of their beingness ("ontologically" in the broader sense).

All the possibilities for comparing the thinking responsive to the history of beyng with "philosophy" will become invalid. (cf. Winter Semester 37/38)[1]

However, what dominates all metaphysics, the interest in the "mind" and the explanation from the "absolute" is only the essentially unrecognizable residue of the unleashing of beings into beingness, which is no longer to be mastered. In this unleashing, being is ἰδέα and i.e., ἀγαθόν – ἐνέργεια – > αἰτία. This primacy of ψυχή and ἰδέα from their reciprocal relationship, which itself stems from what is even found in Heraclitus and Parmenides – certainly ungrounded – is retained in the ταὐτό of εἶναι and νοεῖν, in the ἀλήθεια and the λόγος of φύσις.

[1] *Grundfragen der Philosophie. Ausgewählte "Probleme" der "Logik,"* GA 45, 181ff. {TN: *Basic Questions of Philosophy: Selected "Problems" of "Logic,"* 156ff.}

[167] 160. Truth as Certainty: Modern Metaphysics (Leibniz)

means *assuring* the being of the human being on the basis of itself and for itself.

Indeed, this essence of truth like all history is only developed in sharp thrusts and often eventuates in a forward thrust, which can simply not be recognized in terms of its essential scope, within the realm of this thrust.

Thus, Leibniz stands in many aspects still entirely within the Christian world and far from any displacement of the human being into the unconditional. *Nevertheless*, he is the inventor of "life insurance." This fact contributes more toward the elucidation of his metaphysics than wide-ranging discussions on the Charakteristica univeralis or the pre-established harmony.

III. METAPHYSICS

(cf. The Overcoming of the Metaphysics,
The History of Beyng)[1]

THE BASIC POSITIONS OF METAPHYSICS

(The Consummation of Metaphysics)

Cf. Hegel's Negativity,[2]
Schelling's Treatise on Freedom,[3]
Nietzsche's Metaphysics[4]

[171] **161. From Whence the Appearance that the
Thinking Responsive to the History of Beyng is Only a
Modification of Hegel's Metaphysics?**

From the fact that one neither has a knowledge of the essence of metaphysics as the truth of beings nor attempts to carry out the questioning
responsive to the history of beyng as the inceptual question. If one
falsifies beforehand the ungrasped thinking responsive to the history

---

[1] *Die Geschichte des Seyns*, 1. *Die Geschichte des Seyns* (1938/40), 2. *Κοινόν:
Aus der Geschichte des Seyns* (1939/40), GA 69, ed. P. Trawny (Frankfurt am
Main: Vittorio Klostermann, 1998). {TN: Translated into English as *The History
of Beyng*, trans. William McNeill and Jeffrey Powell (Bloomington: Indiana
University Press, 2015).}

[2] *Hegel*. 1. *Die Negativität* (1938/39), 2. *Erläuterungen der "Einleitung" zu Hegels
"Phänomenologie des Geistes"* (1942), GA 68, ed. Ingrid Schüßler (Frankfurt am
Main: Vittorio Klostermann, 1993). {TN: Translated into English as *Hegel*, trans.
Joseph Arel and Niels Feuerhahn (Bloomington: Indiana University Press, 2015).}

[3] *Schelling, Vom Wesen der menschlichen Freiheit* [*Schelling: On the Essence of
Human Freedom*], GA 42.

[4] *Nietzsches Metaphysik*, GA. 50. {TN: Translated into English as *Nietzsche
III*.}

of beyng into metaphysics and its ungrounded essence, then one can later certainly procure this thinking from there [Hegel's metaphysics], as needed, and "already" rediscover it there.

The thinking responsive to the history of beyng is then only a "Hegel" gone over to the side of caution, who in place of the "absolute spirit" posits finite knowledge.

By such a comparison we can indeed equate anything with anything; where we ourselves land up as a result, we leave unquestioned and take as something settled and assured.

162. Hegel's Concept of History

History is "motion" and motion is progress as transition. The transition is specifically between modes of consciousness, that is to say, between modes of certainty and modes of subjectness. The character of the transition is "dialectical," i.e., determined here by the unconditionality of certainty – absolute knowledge of oneself.

The systematicity of subjectness brought into such motion is the essence of history, according to Hegel.

The fact that the "the philosopher" in his or her knowledge is identical with the world-spirit in this history, taken as the dialectical consciousness of the absolute spirit, has certainly nothing in common with the belongingness of Da-sein to beyng as event.

But this subjectness as spirit is the truth of beings, which has proceeded from the inceptual essence of being. This truth of beings, as [172] the unconditional certainty of beings must be taken for being itself.

163. Beyng – Event – Inception
(Meant from the Standpoint of "Metaphysics")

The inceptual essence of beyng and thus, beyng itself, that it is the throw and the inexplicable is concealed from metaphysical thinking.

The inceptual essence of beyng is also completely inaccessible to the opinion, which is itself an offshoot of metaphysics, which would nevertheless still like to inflate itself into the most up-to-date modernity, as the salvation of the "spirit." This opinion is that fatal mixture of Christianity and scientificity, of the defence of a Christianity, which lacks the power of evidence and the "corroboration" of science, which remains a pure positivism. With this mixture one still invokes ideas, as and when they are apt.

Here we come across an explicability of beings, which is already explained in a "Christian" way. This explicability of beings is the proper enemy of the poetic essence of being.

*

Metaphysics

Descartes to Mersenne, 16-10-1639, Opp. II, 596:[1]
". . . il y a peu de personnes qui soient capable d'entendre la metaphysics."
"Philosophy" – φιλοφροσύνη II. 9, 256[2]
"Nature" – (essence)
[173] Cf. Kant, *Prolegomena* § 2c:[3] "The nature" of pure mathematics "and so to speak, its state constitution."
θεωρία and θεός, cf. Nicholas of Cusa, *De deo abscondito.*[4]

---

[1] Descartes, Correspondence 1638–1639, *Oeuvres de Descartes: Meditations et Principes: Principes de la Philosophie*, Tome II, ed. Charles Adam and Paul Tannery (Paris: Leopold Cerf, 1898), 596. {TN: Translated into English in *The Philosophical Works of Descartes, Vol. III: The Correspondence*, trans. John Cottingham et. al (Cambridge: Cambridge University Press, 1991), 139: . . . there are few who would be capable of understanding metaphysics, translation slightly modified.}

[2] Homer, *Ilias.* 9, v. 256. {TN: Translated into English as *The Iliad*, trans. A. T. Murray (London: William Heinemann Ltd.; New York: G. P. Putnam's Sons, 1928), 401: gentle-mindedness}

[3] Kant, Prolegomena zu einer jeden künftigen Metaphysik, *Werke*, Vol. IV, ed. Ernst Cassirer (Berlin: Bruno Cassirer Verlag, 1922), § 2c, 18 {TN: Translated into English as *Prolegomena to any Future Metaphysics*, revd. edn., trans. Gary Hatfield (Cambridge: Cambridge University Press, 2004), 20, translation slightly modified. The passage to which Heidegger is referring is the following:
Hume, when he felt the call, worthy of a philosopher, to cast his gaze over the entire field of *a priori* cognition, in which the human understanding claims such vast holdings, inadvertently lopped off a whole (and indeed the most considerable) province of the same, namely pure mathematics, by imagining that the nature and so to speak the state constitution of this province rested on completely different principles, namely solely on the principle of contradiction; and although he had by no means made a classification of propositions as formally . . . as I have done here, it was nonetheless just as if he had said: Pure mathematics contains only *analytic* propositions, but metaphysics contains synthetic propositions *a priori*.}

[4] Nicholas of Cusa, "Dialogus de deo abscondito," *Opera Omnia* jussu et auctoritate Academicae Litteratum Heidelbergensis (Leipzig-Hamburg: Meiner, 1932ff), IV, n. 14. {TN: Translated into English as *On the Hidden God: A Dialogue between two [discussants] – one a pagan and the other a Christian, A Miscellany on Nicholas of Cusa*, trans. Jasper Hopkins (Minneapolis: The Arthur J. Banning Press, 1994), 304.}

164. Beings as a Whole and their Entirety
(Metaphysics and Beyng)

does not coincide with the sum-total of beings, not to speak of the difference between sum-total and wholeness as modes of unification.

The whole is not only different and more than the sum-total. It is at the same time also essentially *less* than the sum-total and here our allusion to *beings as a whole* stands resolved.

The differentiation between beings *as such* – whatness – and beings *as a whole* – thatness.

*

"Theology" – The Absolute

The question concerning beings as a whole as the question concerning the "absolute."

The absolute as the cause, the primordial being – the first and comprehensive condition of the enabling of beings as a whole and as such.

*

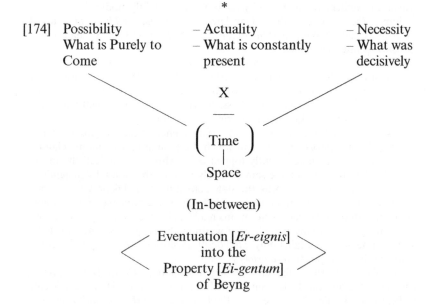

[174]   Possibility   – Actuality   – Necessity
        What is Purely to   – What is constantly   – What was
        Come   present   decisively

X

(Time)

Space

(In-between)

Eventuation [*Er-eignis*]
into the
Property [*Ei-gentum*]
of Beyng

The Essence of Nihilism

[177] The Essence of Nihilism[1]

The name "nihilism" says, if it is to become a naming word and not remain a buzzword, that the *nihil* (nothing) exists essentially in what it names. Nihilism means: there is nothing with respect to a being, and by no means just with respect to this or that being, rather there is nothing with respect to beings as such a whole.

If we venture to think nihilism from this perspective then we stand, knowingly or not, at the place where beings as such open up as a whole and that is to say, where they are thought. This is metaphysics. In it we can experience nihilism. But not every metaphysics has experienced nihilism, only the metaphysics of Nietzsche. It alone asks and tells us for the first time what nihilism is. Nietzsche's concept of nihilism is thus metaphysical. There comes a moment when we must assess the scope of this epoch of thinking. Before that, it is essential to make the first metaphysical experience of nihilism our own and reflect upon it. This requires us to think through Nietzsche's metaphysics. Such a thing cannot be done in a few words. Perhaps it is still not at all possible to do it today, neither in relation to Nietzsche's metaphysics nor in relation to any other metaphysics before him. We must thus content ourselves with a makeshift arrangement.

We will try to indicate the essence of nihilism by means of a commentary on an expression by Nietzsche. The expression is: "God is dead." With this expression Nietzsche gives a theological and, seemingly, only a negative formula for what he, thinking metaphysically, understands under nihilism.

Nihilism, thought positively, is metaphysics understood as the truth of a being (of what is actual) in terms of the will [178] to power from

[1] In the following treatise the talk "of being itself" always means: Being as being. Being itself: 1. Being as being (being in *Being and Time* is conceived as "time," as presence, the present, space of temporal play, event); 2. Being on its own account (The same, identity, essence of identity, event).

the eternal recurrence of the same. What beings are in their ground (principle), the essentia of beings, is the will to power, understood to be that which essentially posits value. Insofar as the will wills itself as command, it wills the same in all the different things it has willed. In willing itself it returns to itself in what is the same each time. It belongs to beings as such to exist in the how of the constant recurrence of the same. The eternal recurrence of the same, which is how the will to power exists as it does, characterizes the existentia of beings as such as a whole. The fact that Nietzsche leaves unthought the ontological relationship of the will to power and the eternal recurrence of the same, is no failure of the metaphysics, which he had to conceive. It is rather the essential failure of all metaphysics that the relationship of the fundamental metaphysical features of beings, of essentia and existentia, remains obscure in its origin and thus in its truth.

This is the reason why neither Nietzsche himself in his metaphysics, nor in any way the philosophical thinking that existed prior to him, can ever satisfactorily think the relationship between the will to power and the eternal recurrence of the same. But from this, it does not follow that the will to power and the eternal recurrence of the same do not belong together as the fundamental basis of beings.

Insofar as the will to power essences in its existence from the eternal recurrence of the same, the positing of value, which belongs essentially to it, is the being fullest in being amongst beings. The positing of value that is grounded in the will to power positively rejects the validity of the hitherto existing values, which in the principle of their positing are ungrounded according to Nietzsche's doctrine. This positive rejection of prior values, which posits the principle of value-positing, is the fundamental feature of metaphysical nihilism, which Nietzsche conceives as the philosophy of the future.

But how then can the negative theological formula for nihilism, the expression "God is dead," still be supposed to count as the formula for nihilism? If it nevertheless counts, and it does [179] count, then a positive tone must in some sense resonate in this expression. If this is so then Nietzsche himself must have emphasized this positive tone. In the entire text of the passage that expresses the formula, only two places are spaced out, i.e., emphasized, in addition to the heading. The first is found in the following context: "The madman jumped into their midst and pierced them with his gaze. "Where is God?" he cried, "I will tell you! *We have killed him** – you and I! We are all his murderers!"[2]

---

* {TN: This sentence is not emphasized in the text. I have emphasized it because Heidegger refers to it in the succeeding paragraph.}

[2] Friedrich Nietzsche, "Die Fröhliche Wissenschaft," in *Nietzsches Werke*

The sentence that is emphasized provides the interpretation of the expression "God is dead." The happening whereby the supersensible world falls away and loses its binding-formative essence is construed as the act of the human being. Nihilism, understood as the history of the devaluation of the highest values, is the work of humans. Yet, how is the emphasized sentence supposed to convey a positive sense for the formula for nihilism "God is dead?" Does not the emphasized interpretation of the characteristic feature of nihilism sound even more negative? It speaks of "murder." It names an act, which manifestly cannot be atoned for through any atonement ceremony. Can the happening "God is dead," can nihilism be construed more negatively than that through which it appears as an irreconcilable act? The formula for nihilism is demonstrated by Nietzsche's own interpretation as something that is only negative and for this reason, as something inadequate for articulating positive nihilism.

Yet, immediately after the sentences "With what water can we purify ourselves? What atonement ceremonies, what sacred games will we have to invent?"*** there follows without transition the question: "Is not the greatness of this act too great for us?"**** Now the act appears as something great. Does its "greatness" only consist in the unthinkability of the crime of murder? If so, it would remain a negative greatness. But Nietzsche must indeed think it positively, if he wants to say through his manner of questioning that we, human beings, [180] are too small for the "greatness of this act." This means: Human beings in their essence do not measure up to this act. Hence, they are also still not capable of grasping this act as such. Hence the lore of this act still cannot indeed even reach their ears.

In the interim we would like to ask: How can human beings then, if everything about them is so small, ever have committed this great act? Nietzsche answers this with one sentence, which like the interpretation of the formula is the only other set of words that is spaced out with it: *"– and yet they have done the very thing!"*****

The human beings of Western history have committed an act, to whose greatness they cannot themselves measure up. When historical

---

(Großoktavausgabe) [*Nietzsche's Works (Großoktav Edition)*], Vol. V (Stuttgart: Kröner, 1921), n. 125, S. 163f. {TN: Translated as *The Gay Science, with a Prelude in Rhymes and an Appendix of Songs*, trans. Walter Kaufmann (New York: Vintage Books, 1974), 181, translation modified.}

** {TN: Ibid., translation modified. Nietzsche's original text says "could" [*könnten*]" and not "can" [*können*], as Heidegger cites it here.}

*** {TN: Nietzsche, *The Gay Science*, 181, translation modified.}

**** {TN: Ibid., translation modified.}

humans have brought to fruition such an act in such a manner, they must indeed have given themselves over to what is great in the greatness of this act. In what does its greatness consist, if it is not all exhausted in the negativity of the excessiveness of a crime? Nietzsche answers through the words of the madman: "There was never a greater act and whoever will be born after us belongs, for the sake of this act, to a higher history than all history hitherto!"****

The greatness of this act consists in its being the beginning of a higher history. Therefore, if we follow this interpretation, the formula for nihilism "God is dead" does say something positive through the sentence: "*We have killed him.*" What sounds like the declaration of an end, when invariably thought from the standpoint of the thinking of Nietzsche's metaphysics, names the beginning of a higher history. The formula thinks nihilism positively.

Yet, what comprises the elevated nature of this history, which begins with what is the greatest historical act so far and which for Nietzsche has already begun? This higher history can indeed only be recognized when we have already thought the determining act sufficiently clearly. This act is the killing of God. We must finally pose the question, to which we know we have been compelled all along: How can God be killed at all? How can human beings ever kill God?

[181] We do not need to direct this question toward Nietzsche alone. He himself has already asked us this question? In the manner in which he asks this question, he already indicates how he wishes his talk of God's death and God's murderers to be thought.

Immediately after the decisive words of the madman: "*We have killed him* – you and I! We are all his murderers."***** Nietzsche lets him ask: "But how have we done this?" What was going on with this murder of God is indicated in the various images: "How were we able to drink up the sea? Who gave us the sponge to wipe away the entire horizon? What were we doing when we unchained this earth from its sun?"*

If we go by the preceding explanation, we know that the name God stands, metaphysically speaking, for the supersensible world. Since Plato, it is the realm of the "ideas." In their light, which is equated to the sun, beings appear as such. The murder of God, metaphysically speaking, consists in wiping away the entire horizon. The horizon of the supersensible is erased. The idea transforms itself from Plato's εἶδος into the perceptio of the ego cogito of the res cogitans, which Descartes

---

**** {TN: Ibid., translation modified.}
***** {TN: Ibid., translation modified.}
* {TN: Nietzsche, *Gay Science*, 181, translation modified.}

conceives as the substantia finita of the terrestrial human being. The earth is unchained from the sun. Everything that is, exists as the objectum of the subjectum. This is how the self-consciousness of the human being makes itself the basis of everything by measuring all objectivity in accordance with the self-certainty of self-consciousness. The truth about all objectivity becomes the certainty of subjectivity. God becomes the object [*Objekt*] of all objects [*Objekte*], i.e., God becomes the absolute subjectivity of the unconditional self-certainty of everything, the object [*Gegenstand*] and the thing. It is for this reason alone that the question can arise as to whether and how this thing in itself is cognizable or not. The entire horizon of the supersensible is wiped away because it has become that which is posited by the representing subject's act of self-positing. However, this positing of the object by the subject accomplished in the self-assurance of itself has already [182] posited certainty and assurance as the condition of itself with the erasure of the prior horizon. Subjectivity is that which posits values as such. The "truth" itself, the being of beings, understood as that which is permanent, reveal themselves as value, posited in the will to power that in essence assesses values. The entire horizon of the super-sensible is, if it is not already wiped away, obliterated. The supersensible is robbed of its power to nourish, support, form and stimulate. It becomes lifeless. God is killed. The killing of God consists in the positing of the idea as the objectum for the subject. In this way, the reign of the appearing of that which comes to presence, which essences from out of itself, is dispelled. The killing of God is itself a history. This history has its decisive turning point at the juncture where human beings establish their essence in the subject–object relationship, upon which every merely possible truth of beings is erected. Human beings have thus committed this act of killing without having any advance knowledge of the ground (principle) from which they acted and henceforth act. In fact, human beings as subjects now know self-certainty as the criterion of all objectivity. However, they cannot yet experience that the ego cogito, taken as the principle itself, remains conditioned by something even more fundamental. Certainty as assurance can only become the principle when assurance is already assessed as the highest value, when the assessment of values is accomplished as such and, that is to say, when the positing of value, for its part, becomes aware of its principle. When this happens, subjectivity succeeds in becoming the ultimate ground of itself. However, this happens when metaphysics experiences the will to power as the actuality of what is actual and assimilates the principle of all value-positing into such an experience. But, as long as this has not happened, the wiping away of the entire horizon of the highest values remains without a principle. The act of killing God remains too great for human beings, who have nonetheless performed it in its entirety, to the extent that they have understood themselves as subjectivity. Human beings lag behind the already reigning principle of their essence. But, insofar as the will to power is posited as the principle of all value-positing, this principle [183] comes to have a higher standing as the actuality of all actual happening. Thus, begins a "higher history."

It begins in principle with wiping away the entire horizon that existed previously. The higher history, however, only really begins when human beings, who were hitherto too small for the greatness of their act, transcend this smallness. Human beings existing hitherto go beyond their hitherto existing essence when they acquire for themselves an essence of the kind that corresponds to the being of all beings, i.e., to the will to power. When they grasp their essence in willing, as the "I will" in terms of the will to power, then they have gone beyond their prior essence, the animal rationale. So little is ratio thus eliminated as their essential feature that it is rather only now placed in the service of the will that wills itself and takes over for this will, the calculated assurance of the continued existence of all beings, i.e., of the "truth." As long as ratio is not grounded in the being of beings in terms of the will to power, neither ratio itself nor the animality of human beings is realized. Hence, Nietzsche calls the human being hitherto existing, whose essence still does not will and simultaneously does not think from the will to power, the "animal that is not yet realized." But insofar as human beings existing hitherto as the rational animal go beyond themselves and take up willing from the will to power, animalitas, the hitherto incomplete essence of human beings, is completed for the first time.

Human beings who go beyond their previous essence and into the "higher history" of the will to power, explicitly experiencing it and taking it up, are "superhumans."

With this oft misinterpreted appellation, Nietzsche does not intend some individual exemplar of the hitherto existing species "human being", in which the individual capacities and intentions of the commonly known human being are exceptionally augmented and intensified into something gigantic. Rather, this appellation names the essential structure of the very humanity that henceforth experiences its own being as the will to power, admitting that it exists in the way it does, insofar as it already belongs to the [184] actuality of the actual already decided in terms of the will to power.

However, the essence of the self-willing subjectivity reaches its consummation in the will to power as the essentia of all beings, with subjectivity being the principle of the epoch called "modernity." At this point,

The Essence of Nihilism 151

humanity in the essential form of the superhuman stands at the beginning of the consummation of modernity. The dominance over the earth unchained from the sun wills itself to be one that is unconditional and total. The struggle for this dominance is conducted by a humanity that transcends the human being hitherto existing and therefore belongs to a "higher history." The appellation under which these instances of humanity emphasize their kind and their will is of no concern because such names stem from what existed hitherto as modernity. This final struggle within this epoch receives its particular acuteness from the fact that the combatants struggle from the actuality of the will to power which always appears the same and yet differently. They thus struggle for the same thing: for the will to power, which is itself that from which this history of the superhumanly human beings originates. "Humanism" appears in a peculiar light, especially when it is understood on the basis of the representations of humankind, still too small for what it does every day.

Superhumanity, in keeping with its historical-earth-dominating determination, has in essence already gone beyond the national. It is just as little international because the international is always just a consequence dependent upon the national and thus in essence still national. "National" and "international" are categories of the hitherto existing humanity.

What is historical is the necessary and variously disguised appearing of the superhuman, which emerges from the will to power as the already essencing actuality of the actual. That is why the superhuman is never a kind of human that could only ever arise from the practical application of the philosophy of "Mr. Nietzsche." Along such a path, there are only [185] half-baked comprehensions and therefore comprehensive misinterpretations of a philosophy, which degenerate into an ill-intention (but not history).

The self-transcending human beings existing hitherto have been on the way to themselves for centuries, that is, on the way to going above and beyond themselves. The humanity of the will to power is already historical before it expresses itself with words originating from the metaphysics of the will to power. It is historical even when and more so when it speaks another language and speaks it from the will to power, which, in accordance with the essence of the empowering power, never says what it wants. Thought from the standpoint of being, the metaphysics of the will to power is simply not ordained to provide the historically acting superhumanity with an "ideology," but rather to prepare the hidden history of being in its inconspicuous arrival.

Let us grant that the essential development of metaphysics indeed exhausts itself and consummates in the metaphysics of the will to power. Let us also grant that metaphysics brings the truth of beings as such to history, but never the truth of being itself. Let us grant, as a final point, that it is being itself that is truly the truth. In that case, the history of being in the epoch of the consummation of metaphysics approaches a unique and seldom noticed turning point, into which there is no transition in the sense of a footbridge.

The appellation "superhuman," when thought metaphysically, signifies the historical humanity which, with the horizon of the supersensible wiped away on account of the actuality of the will to power, conducts the struggle for dominance over the earth that has been unchained from the sun. It understands this struggle as its history and thus establishes all historiography upon this struggle in the form of the appropriate objectification of history.

The superhuman has come out of the superseded and metaphysically half-thought essence of the hitherto existing human being (animal rationale), but only in order to turn back into the essential ground of the ratio and the animalitas, namely, into the will to power. The superhuman, seen from the hitherto prevailing horizon [186] of the hitherto existing humanity and its metaphysical world, is necessarily de-ranged [*ver-rückt*], and that is to say, the madman. That is why Nietzsche's metaphysics gives the now elucidated passage from *The Gay Science*, the sub-heading "The Madman." First, the madman views the will to power as the principle of a "higher history," in virtue of the disarrangement [*Verrückung*] of his essence in the consummation of the subjectivity of the will to power. Only the madman can, in line with his thinking, which is to posit values, cognize and will in a cognizant manner, the greatest act of all history hitherto, which for him is the act of value-positing. This act is the "death of God," interpreted into the knowledge: "*We have killed him* – you and I; we are all his murderers." In the emphasized statement the "we" needs to be emphasized once more. The "you and I" signifies the bystanders, who do not believe in God and the one, who, in search of God, "screams" after God. "We all" signifies not only the ones named, but in accordance with the conclusion of the passage, even those who think that they believe in God. "We all" – this expression thinks of the historical humanity of the West, whose history is grounded in the historical course of metaphysics. "We are all his (God's) murderers."

But this statement, thought in the terms of the madman, says something that is at same time positive, beyond its appearance as something only negative: As a consequence of this act, which without our knowledge has already overrun our essence, we stand under the claim to the truth of beings as such as a whole to which we have not yet caught up. This truth appears as the will to power from the eternal recurrence of the same. This being of beings demands from our human essence the very kind of willing, by means of which the modern humanity of unconditional subjectivity first corresponds to the being of beings in order to be actual in such a correspondence, that is to say, to be truthful from the truth of the metaphysics of the will to power. The ego cogito is that in which subjectivity is for the first time brought to an unconcealedness that is commensurate to it. This ego cogito, as the unthought co-agitare, is already the rounding-up of all beings toward the "I think," the will of the subject, which [187] wills itself. The God in the metaphysical meditations of Descartes is already a dead God, that is to say, a God who has been killed. With the death of God, the will as the will to power comes to life. In principle, this is how the essence of the superhuman is willed. This is why Nietzsche concludes the first part of *Thus Spoke Zarathustra*, which appeared in 1883, a year after *The Gay Science*, with the words: *"'Dead are all the gods: now we will that the superhuman live'* – on the great noon, let this be our last will!"*

Inasmuch as this will wills itself, the superhuman is historically actualized. "The great noon" is the time of the brightest brightness, namely, the brightness of the clara et distincta perceptio of the very self-consciousness, which has guaranteed (co-agitat) its subjectivity unconditionally and in every aspect. This assurance occurs in the knowledge that a will exists by willing the will to power as the objectivity of all that is actual, i.e., as the being of all beings, but i.e., as the subjectivity of all objects.

From its unconditional subjectivity, the superhuman wills itself in the willing of the will to power and in its willing-itself it wills the will to power. Its subjective willing appears to it necessarily as the execution of the objective will to power. In such an appearance it is the yea-saying to what is.

The unconditional subjectivity of the superhuman brings the will to power as the being of all beings into the brightness of its own self. It is a kind of unconcealedness and in this way still a trace of the old essence of truth. We will therefore say: The unconditional subjectivity of the superhuman is the truth of beings, in as much as being appears as the will to power.

Accordingly, the fundamental features of this truth of beings as such must also be determined from this very essence of truth, in such a way

* {TN: Nietzsche, "Thus Spoke Zarathustra," in *The Portable Nietzsche*, ed. and trans. Walter Kaufmann (New York: Penguin Books, 1976), 191, translation modified.}

that subjectivity is the truth of the objectivity within which the being of beings appears in modernity. Subjectivity is, however, this truth of beings inasmuch as the subjectum essences in the self-certainty of knowing oneself. The [188] truth of beings has the character of certainty. In it the self-representing representation of objects is gathered toward itself. This representation of the subject is science [*Wissen*] as con-science [*Ge-wissen*] (conscientia, conscience).

The representing subject guarantees itself of itself and, that is to say, constantly guarantees itself of what it has re-presented as such. This belongs to subjectivity as its first essential determination. In accordance with such a guarantee, the truth of beings as certainty has the character of assurance (certitudo). The knowing-of-oneself, within which certainty as such exists, remains for its part a variation of the hitherto prevailing essence of truth, namely, the correctness (rectitudo) of representing. However, correctness no longer consists of the approximation to something present whose character of being present is unthought. Correctness now consists in basing all that is to be represented, on the standard set in the claim to knowledge of the representing res cogitans sive mens. This claim comes down to assurance, which is based on the fact that all that is to be represented and the act of representing are herded into the clarity and the lucidity of the mathematical idea and gathered together there. The ens is the ens co-agitatum perceptionis. The act of representing is now correct if it is equal to this claim to assurance. Identified as correct in this way and furnished as that which is right [*recht gefertigt*] and available, it is justified [*gerecht-fertigt*]. In the form of assurance (certitudo), the truth of beings in terms of the self-certainty of subjectivity is fundamentally the justifying of representing and what it represents on the basis of its own light. The justification (iustificatio) is the enactment of iustitia and so justice itself. As the subject is every individual subject, it ascertains its own assuring. It justifies itself on the basis of the claim it makes to justice.

At the beginning of modernity, the question arises as to how the human being, in the midst of the entirety of beings and that is to say, before the ground of all beings that is fullest in being (God), can become and be certain of its permanence and that is to say, of its salvation. This question of the certainty of salvation is the question of justification, that is to say, of justice (iustitia).

[189] Within modern metaphysics, Leibniz is the first to conceive of the subjectum as ens percipiens et appetens.* He for the first time sees clearly in the vis-character of the ens, that the being of beings is in

---

* {TN: A being that perceives and desires.}

essence the will. He thinks in the modern way of the truth of beings as certainty. In his 24 theses on metaphysics Leibniz says (n. 20): iustitia nihil aliud est quam ordo seu perfectio circa mentes.** The mentes, i.e., the res cogitantes, are according to n. 22, the primariae mundi unitates.*** Truth as certainty is the assuring of assurance, is order (ordo) and comprehensive establishment, i.e., finishing through and pro-duction (per-fectio). The character of assuring the first and proper being in its being is iustitia (justice).

Kant conceives of the ultimate self-assurance of transcendental subjectivity in his critical grounding of metaphysics as the quaestio iuris of the transcendental deduction. It is the question of the right [*Rechtsfrage*] to justification [*Recht-fertigung*] of the representing subject, that has by itself demonstrated its essence in the self-righteousness [*Selbst-Gerechtigkeit*] of its "I think."

In the essence of truth as the essence of certainty, this certainty as the truth of subjectivity and subjectivity as the being of beings, justice experienced from the justification of assurance is concealed. Justice indeed reigns as the essence of the truth of subjectivity. It is, however, not thought as the truth of beings within the metaphysics of subjectivity. By contrast, "justice," as the self-knowing being of beings, must be encountered by the thought of modern metaphysics as soon as the being of beings appears as the will to power. Will to power knows itself as *that which essentially posits values*, which assures itself in positing values as the conditions for the permanence of its own essence. In this way, it is constantly becoming equal to itself [*selbst gerecht wird*] and in such a becoming, it is "justice" [*Gerechtigkeit*]. In justice and as justice, the will to power's own essence must "represent" and that is to say, conceived in terms of modern metaphysics, exist. In the metaphysics of Nietzsche, the thought of value is more fundamental than the thought of certainty in the metaphysics of Descartes. To that extent, [190] certainty can only be regarded as "the right," [*das Rechte*] when it is considered the highest value. So, in the consummation of Western metaphysics in Nietzsche, the clear self-certainty of subjectivity proves to be the justification of the will to power in accordance with justice, which reigns in the being of beings.

Already in an early and also commonly known text, the second *Untimely Meditations*, "Of the Uses and the Disadvantages of History for Life" (1874), Nietzsche (section 6) puts "justice" in place of the

---

** {TN: Justice is nothing other than order and perfection with respect to the mind.}
*** {TN: primary unities of the world.}

"objectivity" of the historical sciences. However, Nietzsche is otherwise quiet about justice. Only in the decisive years of 1884/85, when *The Will to Power* occurred to him as his major work, does he pen a couple of thoughts on justice, without publishing them.

The first note (1884) bears the title: "The Paths of Freedom." It goes like this: "*Justice* as the constructive, segregating, destructive way of thinking, coming out of the assessments of value; *highest representative of life itself*" (XIII, n. 98, S. 42).[3]

The second note (1885) says: "Justice, as the function of a power that has a wide view, which sees beyond the narrow perspective of good and evil, thus has a wider horizon of *advantage* – the intention, to preserve something that is *more* than this or that person" (XIV, n. 158, S. 80).[4]

A precise explication of these thoughts would go beyond the scope of the reflection attempted here. It suffices here to provide a clue to the essential region within which the "justice" thought by Nietzsche belongs. To prepare an understanding of the "justice" that Nietzsche has in mind, we must bracket out all the representations of justice that stem from Christian, humanist, enlightenment, bourgeois, and social- ist [191] morality. This is because Nietzsche does not at all understand justice primarily as a determination of the ethical and the juridical realm. He thinks it from the being of beings as a whole, i.e., from the will to power. The just remains that which is in accordance with what is right. But what is "right" is determined from that which as a being exists as a being. Thus, Nietzsche says (XIII, n. 462, 205): "Law = the will to eternalize a particular power relationship."*

---

[3] F. Nietzsche, "Unveröffentlichtes aus der Umwerthungszeit (1882/1883–1888) [Unpublished Fragments from the Re-evaluation Period (1882/1883–1888)]," *Nietzsches Werke (Großoktavausgabe) [Nietzsche's Works (Großoktav Edition)]*, Vol. XIII, n. 98, 42. {TN: This fragment will be translated in *The Complete Works of Friedrich Nietzsche: Unpublished Fragments from the Period of* Thus Spoke Zarathustra (Spring 1884–Winter 1884/85), Vol. 15, ed. Alan D. Schrift and Duncan Large (Stanford, California: Stanford University Press).}

[4] F. Nietzsche, "Unveröffentlichtes aus der Umwerthungszeit (1882/1883–1888) [Unpublished Fragments from the Re-evaluation Period (1882/1883–1888)]," *Nietzsches Werke (Großoktavausgabe) [Nietzsche's Works (Großoktav Edition)]*, Vol. XIV, n. 158, 80. {TN: This fragment is actually from the Summer–Fall of 1884. It will also be translated into English in Vol. 15 of *The Complete Works of Friedrich Nietzsche* by Stanford University Press.}

* {TN: Translated in *The Complete Works of Friedrich Nietzsche: Unpublished Fragments from the Period of* Thus Spoke Zarathustra (Summer 1882–Winter 1883/84), ed. Alan D. Schrift and Duncan Large, trans. Paul S. Loeb and David F. Tinsley (Stanford, California: Stanford University Press, 2019), 245, translation modified.}

It may even be true, as is appropriate here, that Nietzsche's metaphysical concept of justice further alienates its familiar representation. Yet, it captures the essence of the justice, which, at the beginning of the consummation of the modern epoch, is already historical within the struggle for domination. Thus, this essence of justice determines all the actions of human beings in this epoch, whether explicitly or not, whether in a hidden way or openly.

Justice, as conceived by Nietzsche, is the truth of beings, which exists in the mode of the will to power. However, Nietzsche had neither explicitly thought justice as the essence of the truth of beings nor had he articulated the metaphysics of a consummated subjectivity from this thought. Justice is, however, the truth of beings determined by being itself. As this truth, justice is metaphysics itself in its consummation as modernity. In this consummation, lie hidden the grounds for Nietzsche's metaphysical experience of nihilism as the history of value-positing, but also his inability to think the essence of nihilism, nonetheless.

Nietzsche's formula for nihilism sounds negative: "God is dead." Positively it says: The superhuman lives. The superhuman lives in the willing that wills from the will to power, which is how being reigns and reigns even when prior "worldviews" still represent reality in prior ways. Yet, we would be thinking too flatly and against the sense of Nietzsche's metaphysics, if we wished to restrict the positive explication of the negative formula to the convenient view that, according to Nietzsche's doctrine, the human being in the [192] form of the superhuman just steps into God's position. This view is misleading because the human being can never succeed to that position and therefore can never take up the position appropriate to God. This position, metaphysically speaking, is the place of the causal production of beings as something created. Indeed, by contrast, the metaphysical place of God can be left empty and, in its stead, a different, i.e., metaphysically corresponding place can be constituted. The superhuman does not step into God's place, but the place, which the superhuman assumes is another realm related to another way of grounding beings in their other being. Since the beginning of modern metaphysics, this other being of beings is subjectivity. Unconditional subjectivity may be conceived as God in terms of the self-knowing will of the absolute spirit, as we see in the metaphysics of absolute idealism, or it may be experienced as the essential form of the self-willing will in the sense of the will to power as the superhuman. This does not change anything with regard to what is metaphysically decisive, namely, that in the former and the latter, being remains posited in subjectivity as the ground of objects with regard to their objectivity.

In a note from the year 1884 (*Will to Power*, n. 614),[5] Nietzsche makes the demand: "'to humanize' the world, i.e., to feel ourselves more and more as masters in it." These words do not mean that all beings are only interpreted in a "humanly" way, according to the prevailing representation of any hitherto existing human being. These words think metaphysically the thought that *hitherto existing* human beings, before anything, first experience their essence from the being of beings as a whole, i.e., from the will to power and as superhumans, who experience themselves in this way, willingly shape beings in the dominant image of the will to power. "To humanize" does not mean dragging being down to the level of the hitherto existing human being and its all-too-humanly ways. It rather requires that the hitherto existing human being be elevated into a "higher history" and beings be represented and produced in terms of the subjectivity [193] of the will to power and brought to shape in such a way.

The superhuman does not eject God from his place in order to usurp it for itself. In that case the superhuman would be an essentially godless human being. However, the superhuman, seen from the standpoint of the hitherto existing human and only from that standpoint, is a human being which is in essence de-ranged. Yet "the madman" does not have anything in common with the ways of any bystander, who does not believe in God. This is because the latter are not unbelievers for the reason that God has for them become something unworthy of belief, but rather because they have themselves given up the possibility of belief as they can no longer seek God. They can no longer seek because they can no longer think. The bystanders in public have abolished thinking and replaced it with chatter, by means of which they can make excuses for their fear of thinking. This is because this fear is the ground for their inability to think any longer. "The madman" by contrast, is clearly according to the first sentence of the passage, and for those who would like to hear, even more decisively according to the last sentences, the one who seeks God because he screams after God.

Seeking means: to approach something, in order to encounter something, which is absent beforehand, as something present, i.e., to find it. In order to experience finding or at least the inability to find from the

---

[5] Nietzsche, "Der Wille zur Macht," Third and Fourth Books, *Nietzsches Werke (Großoktavausgabe)*, Vol. XVI (Leipzig: Kröner, 1911), n. 614, 100. {TN: Translated as *The Will to Power*, ed. Walter Kaufmann, trans. Walter Kaufmann and R. J. Hollingdale (New York: Vintage Books, 1967), 329, translation modified.}

ground up, all seeking must enter into the essential dimension, within which what is sought, if at all, can only be encountered as a discovery.

It remains for us to ask whether the God-seeking superhuman finds or indeed can find what it seeks. Our question asks even further whether this God-seeker brings itself and is capable of bringing itself at all into the dimension of the possible discovery and thus of the only appropriate seeking. For a search for God, this dimension would have to be that of divinity, in which the Godlike essences. This dimension would have to first of all de-termine the seeking as well as the inability to find. Would a thinking, which stands in the experience "God is dead" and understands this as: "We have killed him?" still want to open up the dimension of the divine? [194] For this, the clearing of a possibility of "God living," "God existing" would have to be able to be shown to thinking. And this clearing would be in an entirely distant shape of a divine being. But before that "being itself" would have to have been cleared. Yet, for being itself to be cleared up for thinking in its hardly recognizable essence, it would have to specifically de-termine [*be-stimmen*] thought, if not indeed attune [*an-stimmen*] thought to its essence.

For the seekers of God even to find themselves just in the dimension of the seeking and not yet in that of the portended discovery, they would have to go beyond "God is dead." For, with this event the entire horizon of divinity is already wiped away. If, however, the word "God is dead" now provides the formula for nihilism, then the thought we have just had tells us: For the seeker of God even to be able to seek, nihilism would have to be overcome.

Is nihilism not then overcome according to Nietzsche's own words? Does the life of the superhuman not follow the death of God? Will the negative not be superseded by a positive and in such a way that it is not the human being who assumes the place of God, but rather the position from which beings as such are re-presented and pro-duced, is transformed in its positional character? Could not a new seeking, nevertheless, be directly advanced from this new position that comes from the thinking of the superhuman, which, as the gesture of the de-ranged human being indeed indicates, would be an "incessant screaming" after God? Could the superhuman, who transcends the humans existing hitherto, that is to say, transcends their enlightenment and their ordinary and blind atheism, not come to God again and through such a coming first truly find and through such a finding truly "have" God for the first time, if indeed the human being is capable of "having" God? Nietzsche's quietest thinking certainly goes out into this expanse, and perhaps is the only one that approaches it. We must only abandon our self-righteousness and pay attention to the hidden disposition in the thinking of this ill-reputed [195] atheist. We should not ignore anything about his own tone because of his distraught demeanour. It would be more advisable to reflect upon who it is who screams if Nietzsche's metaphysics is pompously denounced as a naked atheism. Even atheism still remains a screaming if one proves in relation to this thinker that he is in principle not separated from God.

Yet, we ask ourselves a counterquestion: Can thinking in the manner of the superhuman, can the thinking from the standpoint of the will to power ever find itself in the dimension of a God-seeking? Can this thinking think the divine as being, can it think being at all?

But we still showed clearly and in a detailed enough manner that Nietzsche thinks the will to power as the being of beings. Indeed. But what is being to the thinker who experiences beings as such, in terms of the will to power? "Being" is a value posited in the will to power. Being appears in the metaphysics of the will to power as something other than being. Being is not being, but value. As "value," is it more or less than being? If it is a value it seems to be something higher than mere being. However, as value, namely, as the condition of its assurance posited in the will to power, the permanence of the permanent exists by the grace of and under the dominion of the will to power. As value, as posited viewpoint, being is under the will to power, which Nietzsche also calls "becoming" and "life." Yet, did we not hear from Nietzsche himself that the highest will to power is to stamp the character of being upon "becoming?" So, does "being" still become the highest and come to stand above becoming, i.e., above the will to power? But Nietzsche perhaps, in keeping with the kind of representation and thinking that has been common for a long time in metaphysics, means by the name "becoming" that which becomes, on which the character of being is to be stamped and which thus has to be conceived as a being in its being. As a result, being, as this stamp, still remains something posited by the will to power, a value. And the will to power itself, as that which posits values, and this positing of values itself? [196] Is the will to power not the actuality of that which actually effects? However, the actuality of the actual, as the actualitas des ens actu, is the being of beings. In that case Nietzsche still thinks being as being and not as value, if he thinks being as a whole metaphysically as the will to power, to say nothing of the eternal recurrence of the same here. To add to that, if being were only a value, how should the will to power as value ever be able to posit values? Nietzsche indeed interprets being as value at all times, even when he means it in the sense of assuring continued existence within the will to power and for the will to power, as well as when he conceives of being more universally as the most universal determination of "becoming," i.e., of the actual in the sense of the will to power. At the same time, however, Nietzsche's thinking never arrives at the consideration that the will to power, as the actuality of the actual, which posits value, is being. This is attested to by the conclusion of a note which is important in many aspects and therefore already quoted previously in many contexts (*Will to Power*, n. 675, 1887–88, 138):

"All assessments of value are only consequences and narrower perspectives in the *service* of this one will: the assessment of value is *itself* only this *will to power*.

A critique of being on the basis of any of these values is something absurd and misleading. Even if we grant that a process of decline is initiated in it, this process still stands in the service of this will.

To evaluate being itself! But the evaluating is itself still this being! – and in saying no, we still do what we *are*."*

In these statements, which contain a critique of Schopenhauer's metaphysics, there is talk of "being," even of "being itself," of assessment of value, of will to power. In order to understand these statements, we must pay attention to what the most universal determination "being" means. The statement that is cited at the end reveals this: "– and in saying no" – to what and against what? To beings, what they are, and against beings, that they are and how they are. "Being itself" here means: A being with reference to its [197] being. What is in consideration is Schopenhauer's metaphysics, which teaches that beings are really a nullity and thus "critique" requires saying no to beings. "Critique of being" means: Critique of beings as such. "To evaluate being itself," i.e., to pejoratively reject beings as such, is absurd. It goes against the sense of this deed, that, insofar as it is done, it is something like a being.

As metaphysics, philosophy from ancient times always thinks of "a being." Nietzsche writes in another note (*Will to Power*, n. 570, 1887/88, XVI, 69): "If one is a philosopher in the way one was always a philosopher, one has no eye for that which was and that which will be: one only sees a *being that is*."** Here it is made clear that Nietzsche, in keeping with tradition, understands "a being" as that which is permanent-presencing (the present). Yet, Nietzsche continues: "However, because there are no beings that are, only the *imaginary* was left for philosophers, as their 'world.'"*** This means: Philosophy hitherto thought beings and thought them with reference

---

* {TN: Translated in *The Will to Power*, 356, translation modified.}
** {TN: *The Will to Power*, 307, translation modified.}
*** {TN: Ibid., translation modified.}

to being. But, because there is nothing permanent and everything "is" a becoming-having-become, "permanence" remains something only imagined in fancy. Indeed, this imagination is necessary, as the positing of the permanent, for assuring the continued existence of the will to power. The "imaginary" "as being" is only a necessary value. "Being" has no actuality. What is actual is only what becomes. Nietzsche, thus, wants to be a philosopher of the kind that one previously was not. He wants to think what becomes in its becoming and believes he can name Heraclitus and Hegel as his predecessors in such thinking. Nietzsche thinks what becomes in its becoming as the will to power. Yet, did we not hear that the highest will to power is to stamp becoming with the character of being? The note (*Will to Power*, n. 675), however, says even more: In "evaluating" being, we posit values and in assessing values we stand in service of the will to power. What we reject in negating beings as such is what we are in this act of rejection. We are the beings of the will to power. Nietzsche [198] concludes his note with a demand: "One must realize the *absurdity* of this gesture of judging existence; and then seek to figure out *what* really comes to pass in it. It is symptomatic."****
Here Nietzsche uses the name "existence" for "being" and understands this word in terms of metaphysics. "Existence" is the whole of beings in the widest sense of being, according to which even what becomes as such, the will to power, is still a being. Metaphysical language also calls the entirety of existence the world. Nietzsche says at one time (*Will to Power*, n. 1067, XVI, 401f.): "And do you also know, what 'the world' is for me?" He answers: "This world: an enormity of force, without beginning, without end, a fixed, brazen magnitude of force . . ."* Nietzsche thinks of the world as beings as a whole. He finally asks: "– and do you wish a *name* for this world?" He answers: "*This world is the will to power – and nothing other than that*! And even you yourselves are this will to power – and nothing other than that!"**

We speak in the language of metaphysics and say at once that we understand "a being" in the most universal terms as that which becomes: The will to power is beings as such as a whole.

If Nietzsche (*Will to Power*, n. 675, conclusion) demands that we realize that Schopenhauer's negation of beings as such as whole is an "absurdity," he expresses the guiding thought of metaphysics, that thinking, if it does not wish to fall into the unthinkable and thereby lose its essential element, must in advance, i.e., as thinking, already

---

**** {TN: Ibid., 357, translation modified.}
  * {TN: Ibid., 549–550, translation modified.}
 ** {TN: Ibid., 550, translation modified.}

recognize beings as such. Yet, Nietzsche demands that we try to figure out, "what" "really comes to pass" from the absurd negation of beings as such. Nietzsche himself figured it out because he experienced Western history in its occurrence as nihilism. Nihilism, as the process of the devaluation of the highest values, the murder of God, must lead to the revaluation of all values, if everything is not to end in the empty nothingness of what is only a nullity. However, the revaluation of [199] all values can be accomplished as the counter-movement to the devaluation of the highest values only when the process of devaluation is experienced, i.e., when its signs in contemporary history are adequately recognized. Nietzsche recognized in the "gesture of judging existence" of Schopenhauer's metaphysics a "critique of being" (i.e., of beings as such as a whole) – a prominent attempt at comprehensively devaluing the highest values prevailing hitherto. Schopenhauer's metaphysics determines his own metaphysics most acutely because the latter turns against the former, always thinking from this "against" and only so. Nietzsche sees in Schopenhauer's metaphysics a sign of nihilism, which is to be rightly experienced. That is why what happens in this absurd "critique of being" is "symptomatic." However, the symptom can be recognized as such, only if and only because the whole, for which it is a symptom, comes into view beforehand. This means: Nietzsche recognizes the process of the devaluation of the highest values first in all of its appearances, after he has recognized beforehand the posting of value itself in its principle, which is for him, the will to power. This latter is a being as such, a being in its being.

How, we ask again, does the superhumanly thinking of the metaphysics of the will to power stand in relation to being itself? Does this thinker, in whose thoughts and wishes the God-seeking thorn never stops pricking, think beyond into being? Does Nietzsche think being itself, consequent to which he would find himself in the dimension within which the divine can first open up as the realm of the flight and the arrival of God?

Nietzsche recognizes beings in their being as the precondition for thinking. Nietzsche interprets being as the necessary but in no way the highest value. And even where he thinks "being" universally, encompassing even becoming, he interprets being as value. Does Nietzsche, as a consequence of this fundamental disposition to beings and to being, still think being itself as being? He thinks being neither in his former recognition of beings as such nor in his latter interpretation as value.

[200] Yet, did we ourselves not ceaselessly exhibit during the whole course of our reflection that Nietzsche, in thinking beings as will to power, thinks the being of beings? Certainly. But by this we by no

means suggest that Nietzsche thinks the will to power, the being of beings, as being itself, with being as his starting-point. If Nietzsche were to have thought this, he would have had to recognize, at the point where he thinks the will to power in its highest representation and determines it as justice, what justice itself is as being. Yet, Nietzsche just does not recognize this. He does not think justice as being, from being itself, but from the will to power as its admittedly highest representation. Our explanation first showed the extent to which what Nietzsche experiences as justice is the hidden essence of the self-certainty of unconditional subjectivity. Justice, as such a certainty, belongs to the essence of truth in the sense of the unconcealedness of beings as such, which unconcealedness belongs to being itself. Our explanation already thinks from being itself, inasmuch as this thinking experiences Ἀλήθεια, over and beyond Greek thinking, explicitly as the essential feature of being itself. Or do we suppose that Nietzsche still thinks justice in its essential truth when he calls it the highest, which is still the representation of the will to power? Representation, that is: letting-appear, self-clearing, unconcealedness. In fact, Nietzsche's thinking touches upon the essence of the truth of justice, although he does not think of it as the essence of its truth. He does not think justice from being itself. He rather takes justice back into the will to power, i.e., into a being as such. That the situation is so, cannot in any way be attributed to Nietzsche as a deficiency of his thinking. To the contrary. Nietzsche's thinking, despite interpreting truth and being as values, is touched by the being-like essence of truth, that is to say, it lets itself be touched, without knowing it. This attests to his simple belongingness to the essential history of metaphysical thinking. The greatness of thinkers depends upon their enduring this simple belonging, supposing that this talk of [201] great and the small still remains in compliance with this simple at all, which is what we are contesting.

Nietzsche does not think being from being itself. Nevertheless, it remains necessary for our reflection, not for Nietzsche's thinking, to experience this properly and to contemplate at length that and in what way the thinking of being as being is missing from Nietzsche's metaphysics.

Nietzsche thinks beings in their being and experiences beings as the will to power. Accordingly, he can always say: a being as such is the will to power. However, Nietzsche says even more: He insistently and ceaselessly tells us what the will to power is. But in doing so he thinks being. Of course. But he thinks the will to power, what it is as will to power, but not what it is as being *from* the *essence of being* itself. We should certainly never mistake the challenge that lies in such utterances about

Nietzsche's metaphysics. There is always the looming danger of our thinking being too hasty in relation to his thinking. For, the following note appears to disabuse us in relation to the nagging question [concerning being]. In the conclusion of a piece (*Will to Power*, n. 635 from the year 1888 May till June, XVI, 113) Nietzsche writes: "The will to power not a being, not a becoming, but a *pathos* – is the most elementary fact, from which a becoming, an effecting first emerges . . ."*

The note contains two thoughts. The first says: The will to power is "a pathos." Nietzsche characterizes the essential structure of the will to power in this way. It is a passion and indeed in a double sense in accordance with the twofold essence indicated earlier. Reception of power and the intensification of power are particularly characteristic of it. As reception, it sustains, bears and suffers every level of power it reaches. But as intensification it wrenches itself forward toward more power. It propels itself beyond itself. Viewed from this perspective, reception is only a tolerance and an essentially necessary self-acceptance. What the will to power "suffers" (tolerates) in this way, does not cause it harm inasmuch as the will to power is agitated in wrenching forward toward more power. The will to power is passion insofar as [202] it is specifically a suffering [*Leiden*] in the sense of a tolerating and to that extent it is "passionate" [*leidenschaftlich*] in the sense of the agitated wrenching forward of overpowering. Nietzsche certainly does not want to say that the will to power is one pathos among others. For, then it would still be a being as such. Thus, he underlines "pathos" in order to contrast the essential structure of the will to power against that which he names at the end. The will to power is "not being." This statement of Nietzsche's seems capable of toppling our entire interpretation of his metaphysics so far. But let us not forget what "being" ordinarily means in Nietzsche's language and not only in his language. "Being" means: a being [*Seiendes*] and "what is existent" [*seiend*] understood in the sense of what is "present," available, "permanent," if not completely worn out. As "pathos" the will to power is not like this: "not being." But as "pathos" in the sense explained, it is also nothing impermanent in the sense of always being only other, no mere process of transformation: "not becoming." What is the will to power revealed to be, if it is presented in the greatest fullness of its essence as pathos? Pathos propels itself as agitation into the heights. It builds. At the same time, it tolerates what is arrived at and discards what is not commensurate with it. This manner of building, discarding, and consequently annihilating taken together is

* {TN: *The Will to Power*, 339, translation modified.}

what Nietzsche conceives as "justice." Justice also contains the will to power's essential character of fiat and command.

The first thought in the note is supposed to remind us with an essential and emphatic word, of the one thing that the will to power is, in the essential unity of the manifold structure of its essence. The word "pathos" is taken from the realm of "life." It does not think beyond this, but thinks back into this as the realm of the "willing."

The second thought contains what Nietzsche wants really to say in the cited statement: The will to power – and indeed as pathos – is "the most elementary fact." If we speak of something as a "fact," we do not say what it is but how it is. We say that it, in fact, is. In the language [203] of metaphysics, we say: that it exists. If Nietzsche now characterizes the will to power as fact, he conceives of it with reference to "existence," which is a name one also prefers to use for "being." Nietzsche actually says that the will to power is "the most elementary fact," not one among others, but a distinctive fact. *The one that is* distinguished from all others. On what basis is it distinctive? Because it is the fact, "from which a becoming, an effecting first emerges . . ." The will to power is the most elementary fact as the ground for all other facts which are its consequence. If Nietzsche determines the will to power, which is still the being of beings, as "the most elementary fact," he still thinks "being" with reference to existence and thus as being. Does Nietzsche here think of being as being? By no means. Rather he now characterizes the will to power, the being of beings, as that which exists in principle [*Grund*] and as the principle [*Grund*] of all that becomes and effects. Nietzsche here conceives of the will to power as being. However, he not only does not think of it as being from being itself but he also takes "being" here to be a being and only a being. If it were to be said that being is thought as being here, then we could counter by saying that this kind of thinking falls below the standard of what needs to be thought. Nietzsche only says: The will to power is what exists in principle before all beings. About existence as being he says as little as he does about the factualness of the fact. If he were to have already thought being as being, he would have to had to think the factualness of the elementary fact "will to power." In another place, Nietzsche calls the will to power the ultimate factum to which we descend.[6] In going

---

[6] "The will to power is the ultimate factum to which we descend." (*Will to Power* 1885; XVI, 415) {TN: Translated as *The Complete Works of Friedrich Nietzsche: Unpublished Fragments* (Spring 1885–Spring 1886), Vol. 16, ed. Alan D. Schrift and Duncan Large, trans. Adrian Del Caro (Stanford, California: Stanford University Press, 2020), 214, translation modified.} Cf. in this regard: *Nietzsches metaphysische Grundstellung im abendländischen Denken: Die ewige Wiederkehr des Gleichen*

back from fact to fact we finally hit upon the factum "will to power." But in what does the facticity of this factum consist? Let us grant that Nietzsche posed this question and also grant that he [204] gave an answer to this question. In that case, he would only be determining those beings in their being, which have the mode of being of a fact. The question would always remain as to whether factualness as being is to be the essence of being itself. Before this question there stands another question: In what does the truth of being itself rest, and how is this truth to be thought? For, we still think "being." Otherwise, all our is-saying would be a unique "thoughtlessness."

The acknowledgment of beings themselves in terms of their most elementary fact does not lead Nietzsche to the thinking of being. The thinking of being is also not achieved on the way to interpreting being as a necessary value. If Nietzsche enshrines this acknowledgment as the fundamental philosophical insight, he confines himself to characterizing being as a distinctive being of the factual kind. Recourse to this fundamental insight keeps him away from the path to the thinking of being itself. This fundamental insight does not see this path at all.

Having said this, the question concerning being itself cannot arise in Nietzsche's thinking also for the reason that it has already answered the question concerning being (in the only known sense as the being of beings). "Being" is a value. "Being," i.e., here a being as such, namely, as that which is permanent.

Howsoever far and in whatsoever direction we pose counterquestions to Nietzsche, we do not find his thought thinking being itself from its truth and thus truth itself as being itself.

Yet, the reflection we have carried out just now, may give rise to the suspicion overall that we are insinuating that Nietzsche's thinking must in principle think being itself, that it fails to do this, however, and is thus inadequate. Nothing of this sort is implied. Rather, truly speaking, it is only from thinking in the direction of the question concerning the truth of being itself that we bring ourselves into the neighborhood of Nietzsche's metaphysics, in order to experience what he thought from the highest fidelity to his thinking. Yet, this effort remains distant from the intention to disseminate a perhaps more correct representation of Nietzsche's philosophy. We think his [205] metaphysics only, to be able

[Nietzsche's Fundamental Metaphysical Place in Western Thinking: The Eternal Recurrence of the Same], Freiburg of Lecture Summer Semester 1937, GA 44, ed. M. Heinz (Frankfurt am Main: Vittorio Klostermann, 1986), 163. {TN: Translated as *Nietzsche II: The Eternal Recurrence of the Same*, ed. and trans. David F. Krell (New York: Harper and Row, 1984), 156.}

to ask what is worthy of question, namely, this: *In Nietzsche's meta-physics, which experiences and thinks nihilism as such for the first time, is nihilism overcome or not? We judge Nietzsche's metaphysics according to whether it achieves the overcoming of nihilism or not.* No – we even let go of this judgment. We only ask and direct this question at ourselves: whether and how in this metaphysical experience and overcoming of nihilism, the essence proper to nihilism shows itself. What is asked here is whether the essence of nihilism can be experienced in the metaphysical concept of nihilism, whether this essence can be grasped at all. In such a question we, nevertheless, impute that nothingness drives the essence in what is named by the name "nihilism" and indeed in such a way that there is fundamentally nothing with respect to beings as such. We are thus in no way imputing to Nietzsche's thinking, a claim not in accordance with this thinking and asking too much of it. This is because Nietzsche experiences nihilism as the history of the devaluation of the highest values. He thinks the overcoming of nihilism as the counter-movement in the form of the revaluation of all hitherto prevailing values and indeed from the specifically recognized principle of all value positing. Thinking in this manner – he thinks as value what is precisely in the direction of "being," and i.e., of beings as such – he indirectly understands nihilism as a history in which something happens to beings as such.

Rigorously speaking, we are not imputing something different of something different. We are rather subjecting ourselves to a claim of language, which requires us to think the "nihil" in the word "nihilism" in unison with the fact that something happens to beings as such. But language does not only require that we correctly understand the fabricated lexical products that mere words are, but that we also attend to what is in the word and what is said with it. We subject ourselves to the claim of the name "nihilism," to thinking a history, within which stand beings as such. By this we mean a being in its being.

Now Nietzsche's metaphysics is, however, founded on an explicitly [206] accomplished fundamental insight that beings as such are and only beings so recognized guarantee thinking understood as an existent being, whatever it may think. Nietzsche's fundamental experience says: a being is, and as such it is not nothing. As a consequence, nihilism, according to which there is nothing with respect to beings as such, is excluded from the foundations of this metaphysics. Thus, it has over-come nihilism.

Nietzsche recognizes beings as such. Yet, does he also recognize in such recognition the being of beings and indeed being itself, namely, as being? By no means. Being is determined as a value and therefore explained from the standpoint of a being, as a condition posited by the will to power, which is itself a being. Being is not recognized as being. It is for this reason that being is derived from beings. Being is simply not admitted as being. Being remains away in this thinking. It is as if it is nothing: being is a nihil. Let us grant that a being is by virtue of being and being never is by virtue of a being. Let us also grant that being can never be nothing given that beings exist. Does not nihilism also come or perhaps only come into its own where there is nothing not just with respect to beings, but rather with respect to being? Certainly. Where there is nothing just with respect to beings, there one may discover nihilism. But one does not hit upon its essence, which only appears where the nihil concerns being itself.

The essence of nihilism is the history, in which there is nothing with respect to being itself.

Our thinking, or to put it better, our calculation and planning that accords with the rule of avoiding contradiction stands ready to append the comment that a history that exists, but in which there is nothing with respect to being, is simply a contradiction par excellence. But perhaps being itself does not care about the contradictions of our thinking. If being itself had to be what it is by virtue of a lack of contradiction in human thinking then it would certainly be shorn of an essence of its own.

[207] Absurdity is impotent in in the face of being itself and thus even in the face of that which happens to being in history, that there is nothingness with respect to being itself.

More essential than reckoning with absurdities is that we experience on the basis of the path we have travelled hitherto that, and to what extent, there is nothing with respect to being in Nietzsche's metaphysics.

We therefore say: Nietzsche's metaphysics is nihilism proper. But did he require that we retrospectively attribute something such as this to his thinking. In characterizing the manner in which Nietzsche himself sees the various forms and levels of nihilism, we touched upon the concluding sentence of the note (*Will to Power*, n. 14. Spring to Autumn 1887),[7] which is as follows:

"'Nihilism' as the ideal of the *supreme potency* of the spirit, of the most overabundant life, partly destructive, partly ironic." The extended "recapitulation" (*Will to Power*, n. 617, possibly 1885/86, XVI, 101), however, begins as follows:

[7] Nietzsche, "Der Wille zur Macht" Third and Fourth Books, *Nietzsche's Werke (Großoktavausgabe)*, Vol. XV (Leipzig: Kröner, 1911), n. 14, 152. {TN: Translated as Nietzsche, *The Will to Power*, 14, translation modified.}

"To *stamp* becoming with the character of being – that is the *supreme will to power*."[*]

The spirit of Nietzsche's metaphysics accomplishes this stamping as the ideal of its supreme potency. In this way, it corresponds to the just mentioned highest form of "nihilism." In conceiving a comprehensive revaluation of all values prevailing hitherto, Nietzsche's metaphysics completes the devaluation of the highest values that prevailed hitherto. In this way, it belongs "destructively" to the course of the history of nihilism existing hitherto. Inasmuch as this revaluation is executed out of the principle of value positing itself, this nihilism renders itself as that which no longer exists on its own terms. As that which is "destructive," it is "ironic." Nietzsche understands his metaphysics as the most extreme nihilism; indeed, in such a way that it is, at the same time, no more a nihilism. But we said that Nietzsche's nihilism is a proper nihilism. It is for this reason that this nihilism not only does not overcome nihilism but can also never overcome it. For, precisely that [208] in which and through which Nietzsche intends to overcome nihilism – newly positing values from the will to power – is where and how proper nihilism first announces itself, such that there is nothing with respect to being itself, with respect to that being which has now become value. Accordingly, Nietzsche also experiences the historical movement of nihilism as a history of the devaluation of the highest values that prevailed hitherto. On the same grounds, he represents the overcoming as revaluation, accomplishing this not only by positing values anew, but also in a such a way that he experiences the will to power as the principle of the new and fundamentally all value positing. This valuative thinking is now elevated to a principle. Being itself is not principally admitted as being. In this metaphysics, there is fundamentally nothing with respect to being. How could there be anything here with respect to being itself, namely, being itself? How is an overcoming of nihilism supposed to take place here? Indeed, how is it even supposed to rear its head?

Nietzsche's metaphysics is consequently no overcoming of nihilism; it is rather the ultimate entanglement in it. By means of the valuative thinking arising from the will to power, it commits itself to the recognition of beings. But it simultaneously chains itself up with the fetters of the interpretation of being as value, to the impossibility of even getting just a glimpse of being as being itself. Through this entanglement of nihilism in itself, it only completes itself quintessentially into what it is. This quintessentially complete, perfect nihilism is the consummation of nihilism proper.

[*] {TN: Nietzsche, *The Will to Power*, 330, translation modified.}

However, as long as its essence is the history of nothingness with respect to being itself, the essence of nihilism cannot also be experienced and thought, as there is nothing in thinking and for thinking with respect to being itself. The consummated nihilism thus closes itself off conclusively from the possibility of ever being able to think and know the essence of nihilism. Would this mean that the essence of nihilism is closed off to Nietzsche's thinking? How could we assert such a thing? He clearly asks (*Will to Power*, n. 2, until Autumn 1887, [209] XV, 145): "What does nihilism mean?"* He answers succinctly: *"That the highest values are devalued."***

Indeed, this note does not show any less clearly and succinctly that Nietzsche "interpretively" questions what he experiences as nihilism and interprets what is so interrogated from the standpoint of his valuative thinking. His question about the meaning of nihilism is, accordingly, still a nihilistically conceived question. That is why he does not succeed with his kind of question, in entering the realm of that which the question concerning the essence of nihilism seeks: that it is and how it is a history that concerns being itself. To the extent that nihilism for Nietzsche still manifests itself as an occurrence of de-valuation and decline, of weakness and death, his experience appears at the very least to establish the nihil in nihilism. Faced with the no to beings as such, Nietzsche demands a yes. He thinks in the direction of an overcoming of nihilism. But how is this supposed to be possible whilst the essence of nihilism is not experienced? Thus, what is needed before all overcoming is an adversarial engagement with nihilism, which for a start brings its essence into the light.

But if we grant that in this adversarial engagement with the essence of nihilism, which concerns being itself, some portion remains allocated even to human thinking then this thinking must itself by affected by the essence of nihilism. Thus, in the light of this very metaphysics, which first experiences and thinks nihilism holistically as a historical movement and which simultaneously begins to appear to us as the consummation of nihilism proper, we must ask wherein that which is of immediate historical concern for us – the appearance of nihilism proper, namely, its consummation – has its ground.

Nietzsche's metaphysics is nihilistic insofar as it is a valuative thinking and this thinking is grounded in the principle of the will to power as the principle of all value positing. Consequently, Nietzsche's metaphysics becomes the consummation of nihilism proper because it is

* {TN: Nietzsche, *The Will to Power*, 9.}
** {TN: Ibid., translation modified.}

the metaphysics of the will to power. If this is how things stand then [210] metaphysics as the metaphysics of the will to power, indeed, remains the ground of the consummation of nihilism proper. In that case, it can in no way be the ground of nihilism proper as such. Nihilism proper, although still incomplete, must in essence already reign in the preceding metaphysics. This preceding metaphysics is no metaphysics of the will to power, but the metaphysics of the will. It experiences beings as such as a whole as will. It might also be the case that the essence of the will thought here remains obscure in several respects and, indeed, necessarily so. Yet, in the metaphysics of Schelling and Hegel going back through Kant and Leibniz right up to Descartes, a being as such is fundamentally experienced as will. This certainly does not imply that the subjectively lived experience of the human will is transferred to beings as a whole. In fact, it only suggests the inverse: From an experience, still unclear, of beings as such, characterized in terms of a will that has not been thought until now, human beings learn to know themselves for the very first time as willing subjects in an essential sense. An insight into these connections is indeed unavoidable for an experience of the history of nihilism proper, an experience which is responsive to the history of the essence. However, these connections cannot be analysed here. For the moment, this task is also not urgent. This is because what is said about nihilism proper in the characterization of Nietzsche's metaphysics as the consummation of nihilism, must have already provoked a different supposition in those who are reflective: Neither the metaphysics of the will to power nor the metaphysics of the will is the ground of nihilism proper. Rather it is only metaphysics itself that is this ground.

Metaphysics as such is nihilism proper. As metaphysics, the essence of nihilism *is* historical. Plato's metaphysics is no less nihilistic than Nietzsche's. In the former the essence only remains hidden, in the latter it comes to appearance in its fullness, without it ever making itself known from the standpoint of metaphysics or within its bounds.

These are strange statements. Metaphysics still determines the history of the Western age. In all its relationships to beings and that is to say, even to itself, Western [211] humanity is supported and led by metaphysics in all respects. In the equation of metaphysics with nihilism one does not know which is greater, the arbitrariness of our condemnation or the degree to which we condemn all our previous history.

In the meantime, we must also make one observation, that our thinking still hardly approaches the essence of nihilism proper, to speak nothing of already thinking its essence sufficiently in order to reflectively to mull over and then judge the statements just uttered about metaphysics and nihilism. If metaphysics as such is nihilism proper then the latter, in accordance with its essence, is not capable of thinking its own essence. How then can metaphysics itself ever encounter its own essence? The metaphysical representations of metaphysics necessarily lag behind its essence. Metaphysics can never arrive at its essence from metaphysics.

Yet, what does "essence" mean here? We are not taking the idea of "essentialities" from this word. We perceive in the name that which essences? What is the "essence" of metaphysics? How does it essence? How is it related as such to being itself? That is the question. Our attempt to answer this question within the sphere of this reflection, remains necessarily inadequate. In addition, as long as our thinking comes from metaphysics, this attempt always remains questionable. Despite this, we must dare to take a few steps. We persist with the question, which Aristotle had pronounced as the abiding question of metaphysics: What is a being?

Every question as question delimits the scope and the kind of answer required by it. It therefore defines, at the same time, the sphere of the possibilities of responding to it. In order that we reflect sufficiently upon the question of metaphysics, what is needed first of all is to reflect on it as a question, but not the answers, which have fallen to it in the course of the history of metaphysics.

In the question: What is a being? we ask of a being as [212] such. A being as a being is so thanks to being. In the question: "What is a being as such?" we think of being and indeed of the being of beings, i.e., of that which a being is. The being-what, τὸ τί ἐστιν responds to what it is, namely, a being. Plato defines the whatness of a being as the ἰδέα (cf. Plato's Doctrine of Truth).[8] The whatness of beings, the essentia of the ens, one calls "the essence." But this is no accidental and harmless naming. Rather what is concealed in it is that the being of beings, that is, the manner in which it essences, is thought from the standpoint of whatness. "Essence" in the meaning of essentia (whatness) is already the metaphysical interpretation of "essence" that asks about the what of beings as such. Indeed, "essence" is here constantly thought of as the essence of a being. The being of beings is creatively questioned from the standpoint of a being, as that which is thought in the direction of a being. Thought as what? As γένος and κοινόν, as that from which any being in its being so and so receives its common what.

---

[8] *Wegmarken*, ed. F-W. von Hermann, GA 9 (Frankfurt am Main: Vittorio Klostermann, 1976), 203–238. {TN: Translated into English as "Plato's Doctrine of Truth," *Pathmarks*, trans. Thomas Sheehan, 155–182.}

In inquiring into a being as such, it is also already experienced in the following respect: that it simply is. Thus, from the question as to what a being as such is, there simultaneously arises another question: What is it that among all the beings as beings most corresponds to what is defined as the what of beings? A being, which corresponds to the whatness, the essentia of beings as such, is what truly exists. In the question: "What is a being?" being is thought specifically with reference to the essentia and the existentia. A being is, in this way, determined as such, that is to say, in what it is and in the fact that it is. Essentia and existentia of the ens qua ens answer the question: What is a being as such? They determine a being in its being.

How does metaphysics then relate to being itself? Does metaphysics think being itself? No and never. It thinks [213] beings in reference to being. Being is the response to the question in which it is beings that are always the object of interrogation. Thus, being itself remains unthought in metaphysics. And indeed, not incidentally, but in accordance with its own questioning. In thinking beings as such, this question and the answer necessarily think from the standpoint of being but they do not think of being itself and indeed for the reason that in accordance with the most proper sense of the question of metaphysics, being is thought as a being in its being. Inasmuch as metaphysics thinks a being from the standpoint of being, it does not think being (as being) (itself). Here being remains unthought in a thinking and indeed, in the very thinking which is deemed to be thinking par excellence. Consequently, that being itself remains unthought in metaphysics as such, is a remaining-unthought of a peculiar, extraordinary, and unique kind.

Already, the question of metaphysics does not reach being itself. How could we expect it to reflect upon being itself? But can we say that the question of metaphysics does not question far enough and not far enough beyond beings? We leave this question open only for this reason that it is in no way decided as to whether metaphysics does not indeed determine being itself. This is because we cannot forget this characteristic of being, which, right from the beginnings of metaphysics and throughout its history, is thought under the eventual name of the "a priori." The name suggests that being is – indeed in accordance with being – prior to a being. But in this way being is still thought from the standpoint of beings and in the direction of beings and only in this way, even if metaphysics interprets the a priori as that which is actually prior or as that which has priority in the order of knowledge and objective conditions. As long as the being of beings is thought as the a priori, this determination itself will continue to prevent us from thinking being (as being) itself. We need to think being (as being) itself in order perhaps first to experience the extent to which being as being includes a relationship of a priority to beings, whether this relationship merely attaches to being, is hooked into it, so to speak, or whether being itself [214] is this relationship. In that case what does being mean and what does the relationship mean? That all metaphysics, even the inversion of Platonism thinks the being of beings as the a priori only attests to the fact that metaphysics as such leaves being unthought (as being itself).

Metaphysics indeed recognizes: There are no beings without being. But what is hardly said is that it misplaces being in turn into a being, be it the highest being in the sense of the highest cause, be it the distinctive being in the sense of the subject of subjectivity as the condition for the possibility of all objectivity, be it the determination of the highest being as the absolute in the sense of unconditional subjectivity as a consequence of the common bond connecting both the ways in the which the being of beings is grounded [as cause and subject].

When being that is hardly remembered is grounded in what is the fullest in being amongst beings, this grounding proceeds, in accordance with the metaphysical question, from a being as such. This grounding experiences: that beings are. As if in passing, this grounding is lightly touched by the essencing of being. But this experience, in the course of metaphysical questioning, unwittingly manages to ask the question, which in the later formulation of Leibniz runs as follows: Why are there beings at all rather than nothing? This question inquires into the highest cause and the highest ground of beings. It is the question concerning θεῖον which already emerges at the beginning of metaphysics with Plato and Aristotle and that is to say, from the essence of metaphysics. Metaphysics in thinking beings as such continues to be addressed by being. However, it thinks in the direction of beings from the standpoint of beings. Hence, metaphysics as such must speak (λέγειν) of θεῖον in terms of the most eminently existing ground. Metaphysics is in itself theology. It is theology insofar as it speaks of a being as being, the ὄν ἧ ὄν. Ontology is simultaneously and necessarily theology. In order to know the basic onto-theological structure of metaphysics, we do not first need an orientation into the merely scholastic concept of metaphysics. Rather, the scholastic concept is only an erudite embodiment of the metaphysically conceived essence of metaphysics.

The names ontology and theology employed here do not coincide [215] with what these titles name in the scholastic concept of metaphysics. Rather ontology is all the determinations of a being as such in reference to its essentia. It is found in psychology, cosmology, and theology. On the other hand, theology, correctly conceived, disguises itself as much in cosmology and psychology (anthropology) as it does in metaphysica generalis.

As an ontology, even Nietzsche's philosophy, even though it appears to be very far from scholastic metaphysics, is a theology. This ontology of beings as such thinks essentia as the will to power. This ontology of beings thinks the existentia of beings as such as a whole theologically as the eternal recurrence of the same. This metaphysical theology is nevertheless a negative theology of a peculiar kind. Its negativity is exhibited in the words: God is dead. These are not the words of an atheism, but the words of an onto-theology, of the very metaphysics, in which proper nihilism achieves its consummation.

However, if metaphysics as such does not think being and indeed for the reason that it thinks being in terms of beings as such, then ontology and theology, due to their reciprocal reliance on each other, must also leave being itself unthought. Theology takes the essentia of beings from ontology. Ontology, knowingly or not, mislays beings with reference to their essentia, understood as what exists, into the first foundation that theology conceives. The onto-theological essence of metaphysics thinks beings with reference to their essentia and existentia. These determinations of being are only, so to speak, lightly touched in thought [by being] but not thought from being itself, neither each for themselves nor the two in their difference. This difference, along with everything that it encloses in the unthought, is suddenly there in the thinking of metaphysics as if it had fallen from the bright skies. Perhaps this is how it really is, in which case, one would only have to reflect upon what this means with regard to being itself.

This multi-faceted and still hardly clarified togetherness of ontology and theology in the essence of metaphysics, [216] manifests itself particularly clearly where metaphysics, in keeping with the style of its own name, names that fundamental feature from which it becomes familiar with beings as such. That feature is transcendence. This word names the surmounting of beings toward that which they are in their constitution as beings. The surmounting of beings toward essentia is the transcendence as the transcendental. Kant, in keeping with the critical restriction of beings to objects of experience, equated the transcendental with objectivity. Transcendence, at the same time, means the transcendent, that in the sense of the first existing ground of beings – the ground of that which exists – surpasses them and in towering over them, towers around with the entire fullness of the essential. Ontology represents transcendence as the transcendental and theology represents it as the transcendent. This unified ambiguity of what is called transcendence is grounded in the difference between essentia and existentia, which is obscure with respect to its provenance. This unified ambiguity of transcendence mirrors the onto-theological essence of metaphysics. On the strength of its essence, metaphysics thinks beings by surmounting them in a transcendental-transcendent manner, but surmounting them only in order to re-present beings themselves, that is to say, to turn back toward beings. In this transcendental-transcendent surmounting, being is, so to speak, touched by way of representing. This thinking which surmounts constantly passes being by in thinking, not by missing the mark, but by not engaging with being. The thinking of metaphysics does not engage with being because this thinking has already thought being in its own way, namely, as a being insofar as it is a being.

Being itself remains unthought in metaphysics as a matter of essential necessity. Metaphysics is the history in which there is essentially nothing with respect to being itself.

Metaphysics as such is nihilism proper.

The experience of the nihilistic essence of metaphysics just indicated is still not enough by far to do justice to the proper essence of metaphysics. What [217] we require here before anything is to experience the essence of metaphysics from the standpoint of beyng itself. But if we are also assuming that a thinking coming from afar is on its way to this essence then it would have had first of all to learn to know what the following means: Beyng itself remains unthought in metaphysics. Perhaps thinking first has to learn only this.

Beyng itself remains unthought in metaphysics because it thinks beings as such. What does this mean: Beings as such are thought? It implies: Beings themselves come to appear. They stand in the light. Beings are illuminated. Beings themselves are unconcealed. Beings stand in unconcealedness. This is the essence of truth that appears at the inception only to recede away again at once. In what truth do beings stand when they are thought in metaphysics as beings themselves? Obviously, metaphysics itself is the truth of beings as such. What kind of essence does this unconcealment have? Does metaphysics ever say anything about the essence of truth, in which and from which it itself thinks beings, given that metaphysics itself indeed essences as this truth? Never. Or do we only speak like this – which seems arrogant – because we have so far sought in vain for what metaphysics says about the essence of truth within which it also stands? And have we sought in vain only because we still continue to question in an inadequate fashion? We must correct ourselves when the chance presents itself. Provisionally, the reference to Nietzsche's metaphysical concept of justice showed us though that Nietzsche was neither able to cognize the justice conceived by him in its essential truth nor as the essential structure of the truth of his metaphysics. Does this inability lie in the fact that this metaphysics is the very metaphysics of the will to power or does it lie in the fact and only in the fact that it is metaphysics?

It lies in the latter. As metaphysics, it leaves beyng itself unthought. In thinking beings as such, it touches upon being by way of thinking, in order quickly to pass over it in favor of *beings*, to which it returns and among which it comes to rest. That is why metaphysics thinks beings as such. However, [218] it does not reflect upon the "as such" itself. In the "as such" it is said: Beings are unconcealed. The ᾗ in ὂν ᾗ ὄν, the qua in ens qua ens, the "as" in "beings as beings" name the unconcealedness that as such is unthought. Language secures something so essential so inconspicuously in such simple words, if they are words at all. This "as such" touches upon the unconcealedness of beings in their being by way of naming. However, since beyng itself remains unthought, even the unconcealedness of beings remains unthought.

What if in beyng and unconcealedness, which is unthought in each case, were the same? The unconcealedness of beings that is unthought would then be the beyng itself that is unthought. Beyng itself would then essence as unconcealedness.

Once again, we have shown even more essentially what it is that remains unthought in metaphysics, which is the truth of beings itself as such. It is therefore now time for us to finally ask how this "unthought" itself is to be thought. In addition, along with what remains unthought, we are citing the history of nothingness with respect to beyng itself. In reflecting upon the "unthought" in its essence, we come closer to the essence of nihilism proper.

If beyng itself remains unthought, then it seems that the responsibility for this rests with thinking because for thinking, beyng itself is responsible for nothing. Thinking neglects something. Meanwhile, metaphysics thinks the being of beings. It is familiar with being through its fundamental concepts essentia (essentiality) and existentia (existence). But it is familiar with being only in order to cognize a being itself as such from it. In metaphysics, being is neither passed over nor overlooked. *Its* manner of looking at being does not permit being to be thought on its own. For this, metaphysics would have to permit being to be itself and in this way to be addressed in thought by metaphysics. Being remains in view, even in the view of concepts and still remains unthought. In that case metaphysics must reject being as that which is to be addressed in thought by itself.

Surely, such a rejection already presupposes that metaphysics [219] had somehow admitted and permitted beyng itself into its domain, as that which is to be addressed by it in thought. We find no trace of such a rejection even in the thought of metaphysics. Metaphysics validates and knows itself, even where it expresses itself not as onto-theology, but as the thought that constantly thinks "being" pervasively, even if only in terms of beings as such. Nevertheless, metaphysics is not familiar with this "even if only . . ." And it is unfamiliar with it not because it rejects beyng itself as that which to be addressed in thought, but because beyng itself stays away. If this is how things stand, then the "unthought" is not due to thinking or neglecting something.

How ought we to understand beyng itself staying away? Perhaps in this way: Beyng itself resides somewhere like a being of some kind, not arriving for some reason (perhaps it has lost its way)? But being is still in metaphysics and remains in view for it.

In the meantime, the following has become clearer: Beyng itself essences as the unconcealedness in which a being comes to presence. Unconcealedness itself, however, remains concealed as unconcealment. On its own terms, namely, those of unconcealedness, unconcealment stays away in relation to itself. The "un" of unconcealedness stays away in relation to unconcealedness. It remains with the concealment, namely, of being as such. Beyng itself stays away. This means: It stays with the concealedness of beyng itself, indeed in such a way that this very concealedness is concealed within itself. The staying away of beyng is beyng itself as this staying-away. Beyng is not isolated somewhere by itself besides staying away. Rather, beyng itself is the staying away of being as such. In staying away, beyng is veiled by its very self. This veil, disappearing into itself, is nothingness as beyng itself. It is the form in which beyng itself essences in staying away. Do we have an intimation of what essences in nothingness? If we did, there could be something other than just a negative assertion in the characterization of the essence of nihilism proper, according to which, there is nothing with respect to beyng itself.

Being itself remains unthought in metaphysics as such. [220] This now means: Being itself stays away and being itself essences as this staying-away.

Since its own "un-" stays away in unconcealedness with respect to itself and remains with the concealedness "of" being itself, the staying-away exhibits the characteristic feature of concealment. In what sense may we indeed think of concealment? Is this concealing just a veiling or simultaneously a stashing-away and keeping-safe? The staying-away "of" being itself (being as staying-away) is such always in relation to beings. Are beings deprived of being in this staying-away? Is this depriving in fact a *refusal*? We only ask and ask what we have to surmise in relation to the *staying-away* of being itself. Let us grant that the *staying-away* is being itself. Will it then depend upon beyng itself and how it strikes [*anmuten*] our own thinking for us to *surmise* [*vermuten*] from it the specific features that essence in staying-away? First and foremost, we must pay attention only to that which belongs to the staying-away of being.

The concealment may or may not be a self-refusing safekeeping of being itself. However, what essences in it is something like a self-withdrawal of being itself, indeed, in such a way that it simultaneously remains in view as the being of beings. The withdrawal, which is how being itself essences, does not rob beings of being. Nevertheless, a being stands, precisely if it is a being and only a being, in the withdrawal of being itself. We say: Beings are abandoned by being itself. Nevertheless, the abandonment by being allows beings themselves to be. Yet, the abandonment by being concerns beings as such, not only beings of the kind called human, who represent beings as such, in which representing we have the withdrawal of being itself in its truth.

Being withdraws itself. This withdrawal happens. The abandonment of beings as such by being happens. When does this happen? Now? Only today? Or since a long time? For how long a time already? Since when? Ever since beings came into unconcealedness as beings themselves. Ever since this unconcealedness happened, [221] we have had metaphysics because metaphysics is the history of this unconcealedness of beings as such. Ever since there is this history, there is historically the withdrawal of being itself, there is the abandonment of beings as such by being, there is the history of nothingness with respect to being. Since then and consequently, being itself remains unthought.

Nihilism proper has essenced ever since, but has at the same time been concealed in keeping with its essence. We are thinking this name now, insofar as it names the nihil. We are thinking the nothing, insofar as it concerns being itself. We are thinking this "concerning" itself as history. We are thinking this history as the history of being itself. The essence of nihilism proper is being itself in the staying-away of its unconcealedness. This unconcealedness exists as the 'it' itself of being and in staying away, determines its "is."

Now indeed, it could perhaps become clear to us, at least in certain respects, that this remaining-unthought of being as such that was initially mentioned, is due to the staying away of being. This staying away is being itself. Yet, we said too much and in view of this, we wanted to make the following assertion: Being itself is responsible for its remaining-unthought, not thinking. Thus, thinking belongs to the staying-away of being. This statement can, as soon as it is thought, hit upon something essential. But it can also miss it. In the same way, the statement: Being itself is responsible for the remaining-unthought can say too much. Yet, it can also say what is alone essential.

Thinking belongs to the staying-away of being as such. But thinking belongs, not by way of asserting this staying-away or rather, not by way of yet asserting it, as though being itself were somewhere there as one separate thing and thinking somewhere here as another separate thing, which, left to itself, either takes care of being in its unconcealedness as such or does not. Thinking is in no way this activity in opposition to being, standing above and for itself, not even as the representational activity of the subject, carrying being already with itself and in itself as the most universally represented. Characterizing it in this way, [222] misconceives the simple appearance and the distinct meaning of thinking. Apart from this, by locating being in the region that is under the control of the representing subject, we would neither be able to see nor understand how being as such in its unconcealedness and with its unconcealedness, eludes thinking while and insofar as thinking always already represents beings as such and, that is to say, being. In sharp contrast, thinking belongs to being itself, insofar as thinking, in accordance with its essence, is involved in that which never comes to being as such only from somewhere outside, but which comes from being itself and indeed as 'it' itself and being is always with it. What is this?

What we are inquiring here and what needs to be experienced in its simplicity, we have already unwittingly mentioned as we were about to distinguish the staying-away of being as a feature of being itself. There we were talking about how being itself does not stay isolated in some place. From what indeed should being isolate itself? Not from beings, which have their basis in being, even though being continues to be distinct from beings. Not from being since this is how being itself is an "it itself." However, in the staying-away from, there essences the relation to something like *place*, away from which the staying-away remains what it is: the staying-away of unconcealedness as such. This *place* is the place to stay [*Bleibe*] in which the staying-away [*Ausbleiben*] of the unconcealedness essentially continues its stay [*verbleibt*]. However, if in the staying-away of unconcealedness as such, concealedness stays on, then the staying-on of concealedness also maintains its essential relation to the same place. The staying-away of unconcealedness as such and the staying-on of concealedness essence in a single place to stay, which is already the accommodation for the individual essence of both. However, the staying-away of unconcealedness and staying-on of concealedness do not look around subsequently for an accommodation. This accommodation [*Unterkunft*] rather essences with them as the arrival [*Ankunft*], which is what being itself is. This arrival is in itself the arrival of their accommodation. The locality [*Ortschaft*] of the place [*Ort*] of being as such is being itself.

This locality is, however, the essence of the human being. The [223] locality is not the human being itself (not the for itself as subject), insofar as human beings only dabble in their humanity, taking themselves to be a being among other beings and explain being, in case it specifically strikes them, instantly and always only from beings as such. However, to the extent that human beings also only comport themselves toward being by knowing of it exclusively from beings as such, they comport themselves toward being itself. Human beings themselves stand in the relation to being itself insofar as they comport themselves, as human beings, to beings as such. However, being makes a gift [*begabt*] of itself in coming to pass [*begibt*] in its own unconcealedness. Only in this way is "it" being, with the locality of its arrival being the accommodation of its staying-away. As the "there" [*Da*] of the place to stay, this "where" belongs to being itself, "*is*" being [*Sein*] itself and is therefore called Da-sein [being-there]. "The Dasein in the human being" is the essence, that belongs to being itself. It is, however, the essence to which human beings belong, indeed in such a way that they have to be this being. Da-sein concerns human beings. As their essence, it is in each case their own. It is the very essence to which they belong. But it is not something that they themselves have created and perpetuated as their accomplishment. Human beings become essential by specifically assuming their own essence. They stand in the unconcealedness of beings as such as the hidden locality of being itself (locality, which is how being exists as an "it itself"). They stand in this locality. This means that they are ecstatic in it as they are how they are, at all times and places, from the relation of being itself to their essence, i.e., to the locality of being itself. The ecstatic standing-within the openness of the locality of being as the comportment to being, whether it be to beings as such or to being itself, is the essence of thinking. Such an essence of thinking, namely, that which is experienced by taking one's departure from being itself, is not determined by demarcating thinking from willing and feeling. It should also therefore not be set apart from the practical as just a theoretical attitude and curtailed in its essential implications for the essence of the human being. When we speak of the unthought in our reflections on the essence of nihilism, it is always the unthought of a thinking conceived in such an essential way. [224] Thinking is regarded as the activity of the understanding. The subject matter of the understanding is an understanding appreciation. The essence of thinking is the understanding appreciation of being.

Being itself concerns human beings, along with their essence from the accommodation of its arrival – it being this accommodation. As someone who has been concerned by being in this way, the human being is the one who thinks. This "whether it be . . ., whether it be . . .," in which the essential possibility of something or the other shows itself for thinking, is found in a *certain* way in the thinking of the *human being*, but it has its basis in being itself, which can as such withdraw and does withdraw in showing itself in beings as such. However, because it concerns the essence of the human being, even this possibility of thinking has its basis in the essence of the human being and with it being the locality of being, in beyng itself.

Thus, the human being as the one who thinks can keep sight of beings as such. Thinking then brings being to language in the form of beings as such. This thinking is metaphysical. It leaves being itself unthought. For, it has already thought being as a being as such and thinks at all times and all places on the basis of what is thought in this way, in the mode of representation. Thinking does not reject being itself in this way. However, it also does not keep sight of the staying-away of being as such. Thinking itself does not by itself respond to the withdrawal of being. This two-fold failure related to not rejecting [being] and not responding [to the withdrawal] is however not nothing. In fact, what happens here is that being as such not only stays away but thinking also thoughtlessly obstructs and covers up this staying-away. The more decisively metaphysics assures itself of beings (truth as certainty), assuring itself as the truth "of being," in beings and on the basis of beings themselves (assurance as the highest value), the more decisively is it already done with being as such. Beings as such posit being as the condition of their existence and as this condition it is a value among other values.

Nihilism is now, in keeping with its essence, historically consummate. The staying-away of being itself is explicitly and yet, unknowingly obscured in its staying-away by this type of [225] metaphysical thinking, of thinking in values. Moreover, this obscuring is not recognized as such. Even the nothingness of being is stamped as value in this interpretation of beings. It belongs to this stamping to understand itself as the new yes to beings as such, in terms of the will to power, i.e., as the overcoming of nihilism. Thought from the essence of nihilism, this overcoming is nothing but the consummation of nihilism. In this consummation, the full essence of nihilism is certainly manifested to us more clearly than otherwise in metaphysics. What is proper to nihilism is the staying-away of being itself. But insofar as this staying-away occurs in metaphysics, this aspect proper to nihilism will not be admitted as that which is proper to nihilism. Rather the staying-away as such will be omitted in the thinking of metaphysics, indeed in such a way that metaphysics will even omit this omission as its proper doing. Through this omission the staying-away will be abandoned to itself, and indeed in a hidden manner. Precisely in the manner in which nihilism occurs, what is proper to it is not what is proper. In what way? Nihilism occurs as metaphysics because it is improper to itself. But this improperness is not a lack of the proper, but the consummation of what is proper insofar as the proper is the staying-away of being itself and it is due to this that it, this staying-away, stays on fully as itself. What is proper to nihilism is historical in the form of the improper, which brings about an omission of the staying-away by omitting even this omission. In all its boisterous affirmation of beings as such, nihilism is not involved and also cannot get involved with anything that could concern being itself. The full essence of nihilism is the original unity of what is proper to it and what is improper.

Therefore, when nihilism is experienced and brought to concepts within metaphysics, metaphysical thinking can only encounter what is improper to nihilism. Even this is encountered only in such a way as to not experience what is improper as such, but it is rather explained on the basis of the procedure that is intrinsic to [226] metaphysics. The omission of the staying-away of being as such appears in the form of the explanation of being as value. Being that is omitted for the sake of value, is derived from beings as such as their condition. Nihilism, which is nothing with respect to being itself, always signifies for metaphysical thinking only one thing: that it is nothing with respect to beings as such. Metaphysics itself thus blocks the path toward the experience of the essence of nihilism. Metaphysics, at any time, puts the affirmation or the denial of beings as such up for decision and sees its alpha and omega in the relevant explanation of beings on the basis of their ground, a ground that also exists as a being. Insofar as it does this, it has indeed unknowingly overlooked that being itself already stays away in the priority given to the question concerning beings as such. In staying away, being abandons its own nature to the thinking of metaphysics, which omits this staying-away as such and also does not admit to this omission. Insofar as this thinking that has become historical as metaphysics essentially belongs to beyng itself, and thinks from the standpoint of the unconcealedness of beings as such, even that which is improper to nihilism has its existence from beyng itself.

Improper nihilism is what is improper in the essence of nihilism, insofar as it precisely completes what is proper. A difference essences in the essential unity of nihilism. What is improper to nihilism does not fall outside of its essence. What this shows is that the corrupted essence belongs to the essence. One could opine that the exhibited relationship of the improper to the proper in nihilism is a special case of the universally valid relationship between essence and corrupted essence, so that the former could act as an example of the latter. However, the proposition: "The corrupted essence belongs to the essence," is no formal universal statement of an ontology about the essence that is metaphysically represented as "essentiality" and standardly appears as the "idea." The proposition thinks being itself in the verbally understood word (verbum) "essence" in terms of how "it," being, is. But being is in the "how" of the staying-away of itself, which as such finds [227] accommodation in an omission and is preserved in this way. However, this omission itself essences in what has withdrawn (in withdrawal), in keeping with the concealedness of the unconcealedness of being. Thus, the thinking, which as metaphysics, represents beings as such in the mode of omission, admits so little of the omission that it is incapable of experiencing the abandonment of beings as such by being itself.

If we think of the essence of nihilism in the way we have attempted, we think it, on the basis of being itself, as the history of being, which is how being itself is being. However, the essence of nihilism that is based on the history of being does not now exhibit those features that normally characterize what one understands by the familiar word "nihilism:" The degrading and the destructive, decline and fall. The essence of nihilism contains nothing negative of the destructive kind that finds its place in human disposition and plagues human action. The essence of nihilism is not a matter pertaining to human beings at all, but to beyng itself. For this reason, it is, nevertheless, also a matter pertaining to the essence of the human being and only as a consequence *of this*, is it a matter pertaining to the human being; presumably not just one matter among others. If this negativity we have mentioned within the immediate appearance of the commonly understood nihilism does not belong to its essence then this does not mean that the actuality of destructive phenomena should be overlooked, denied or explained away as superfluous. Rather we need to ask about where these destructive phenomena, not just in terms of their causal nexus, have their essential origin. But how do we intend to even pose this decisive question if we have not reflected beforehand on the essence of nihilism and in unison with it have not been confronted with the following question: Does the staying-away of the question concerning the essence of nihilism not co-determine the dominance of these destructive phenomena and does this dominance of the destructive, our refraining from posing the question and our inability to question the essence of nihilism not ultimately stem from the same common root? If this should be the [228] case, then little would be gained if one wanted to believe that the essence of nihilism, if it does not consist of this negativity, is indeed something positive. However, the positive and its opposite share the same space. Ascent against fall, rise against decline, ennoblement against degradation, construction against destruction, play out as counter-phenomena in the realm of beings. The essence of nihilism, however, concerns beyng itself, to put it more appropriately, the latter concerns the former, insofar as being itself has come to pass in history in such a way as to be nothing with respect to itself.

We could now, especially if we have sufficiently thought through the preceding explication of nihilism, concede that the above-mentioned negative phenomena do not immediately belong to the essence of nihilism because they are not sufficient for it. Nevertheless, we will concede that something "negative" must reign in the essence of nihilism. How else could the name, which we would like to take seriously as a name, still say something? The preceding determination of the essence of nihilism places all the emphasis on the difference between the proper and the improper in nihilism. The "im" of the improper brings the negative to the fore. Certainly. Yet, what does "the negative" mean here? Do we not in fact invoke here a familiar, but still only a crude idea? Do we mean the improper in nihilism to be the bad and even the evil in opposition to the proper as the right and the good? Or does one take proper nihilism to be the evil and bad and the improper to be, if not the good, then still not evil? Discounting their hastiness, both the former and the latter opinion would be equally erroneous. Both judge the two features in the essence of nihilism from the outside. In addition, they utilize standards of judgment, whose applicability in this case is to be first decided. Meanwhile, this much would had to have become clear: here we are moving in the essential realm of being itself, which we can no longer explain and judge from some other standpoint, [229] assuming both these ways of thinking to be still appropriate in this context. If the "im" emerges between the features of the proper and the improper in the essence of nihilism then we can think it only from the unity of this essence. This unity shows a difference, which the "im" brings out. However, it still remains hidden as to whether the "im-" and the "not" have their essence in the difference or whether the negative of the "im-" informs the difference first and only as a consequence of a negation. Yet, what is it in the essential unity of nihilism which gives this negation its source and support? Since something questionable persists here, we will satisfy ourselves with the insight that the differential reigns in the essence of nihilism – the differential concerning being itself. For this reason, the "im" does not depend primarily and only on a negation and its negative. However, if the fundamental feature of the negative in the sense of the destructive is completely lacking in the essence of nihilism, then the intention to want to immediately overcome nihilism as something alleged to be just destructive, begins to appear very strange. What would certainly be even stranger is the view that a thinking rejecting the immediate overcoming of the nihilism, thought in terms of its essence, would need to accept nihilism in the commonly understood sense.

What does overcoming mean? Overcoming means: bringing something under one's sway and bringing what has been so surmounted under one's sway in such a way that it will have no determining power henceforth. Even if overcoming does not aim at elimination, it remains an impetus against. . . . To overcome and want to overcome nihilism which has been thought in terms of its essence, means that human beings by themselves take measures against being itself as it stays away. Yet, who or what would be capable of taking measures against being itself, in whatever aspect and with whatever intent, and of indeed bringing it under the sway of human beings? Yet, an overcoming of being itself is not only never achievable, but also the attempt to do it already reflects the intention to pull the essence of the human being off its hinges. For, the hinge of this essence consists in this: that being itself, [230] whatever its mode, even if in the mode of staying-away, lays claim to the essence of the human being. This essence is the accommodation with which being gifts itself in order to come to pass in such an accommodation as the arrival of unconcealedness. To want to overcome being itself means to want to pull the essence of the human being off its hinges. One could understand the impossibility of this intention as follows: it would be an absurd gesture of thinking that, as such, thinks from the standpoint of being in wanting to take measures against it. This intention would be even more absurd – in case there were levels of absurdity – than the attempt to deny beings as such in an act of thinking, which is still a being. However, what is at stake here is not only whether thinking, taken on its own, contradicts itself in its own activity and thereby transgresses its own fundamental rule, falling thereby into absurdity. How often is human thinking not suffocated in contradictions, and yet remains on a worthy course.

Thinking when taking measures against being itself does not primarily and only fall into logical impossibility. Rather, when taking measures against being itself, thinking arises in the turning away from being itself and perpetuates the surrender of the essential possibility of the human being, which could become or indeed already could be fatefully actual, despite its absurdity and logical impossibility.

The attempt at taking measures against the staying-away of being as such and thus against being itself is not responsible for neglecting a rule of thinking. It is rather responsible for not admitting being itself as being. In fact, it omits being. We, however, recognized an essential trait of nihilism in such an omission. To want to directly take measures against the staying-away of being itself would mean not heeding being itself as being. The overcoming of nihilism intended in this manner would only be a more terrible relapse into what is improper in its essence, obscuring what is proper to it. What if overcoming were not to take immediate measures against the staying-away of being? [231] What if it were to refrain from measuring up to being itself, by refraining from taking measures against the omission of the staying-away? This omission in the form of metaphysics is still the work of human thinking. How should human thinking not take measures against its own failure to think being itself in its unconcealedness? No one will dispute the necessity of this effort if this necessity is experienced beforehand. What this involves is the human being experiencing this omission as such, i.e., experiencing what is improper in the essence of nihilism. How could this happen without being touched beforehand by what is proper? The proper, is however, the staying-away of being in its unconcealedness. But being does not only keep its unconcealedness to itself, retaining it only for itself, so to speak. It also co-determines that its omission happen in and through the thinking of the human being, in keeping with its essential relationship to the essence of the human being. The overcoming of the staying-away can happen only indirectly from the side of the human being. It can only happen if being itself directly demands in advance that the essence of the human being first experience the staying-away of the unconcealedness of being as such as an arrival of being itself and reflect first upon what is so experienced. If we pay attention to the essence of nihilism as a history of being itself then the intention to overcome nihilism becomes invalid if, by it, we mean that human beings by themselves bring this history under their sway and force it in the direction of what they merely wish. But it is also erroneous to speak of the overcoming of nihilism if we mean by it that human thinking takes measures against the staying-away of being. Instead, only one thing is needed: that being itself first appear to thinking, that thinking approach being in its staying-away as such. Such thinking that approaches is based, first of all, upon the recognition that being itself withdraws. As this withdrawal, being is, however, precisely the relationship that lays claim to the essence of the human being, as the accommodation of its (of being's) arrival. With this accommodation, the unconcealedness of being as such already comes to pass. This thinking that approaches [232] does not omit the staying-away of being. It also does not attempt to take possession of the staying-away, so to speak, in order to eliminate it. This thinking that approaches being follows being in its self-withdrawal. Thinking thinkingly follows being by letting being itself go, while for its part, staying behind. Where does thinking linger? No longer in the place where it lingered as the hitherto thinking of metaphysics that omits. Thinking remains behind by taking a decisive step back, back from the omission. Where to? Where else than into the realm which being itself has, for the longest time, left for thinking, left it in the nevertheless veiled form of the essence of the human being.

The thinking touched by the essence of nihilism does not hurry into an overcoming of nihilism that it has always all too quickly calculated. It lingers instead in the arrival of the staying-away and waits on it, in order first to learn to ponder the staying-away of being with regard to what this staying-away might be from its own standpoint. The unconcealedness of beings is concealed in the staying-away of being as the essencing aspect of being itself. However, insofar as being is the unconcealedness of beings as such, being is, nevertheless, already granted to the essence of the human being. Being itself has already announced itself and spoken from within the essence of the human being, by holding itself back and saving itself in the unconcealedness of its essence. Being which grants [*zusprechen*] itself in this manner but holds itself back in staying-away is the promise [*Versprechen*] of itself. To thinkingly approach being itself in its staying-away now means: to become aware of this promise, which is what being itself is. It exists, however, in staying away, that is to say, insofar as it is nothing with respect to itself. This history, i.e., the essence of nihilism, is the destiny of being itself. Nihilism, thought in terms of its essence in relation to what is proper, is the promise of being in its unconcealedness, such that being conceals itself as this promise, simultaneously provoking its [being's] omission by staying away.

But what then is the essence of nihilism when what is proper [233] to it is, at the same time, to be thought in relation to what is improper to it? What is improper to the essence of nihilism is the history of the omission and that is to say, the concealment of the promise. If we grant, however, that being itself is saved in its staying-away, then the history of the omission of the staying-away is precisely the preservation of this self-saving of being itself.

What is essential to the improper aspect of nihilism is nothing inadequate and base. What essences as the corrupted essence in the essence is nothing negative. The history of the omission of the staying-away of being itself is the history of the safekeeping of the promise, indeed such that this safekeeping is concealed from itself as to what it is. It remains concealed because it occasions from the self-concealing withdrawal of being itself and is endowed by this withdrawal with its essence that keeps it safe in this way. What essentially conceals in safekeeping and in so doing, remains in essence concealed in itself and thus absolutely concealed, and nevertheless appears in some manner, is in itself what we call the secret. The secret of the promise occurs in what is improper to the essence of nihilism. This is how being is the "it itself" in saving itself as such. This history of this secret, this secret itself in its history, is the essence of the history of the omission of the staying-away of being. However, the omission of being itself in the thinking of beings as such is the history of the unconcealedness of beings as such. This history is metaphysics as such.

The essence of metaphysics consists in the fact that it is the history of the secret of the promise of being itself. This essence of metaphysics, thought from the standpoint of being itself in its history, is the essential nature of the corrupted essence that belongs to the unity of the essence of nihilism. Just like the essence of nihilism, the essence of metaphysics also does not allow for a positive or a negative evaluation. Now if the plan to directly overcome nihilism already precipitates its essence, then even this intention to overcome metaphysics lapses into a nullity. Unless this talk of overcoming [234] metaphysics contains a sense that neither aims at a degradation nor an elimination of metaphysics. If metaphysics, in the manner attempted just now, is thought in relation to the history of being, it arrives at its essence for the very first time. This essence continues to elude metaphysics itself and indeed in keeping with its very essence. Every metaphysical concept of metaphysics sees to it that metaphysics is itself sealed off from its own essential depth.

Thought in relation to the history of being, the "overcoming of metaphysics" always means only this: Abandoning the merely metaphysical interpretation of metaphysics. Thinking evacuates metaphysics of mere metaphysics by taking a step back, back from the omission of being to its staying-away. In this step back thinking already finds itself on the way toward thinkingly approaching being itself in its self-withdrawal. This self-withdrawal as such belongs to being. It still remains a mode of being – that of the arrival. In thinkingly approaching being itself, thinking does not omit being anymore, but rather lets it in: into the unconcealedness of being which is unveiled for the first time, an unconcealedness which is being itself.

We initially said that in metaphysics being itself remains unthought. In the meantime, we have shown more clearly as to what happens in this remaining-unthought and what form this happening itself takes. It is the history of being itself in its staying-away. Metaphysics belongs in this history. Metaphysics in its essence first approaches thinking from its provenance in the history of being. This essence is the improper aspect in the essence of nihilism and it issues from the essential unity with the proper aspect in nihilism.

To this day, there chimes in the name "nihilism" the discordant note of the negative in the sense of the destructive. To this day metaphysics is taken to be the highest realm, in which we think the deepest. Presumably, the discordant note in the name "nihilism" as well this prestige of metaphysics is an authentic and, in this way, a necessary illusion. This appearance is unavoidable. [235] Metaphysical thinking cannot overcome it. Does it also continue to be impossible for the thinking that is responsive to the history of being to get over it? This appearance of a discordant note in "nihilism" could point to a deeper resonance which may resonate, not from the heights of the metaphysical but from another realm. The essence of metaphysics reaches deeper than metaphysics itself and indeed into a depth that belongs to this other realm where the depth does not correspond to a height anymore.

Nihilism is essentially the history of the promise, of how being itself is saved in a secret. This secret is itself historical and keeps safe the unconcealedness of being on this basis of this history that takes the form of metaphysics. Inasmuch as the entire essence of nihilism, as the history of being, comes to pass as the accommodation in the essence of the human being, it gives thinking everything to think. What is given to thinking in this form, as that which is to be thinkingly addressed, is what we call mystery.

Being, the promise of its unconcealedness as the history of the secret, is itself the mystery. Being is that, which on the basis of its essence alone, makes this essence the occasion for thinking. It is a trait of being itself, that "it," being, is the occasion for thinking, and not sporadically and in some respect, but always and in every respect because it essentially gives its essence over to thinking itself. Being itself is the mystery. This does not mean, in case such a comparison is still applicable here, that being is irrational, which repels everything rational in order to slump into the incapacity to think. In fact, being, as the occasion for thinking, is what is to be thinkingly addressed. Being is also the only one that from out of itself, lays claim to being the only one that is to be thinkingly addressed as this very claim. Confronted by being itself, the insalubrious game of hide-and-seek that is meant to play out between the irrational and the rational becomes completely pointless in its thoughtlessness.

However, doesn't the essence of nihilism in relation to the history of being still remain the mere thought of a mystical thinking in which a romantic philosophy [236] takes flight from what is actually true? What does this essence of nihilism that has been thought here mean in contrast to the only effective actuality of actual nihilism, which spreads confusion and ruin everywhere, fomenting crime and despair? What is this nothingness of being that we have thought supposed to be, in the light of the actual annihilation [*Vernichtsung*] of all beings, which with its violence creeping in everywhere, almost renders any resistance futile, additionally turning it into the ultimate provocation for the most extreme paroxysm of violence? Yet, we hardly need a broad depiction of the violence of actual nihilism running rampant all around, which can also be experienced concretely enough without an unrealistic definition of its essence. In addition to this, in all the one-sidedness of his interpretation, Nietzsche's experience already encountered actual nihilism so deeply, that the now attempted definition of the essence of nihilism appears schematic by contrast, to say nothing of its uselessness. For, who, in the midst of the danger to all the divine, human, thing-like and natural assets, would like to attend to something like the omission of the staying-away of being itself, assuming something like this indeed happens and is not just the chatter of a despairing abstraction?

If only a connection between the actual or even the nihilism experienced by Nietzsche and the essence of nihilism that was thought above would become visible. Then we could get rid of the overt appearance of absolute non-actuality from this essence. For, this appearance of absolute non-actuality seems to be much greater than the admittedly mysterious nature of this essence.

However, "essence" does not mean here what previous reflections unthinkingly assumed. "Essence" does not mean an essentiality which as something non-sensuous and abstract floats over the actual, understood as the sensibly perceptible. "Essence" thought verbally, and that is to say, experienced in thinking, is the essencing being itself, that occasions all beings into beings as such. Yet this is the question that arises first: whether the "essence" of being ever comes from beings; whether the actual as a being in all its activity is capable [237] of determining actuality, being or whether it is from being itself that effectiveness already occasions everything actual.

Does that which Nietzsche experiences and thinks, namely, the history of the devaluation of the highest values stand on its own? Does the essence of nihilism founded on the history of being not essence in this history? The interpretation of being as a value by Nietzsche's metaphysics is the effective and actual omission of the staying-away of being itself in its unconcealedness. What comes to expression as value in this interpretation of being, is the occurrence of what is improper in the essence of nihilism. That which is improper in the essence of the nihilism does not recognize itself and, nevertheless, only has its existence from the essential unity with what is proper to nihilism. If Nietzsche actually experienced a history of the devaluation of the highest values, then what is so experienced along with the experience itself is the actual omission of the staying-away of being in its unconcealedness.

The omission exists as actual history and occurs as this omission only from the essential unity of what is proper to nihilism with what is improper. This history does not exist alongside the "essence." This history is the essence itself and only this.

Nietzsche adds a comment to his interpretation of nihilism (*Will to Power*, n. 2, XV, 145) "that the highest values are devalued." It is as follows: "What is lacking is a goal, what is lacking is an answer to the 'why?'"*

Let us reflect upon the question, which asks "why?" here, more precisely with regard to what it interrogates and what the question concerns. It interrogates beings as such as a whole, why there are beings, and questions in the form of this metaphysical question about a being, which could be the ground for that which exists and how it exists. For what reason is this question concerning the highest values the question concerning the highest? Is this question only lacking an answer? Or is this question itself lacking in something? Is the question itself lacking as the question that it is? It is lacking as a question, insofar as it, asking about the ground of beings, itself existing as a being, questions past being itself and its truth and omits being. The question already fails as a question, not just [238] because it lacks an answer. This question that fails is no mere mistake, as if something incorrect crept into it. The question fails itself. It surrenders to hopelessness, within whose ambit all of the only possible answers fall far short from the very outset. But now, as Nietzsche asserts, the answer to the "why?" is really lacking. This means that in the very place where the answer is still provided, it is ineffective from the standpoint of the whole of beings. For, the fact that this whole exists and exists in the way that it exists, implies something different. It implies that this question dominates all questions, even when it remains without an answer. The exclusively actual dominance of this question is however nothing other than the actual omission of the staying-away of being itself. Is the essence of nihilism something

---

* {TN: Translated as Nietzsche, *The Will to Power*, 9, translation modified.}

abstract? Or is what essences in the history of being itself the happen-ing from which all history now happens? Is the fact that historiography, even that with the scope and wide vision of Jacob Burckhardt, does not and cannot know of all this, proof enough that this essence of nihilism does *not* exist?

However, Nietzsche's metaphysics does not only interpret being from beings in terms of the will to power as a value, but also thinks the will to power as the principle of a new positing of values. He understands and also wills this positing of values as the overcoming of nihilism. In so doing what comes to expression in this will to overcome is the most extreme entanglement of metaphysics in what is improper to nihil-ism such that this entanglement seals itself off from its own essence. Consequently, this entanglement, in the form of an overcoming of nihilism, only displaces metaphysics into the potency of its unfettered corrupted essence. The putative overcoming of nihilism establishes for the first time the dominance of the unconditional omission of the staying-away of being itself in favor of a being of the kind that is a value-positing will to power. In this withdrawal, which nevertheless remains a relation to beings, which is how "being" appears, being itself is unleashed into the will to power, which takes the form of beings seemingly reigning before and over everything concerning being. The staying-away of being itself essences in this reigning and appearing of [239] being that is covered over with respect to its truth. It essences in such a way that it tolerates the most extreme omission of itself, abetting the rush of the merely actual, which spreads itself as that which exists. The merely actual does so by arrogating, at the same time, the criterion for the decision that only the potent (the tangible and the impression, utility and success) is to be considered a being.

The essential unity of nihilism in its relation to the history of being essences in this most extreme form of what is improper to nihilism, which seemingly appears on its own terms. Let us grant that the unconditional appearing of the will to power in the entirety of beings is not nothing. In that case, is the essence of nihilism in relation to the history of being, which reigns in a concealed way in this appearing of the will to power, if not as this very appearing, only something imagi-nary or simply fantastical? If we should so quickly speak of fantasy, is it not precisely due to the fact that we wallow in the habit of deeming actual only the appearances of the consequences of nihilism taken up for themselves and interpreted negatively, a nihilism which has not been experienced in its essence, and scattering to the winds that which essences in this actuality as a nullified nothing? Now, what if this, nev-ertheless, fantastical opinion were of the same kind as the nihilism from which it imagines itself to be untouched or absolved through showing good faith and being permeated with the will to order?

The essence of nihilism in relation to the history of being is neither only something imaginary, nor does it float over actual nihilism completely cut off from it. Rather, what one deems to be actual only exists as a being from the essential history of being itself. Now the difference between the proper and improper that reigns in the essential unity of nihilism could certainly unravel into the most extreme breakaway of the improper from the proper. In that case the essential unity of nihilism itself would have to be concealed in the most extreme manner, in keeping with its own meaning. It would have to disappear as the nullified nothing within the unconcealedness of beings as such, which everywhere counts as being itself. It would have to then appear as though there were actually nothing with respect to being [240] itself, in case one gave some thought to it at all. Who would not want to suppose, if they reflected upon what has been said hitherto, that being itself is capable of this possibility [of being nothing with respect to itself]? Who, if they think, could avoid being struck [*angemutet*] by this most extreme withdrawal of being, so as to surmise [*vermuten*] an imposition [*Zumutung*] by being in this withdrawal, where being itself is such an imposition concerning human beings in their essence? However, this essence is nothing human. It is rather the accommodation of the arrival of being. As the arrival, being gifts us with the accommodation, coming to pass in it such that, "it" thus "grants being" only in this way.

The essence of nihilism in relation to the history of being occurs as the history of the secret, which is how the essence of metaphysics occurs. The entire essence of nihilism is a mystery for thought. We continue to admit this. This admission, however, does not grant something additionally from out of itself, which could be available for itself. This admission [*Eingeständnis*] only turns into persistence [*Inständigkeit*]. This persistence is the standing and awaiting in the midst of the truth of being that veils itself. For, it is from this persistence alone that human beings are capable of retaining their essence as thinkers. When thinking prepares itself to think, it already stands in the admission of the mystery of the history of being. This is because as soon as it thinks it is addressed in thought by being. The manner in which we are inceptually struck by being is the staying-way of its unconcealedness from what is unconcealed in beings as such. Thinking pays no heed to this initially and for a long time after, which bars it from experiencing the fact that the manifestations of the nihilism commonly understood are triggered due to being getting unleashed. This unleashing surrenders the staying-away of its unconcealedness to the omission by metaphysics, which, at the same time, in a hidden way, bars the arrival of self-concealing being. Inasmuch as these nihilistic manifestations emerge from being getting unleashed, they are occasioned by the prevalence of beings and perpetuate the turning way of beings from being itself. In this occurrence of the staying-away of being, [241] human beings are themselves thrown into this unleashing of beings, which proceeds from the self-withdrawing truth of being. By representing being as a being as such, human beings fall for beings, erecting themselves as beings from the standpoint of beings as they fall for them, taking possession of beings as objects by representing and producing them. Human beings on their own invest their essence in assurance amid beings, in favor of and against them. They seek to bring about this assurance in beings by a comprehensive ordering of all beings on the basis of unconditional systematic planning, by means of which the correctness of assurance is supposed to be consummately established. This objectification of all beings as such from the radical emergence of the human being in the exclusive self-willing of its will is the essence of the process in relation to the history of being, through which human beings construct their essence in subjectivity. Accordingly, human beings and what they represent as the world are established within the subject–object relationship that is supported by subjectivity. All transcendence, be it ontological or theological, will be represented relative to the subject–object relationship. With this radical emergence within subjectivity, even theological transcendence – the being fullest in being, what one characteristically enough calls "being" [*das Sein*] – turns into a kind of objectivity, namely into the subjectivity of moral-practical faith. Whether human beings take this transcendence seriously as providence for the sake of their religious subjectivity or just as a pretext for the will of their own only self-centred subjectivity, changes nothing for the essence of this fundamental metaphysical position concerning the human essence. The astonishment over the fact that two contradictory opinions about providence, understood on their own terms, prevail simultaneously alongside each other, is groundless. This is because both stem from the same root – the metaphysics of subjectivity. As metaphysics, it leaves being itself unthought in its truth from the very beginning. As the metaphysics of subjectivity, however, it turns being, in the sense of a being as such, into the objectivity of re-presenting and [242] fore-grounding. The fore-grounding of being as one of the values posited by the will to power is only the final step of modern metaphysics, in which being is manifested as will.

As the history of the unconcealedness of beings as such, this history of metaphysics is still the history of being itself. The modern metaphysics of subjectivity is the admittance of being itself, which in the staying-away of its truth occasions the omission of this staying-away. The essence of the human being is in a concealed way the accommodation of being in its arrival, this accommodation belonging to being itself. However, this essence of the human being is increasingly omitted, the more essentially this arrival is barred in the form of the withdrawal of being. Human beings become unsure regarding their own essence, which remains in its withdrawal with being itself, without being able to experience the whence and the essence of this unsurety. Instead, they seek what is only true and permanent in their self-assurance. Hence, they strive toward assuring themselves amid beings, an assurance that can be organized by human beings themselves. Beings can thereupon be investigated as to what they themselves offer in terms of new and always reliable possibilities of assurance. We can now see that among all beings, the human being is cast in a peculiar way into the unassured. From this we can surmise that human beings, indeed in the relationship to their essence, are most likely caught in a risky play. Thus, there dawns the possibility that beings as such could essence in such a way as to put everything in risky play: this alone is the "play of the world:" . . .

In this sometimes clear, sometimes unclear throng, beings as such are unveiled sometimes as the will to will, at other times concealing themselves again. However, a being as such is always brought into an unconcealedness, which makes it appear as that which puts itself upon itself and brings itself before itself. This is, however, the fundamental trait of subjectivity. Beings as subjectivity omit the truth of being in a decisive way, such that subjectivity [243] posits the truth of beings as certainty from its own will to assurance. Subjectivity is no accomplishment of the human being. The human being rather assures itself as the being which conforms to a being as such, insofar as it wills itself as the I- and We-subject, accordingly representing itself and summoning itself to itself. Beings as such exist in the mode of subjectivity and the human, accordingly, seeks and traverses all the paths assuring its assurance in the midst of beings, all of which only attests to the following: Being keeps to itself with its unconcealedness in the history of its staying-away. Being itself essences as this keeping-to-itself. This essencing of being itself happens, but not after or over beings, but, if anything, before beings as such, if at all the representation of a such a relationship remains appropriate here. Thus, even what is supposedly actual in the nihilism commonly imagined lags behind its essence, not the other way round. The fact that our thinking, steeped in metaphysics for millennia, does not perceive this, is no proof of the opposite view. We could very well ask here whether what is essential are the proofs of thinking, whatever the form they take, or the hints of being. Yet, how can we be sure of these hints? Perhaps this question, which sounds so earnest and ready, comes from a will to know, which still belongs to the realm of the metaphysics of subjectivity. This does not mean we ignore it. It only means that we would do well to reflect upon whether this call for the criterion of certainty considers and has considered everything that belongs to the sphere in which it wishes to create a clamour.

What essences in nihilism is the staying-away of being as such. In staying-away, however, being promises itself in its unconcealedness. The staying-away is given over to the omission of being itself in the secret of history, which is how metaphysics keeps the truth of being concealed in the unconcealedness of beings as such. As the promise of its truth, being keeps to itself along with its own essence. The admitting of the omission of the staying-away happens from this keeping-to-itself. [244] The keeping-to-itself emerging from the particular distance of the withdrawal, which conceals itself in the related phase of meta-physics, determines each epoch of the history of being as the epoch of being itself.

However, if being itself withdraws by holding itself back the farthest, beings as such arise, unleashed in the entirety of their dominance, as the exclusive criterion for "being." Beings as such manifest as the will to power, wherein being as the will consummates in its subjectness. The metaphysics of subjectivity omits being itself so decisively that it remains covered up in the thinking of value, which itself can hardly be known and considered as metaphysics anymore. As metaphysics gets pushed around in the swirl of its omission, this omission becomes unrecognizable as such, is organized in the direction of the truth of beings as such, which is completed by sealing off the truth of beings as such from the truth of being. In keeping with the prevailing blindness of metaphysics toward itself, this sealing off appears as freedom from all metaphysics (cf. *Twilight of the Idols*. How the "True World" finally became a Fable).[9]

In this way, what is improper to nihilism succeeds in gaining uncon-ditional predominance, behind which the proper and its relationship to the improper, along with the essence of nihilism remain invisible in what is inaccessible and unthinkable. In this epoch of the history of being, these consequences and these consequences alone, of the

---

[9] *Nietzsches Werke (Großoktavausgabe)*, Vol. VIII (Leipzig: Kröner, 1919), 82. {TN: Translated as Friedrich Nietzsche, "Twilight of the Idols," in *The Portable Nietzsche*, ed. and trans. Walter Kaufmann (New York: Penguin Books, 1954), 485.}

predominance of the improper in nihilism, come into their own, but never as consequences, but rather as nihilism itself. That is why nihilism only exhibits destructive traits. They are experienced, demanded or combatted in the light of metaphysics. Anti-metaphysics, the inversion of metaphysics and even the defence of the hitherto existing metaphysics constitute one single affair within the long occurring omission of the staying-away of being itself. The struggle around nihilism, for or against it, takes place [245] in the field marked out by the predominance of the corrupted essence of nihilism. Nothing is decided by the struggle. It only stamps the predominance of what is improper to nihilism. This struggle, even when it believes it is standing on the opposing side, is always and fundamentally nihilistic and that too in accordance with the usual destructive meaning of the word.

The will to overcome nihilism misrecognizes itself because it shuts itself out of the manifestness of the essence of nihilism as the history of the omission of being, unable to recognize its own deed. The misjudgment of the essential impossibility within metaphysics of overcoming nihilism, even if it is through its inversion, can go to such lengths as to take the denial of this possibility [of overcoming nihilism within metaphysics] immediately for an affirmation of nihilism or indeed for an indifference, which looks on at the course of nihilistic decay without intervening in any way.

Because the staying-away of being is the history of being and so the history that properly exists, beings as such fall into the unhistorical, particularly in the epoch of the dominance of the corrupted essence of nihilism. The sign of this is the emergence of historiography, which claims to be the authoritative idea of history. It takes history to be the past and explains the past in its emergence as a causally demonstrable nexus of effects. The past that is objectified in this way through narration and explanation appears within the horizon of the very present, which in each case accomplishes this objectification and, if it comes up, explains itself as the product of past happenings. One is also under the impression that one knows what facts and facticity are, what beings of the kind called past, what beings of kind which emerge, are. This is because objectification through historiography always knows how to bring to the fore some kind of material consisting of facts and to place them in a reasonableness that is commonly understandable and most of all close to the present. The historiographical situation is always dissected because it is the outcome and the goal of mastering [246] beings in the sense of assuring the position and the relationships of human beings in the midst of beings. Historiography stands consciously or unconsciously in the service of the will of the instances of humankind, to establish themselves in beings, in accordance with an order that is easily visible. The will to the nihilism commonly understood, along with its activity, as well as the will to overcoming nihilism, move in the realm of the historiographical accounting of historiographically analysed spirit and world-historical situations. What history is, is sometimes also asked in historiography, but always only as an "also," and hence, at times belatedly, at times as an addition and always as if historiographical representations of history with a sufficiently expanded generalization could yield us the definition of the essence of history. However, where philosophy interrogates and an ontology of the occurrence of history is interrogated, there one remains within the metaphysical interpretation of beings as such. History as being, proceeding simply from the essence of being itself, remains unthought. Thus, any historiographical reflection of human beings on their situation is a metaphysical one and therefore one that essentially omits the staying-away of being itself and thus unhistorical. We need to reflect upon the metaphysical character of historiography, if we have to measure the scope of historiographical reflection, which at times thinks it is called upon, if not to save, then to enlighten human beings who are at risk in the age of the self-consummating corrupted essence of nihilism. In the meantime, following the claims and the demands of this age, the job of doing historiography effectively has been passed over from the academic discipline to journalism. The name "journalism" names, correctly and not in a pejorative sense, the metaphysical assurance and the establishment of the everydayness of the incipient age in the form of a historiography of which one can be sure, that is to say, the hastiest possible historiography which works reliably and which serves everyone with a useful objectification of their respective day. This historiography contains at the same time the reflection of the continuing objectification of beings as a whole.

[247] This is because with the self-consummating metaphysics of subjectivity, which corresponds to the most extreme withdrawal of the truth of being as it covers it up to the point of unfamiliarity, we commence with the epoch of the unconditional and comprehensive objectification of everything that is. In this objectification, human beings themselves and everything pertaining to humanity becomes a mere stock, which accounted for psychologically are classed under the process of the will to will. Even if some individuals still appear to themselves to be free, tomorrow some other individuals will interpret this occurrence as something purely mechanical. Both misunderstand the hidden essence related to the history of being, that is to say, the nihilistic essence, which, spoken in the language of metaphysics, always remains

something spiritual. Humanity has indeed become human material, subordinated to raw material and construction material in the process of the unconditional objectification of beings as such. This is not due to a putative materialistic preference for matter and force over the human spirit. It is rather grounded in the unconditional aspect of objectification itself, which must bring everything that exists, whatsoever kind it may be, into its possession and assure itself of this possession.

The unconditional objectification of beings as such arises from the self-consummating domination of subjectivity. This domination essences from the most extreme unleashing of beings as such into the omission of being itself, which, in the form of this omission, refuses its staying-away indefinitely. As this refusal it dispatches being in the form of beings as such into the destiny of the complete concealedness of being in the midst of the complete assurance of beings. This history that is concealed in its historicity is interpreted historiographically, that is to say, always metaphysically, perhaps from different, if not indeed necessarily contradictory standpoints. Setting-up goals for all kinds of ordering, estimating the value of what is human are established in their public character in accordance with the position of valuative thinking, granting this public character its validity. Just as the uncon-cealedness of beings, which is their truth, became a value, [248] in the same way, the kind called unconcealedness signifying public character will become an essential value of assuring the continued existence of the will to power. This happens in the course of the essential progress of this interpretation of the essence of truth. On every such occasion, there are metaphysical or, what is here the same, anti-metaphysical interpretations, of what is to be considered a being and what is to be considered a corrupted being. However, a being that is objectified in this way is, nevertheless, not that which is. It is hardly that which is, just as value and the value-character of being are hardly capable of unveiling the truth of being itself.

What is, is that which happens. What happens has already happened. This does not mean that it is now in the past. What has already happened is alone that which has been gathered in the essence [*Wesen*] of being, that which was [*Ge-Wesen*], from which and as which the arrival of being itself is, and is said to be in the form of the self-withdrawal that stays-away. This arrival keeps beings as such in their unconcealedness and allows them this unconcealedness as the unthought being of beings. What happens, is the history of being. What happens is being as this one history and its history of staying-away. This staying-away touches the essence of human beings. It touches the human beings of this age insofar as they are neither familiar with nor succeed in standing in acknowledgment in their essence withheld from them and are thus historical. The staying-away of being touches the essence of human beings in such a way that human beings in their relationship to being, i.e., to beings as such, shun this essence without acquiring any familiarity with it. They understand being from the standpoint of beings, wanting to understand every question concerning "being" only in this way. If it were to have already happened that human beings stood in acknowledgment in their essence related to the history of being, then they would have been able to experience the essence of nihilism. This experience would have allowed them to reflect upon the fact that the nihilism commonly understood, is what it is due to the consummation of the dominance of the corrupted essence of its essence. It is due to the essential provenance of the nihilism understood metaphysically that it cannot be overcome. However, it cannot be overcome not because it is impossible to overcome it, but rather because every willing-to-overcome is incommensurate with its essence.

[249] The historical relationship of human beings to the essence of nihilism can only rest upon the fact that their thinking is committed to approaching the staying-away of being itself in thinking. This thinking responsive to the history of being brings the human being face to face with the essence of nihilism; in opposition to which all willing-to-overcome puts nihilism behind us but only so far behind, that it rises around us unnoticed in the persistently dominant horizon of metaphysically determined experience, even more troublingly potent and beguiles opinion.

The thinking responsive to the history of being lets being come into the essential space of the human being. Since this essential realm is the accommodation with which being gifts itself as being itself, it means that: The thinking responsive to the history of being lets being exist as being itself and only as being. Being is cleared up as the arrival of the keeping-to-itself of the refusal of its unconcealedness. What is named by "clearing," "arriving," "keeping-to-itself," "refusing," "unconcealed" is one and the same that essences: being. When metaphysical thinking is sent a step back, it steps forward to open up the essential space of the human being. However, such an opening up is only occasioned from being, to approach the arrival of its staying-away in thinking. The step back does not throw metaphysics to the side. Rather thinking has the essence of metaphysics before itself and around itself now for the first time in the sphere of experiences of beings as such. This provenance of metaphysics in the history of being remains that which is to be addressed in thinking. It is in this way that its essence is preserved as the secret of the history of being.

The staying-away of being is its withdrawal in keeping to itself with its unconcealedness, which it promises in its refusing self-concealing. Thus, being essences as the promising in withdrawal. However, withdrawal remains a relationship [*Bezug*], which is how being itself let its accommodation approach it, i.e., it moves into it [*be-zieht*]. As this relationship, being never gives up unconcealing even in the staying-away of its unconcealedness, which is only unleashed in the keeping-to-itself, as the unconcealedness of beings as such. Being, [250] as this arrival which never gives up [*ab-lassende*] on its accommodation, is the un-relenting [*Un-ablässige*]. In this way it is what urges [*nötigend*]. Being essences in this way because being, as the arrival of the unconcealedness, needs [*be-nötigt*] this arrival itself, not as something alien but as being. Being requires accommodation. It makes a claim to it by needing it. Being urges in a twofold, yet unified sense: the unrelenting and the requiring in relation to the accommodation, which is how the essence, to which the human being belongs as the historical, essences. What urges [*das Nötigende*] in this twofold manner exists and is called urgency [*Not*]. In the arrival of the staying-away of its unconcealednes, being itself is urgency.

But urgency is veiled in the staying-away, which, at the same time, remains covered up on account of the omission of the truth of being in the history of metaphysics. Within the unconcealedness of beings as such, which is how the history of metaphysics defines the fundamental happening, the urgency of being does not appear. Beings are, as if being existed without urgency [*Not*]: lacking in urgency [*notlos*].

Yet, this lack of urgency [*Notlosigkeit*], which establishes itself as the dominance of metaphysics, brings being itself into its most extreme urgency [*Not*]. This extreme urgency does not just remain an urging in the sense of a never ceasing demand, which claims accommodation, that is to say, a demand which requires accommodation as the unconcealedness of the arrival, that is to say, which lets it essence as the truth of being. The unrelenting nature of being's requiring extends so far into the staying-away of its unconcealedness, that the accommodation of being, which is the essence of the human being is omitted, threatening human beings with the annihilation of their essence and endangering being itself, which requires its accommodation. Extending so far into its staying-away, being endows itself with the danger that the urgency, which is the form in which being essences in urging, historically never becomes the urgency that it is for the human being. At its most extreme, the urgency of being becomes the urgency of the lack of urgency. There is a predominance of the lack of the urgency of being, a lack that continues to be veiled as such. Being in its truth continues to be the doubly urging urgency of the unrelenting requirement for accommodation. This predominance of the lack of urgency is nothing other than the unconditional supremacy of the completely unfolded corrupted essence in the essence of nihilism.

[251] However, the lack of urgency dominates as the veiled, most extreme urgency of being in the age where beings are obscured and there is confusion, in the age where humanity is violent and in despair, where the will has disintegrated and become impotent. Boundless suffering and measureless suffering openly proclaim the state of the world, remaining silent everywhere as the distressingly urgent and this situation, in the very basis of its history, nevertheless lacks urgency. This is however, in relation to the history of being, both its highest and its most hidden urgency. This is because it is the urgency of being itself.

How can this urgency as such specifically strike human beings, and in the distance of their essence from themselves? What is the human being capable of, if the urgency is the urgency of being itself? The urgency of being itself, which is how the essence of nihilism is historical and perhaps initiates what is proper to it, is manifestly no urgency of the kind that human beings encounter and which they regulate and prevent. How are they supposed to do this if they do not recognize it, even accepting that resistance is not a disposition that is in any case contrary to the essence of this urgency?

To respond to the urgency of the lack of urgency, can only mean to facilitate, for a start before everything else, the experience of the lack of urgency as the essencing of urgency itself. To this end, it is necessary to point into the urgency's lack of urgency. This means: to experience the omission of the staying-away of being itself. It belongs to this experience to think the essence of nihilism as the history of being itself in what has been so experienced. This however means: to thinkingly approach the arrival of the self-withdrawing of being in relation to its accommodation, that is to say, in relation to the essence of the historical human. But what vista opens up here? To approach the most extreme urgency of being in thinking means: to engage with the most extreme endangering of human beings, namely, the danger of the annihilation of their essence and thus to think the dangerous. In that case, the course of reflection would be happy with this "dangerous thinking," which the human world, already confused enough, still bases on the venturesome and the groundless. Glorification of danger and the misuse of violence – does the one not reciprocally intensify the other? [252] The Nietzschean phrase "living dangerously" often bandied about by the comfort-loving bourgeoisie belongs in fact to the realm of the metaphysics of the will to power and demands active nihilism, which now has to be conceived as the unconditional dominance of the corrupted essence of nihilism. But danger as the risk of the unconditional exercise of violence, and danger as the threat of the essential annihilation of the human being, stemming from the staying-away of being itself, are not the same. Indeed, by contrast, not thinking of the omission of the urgency of being itself, which happens as metaphysics, is the blindness toward the lack of urgency as the essential urgency of the human being. This blindness comes from the unadmitted anxiety toward anxiety, which experiences the staying-away of being itself as terror. Perhaps, the blindness toward the most extreme urgency of being, in the form of the prevailing lack of urgency in the midst of all the distress of beings, seen from the standpoint of the duration of history of being, is still more dangerous than the boorish adventures of the merely brutal will to violence. This more dangerous aspect consists in the optimism, which only permits pessimism as its opponent. Both are however assessments of value in relation to beings within the sphere of beings. Both operate in the realm of metaphysical thinking and perpetuate the omission of the staying-away of being. They intensify the lack of urgency and perpetuate, without a possible reflection, only this, that the lack of urgency will not be experienced and will be incapable of being experienced as urgency.

What kind of damage can a thinking inflict which only thinks one thought, to point into the provenance in the history of being, which is ascribed to and kept open for the essence of the human being from the arrival of the staying-away of being itself?

The urgency of being is based on the fact that it urges in a twofold manner, but in its staying-away, brings with it the danger of the essential annihilation of the human being, inasmuch as being occasions the omission of the staying-away of itself. The lack of urgency means: The urgency, in the form in which being itself essences, remains veiled, which is the destiny that escalates the urgency to its utmost limit, into the danger to this urgency itself, bringing it to consummation as the urgency of the lack of urgency.

[253] However, if the historical human being were capable of thinking the lack of urgency as the urgency, then it could indeed experience what it is to belong to the history of being. The human beings of the age of the consummated corrupted essence of nihilism would only then experience that what is, exists as an "is." Since they would have had already thought from the standpoint of being itself. The human being would experience what stems from the history of being, from the lack of urgency as urgency and what has already come in this way from its provenance, but comes into presence [*anwest*] in a concealed arrival,

that is to say, still continues to be absent [*abwest*] for the horizon of metaphysical experience. To continue to be absent, thought metaphysically, means the mere contrary of coming into presence as being: Non-being in the sense of the nihilating nothing.

What arrives from the urgency of the lack of urgency into the unthought of being itself, and that is to say, into the midst of beings as such, in such a way that it counts for nothing?

The staying-away of the unconcealedness of being as such triggers the disappearance of everything wholesome in beings as such. This disappearance of the wholesome takes with it and seals off the opening to the holy. Sealing off the holy obscures any illumination of the divine. This obscuring reinforces and conceals the deficit of God. The dim deficit makes all beings stand in the uncanny. Nevertheless, beings as the objectivities of limitless objectification appear to be an assured possession and trusted everywhere. The uncanny in beings as such brings to light the homelessness of the historical human being within beings as a whole. The where of a dwelling in the midst of beings as such appears annihilated because being itself – that which essences all accommodation – fails. The half admitted, half denied homelessness of the human being with regard to its essence, is supplanted by organizing the conquest of the earth as the conquest of one planet and its atmosphere among other planets. Through the success of its achievement and the organization of ever greater populations of its kind, the homeless human being can be propelled into the flight from its own essence, in order to represent this flight as the return home into the true [254] humanity of the Homo humanus and incorporate it into its own operations. The rush of the actual and the effective intensifies. The lack of urgency in relation to being is reinforced in and through the increasing need for beings. The needier a being becomes for beings, the less it hungers after beings as such, to say nothing of it having to pay attention to being itself. The poverty of beings with regard to the unconcealedness of being has reached its consummation.

The epoch of the concealedness of being in the unconcealedness of beings of the type called the will to will, is the age of the consummated poverty of beings as such. However, this age first begins to establish the dominance of the corrupted essence of nihilism in its totality. This historical course of this age gives the impression of human beings, liberated in their humanity, having freely assimilated the order of the universe into their capacity and disposal. What is right [*das Rechte*] seems to have been found. It is now only a question of establishing it correctly [*richtig*] and therefore establishing the dominance of justice [*Gerechtigkeit*] as the highest representative of the will to will.

The essence, related to the history of being, of what is impoverished in this age, is based on the urgency of the lack of urgency. Since it essences more and is older, the destiny of being, which is how the truth of being is refused in the midst of the throng of beings and only beings, is uncannier than the deficit of God. What is uncanny in this urgency, which goes out of presence and comes into presence, is enclosed within the fact that everything actual, which concerns the human beings of this age and sweeps them along, beings themselves, is completely familiar to them. It is rather due to this that they remain unfamiliar not only with the truth of being, but also wherever "being" comes up, it is taken as a spectral being of mere abstraction and is thus thrown away, misconceived as the nihilating nothing.

What is uncanny in the urgency of the lack of urgency is enclosed in the omission of being itself and disseminates its misinterpreted reign in this omission. But what is uncanny in this urgency comes from [255] the simple, which is how the tranquility of the staying-away of being remains tranquil. However, human beings in the age where metaphysics has reached its consummation hardly approach this simple in thinking. This is because they burden it, provided they are able to think being as such at all, immediately with a surfeit of metaphysical concepts, whether they take this seriously as the work of narrow conceptualization or whether they treat it unseriously as the mere play of a futile fingering. In any case metaphysical cognition is enriched, be it in positive application, be it in negative retraction, both of which stem from the fullness of scientific knowledge, which is spurred by a disgust toward the thinking of being, not only in its impressive results, but also in its very foundations. However, the thinking that approaches the staying-away of being in questioning is neither grounded in science nor can it ever find its way by demarcating itself from science. Thinking exists, if it exists, only in being occasioned by being itself and as this occasion [*Anlaß*], insofar as it engages [*einläßt*] with the unconcealedness of being.

A thinking of being, following from its own essence coming from the history of being, can experience what remains for it to experience only in the midst of the urgency of the lack of urgency, namely, the urgency itself as the destiny of the staying-away of being in its truth. In being able do this, it prepares itself necessarily – under the dominance of metaphysics and within its unrestricted realm of dominance – for the first steps, following which brings it face to face with the relationship of being to the essence of the human being in the form of withdrawal.

The thinking of being is so decisively caught in the metaphysical thinking of beings as such that it can pave and go its way only with the sticks and stones borrowed from metaphysics. Metaphysics is both a help and a hindrance. But it does not weigh down progress because it is metaphysics, but because in keeping with its essence, it holds its own essence to be unthinkable. This essence of metaphysics, however, because it shelters the unconcealedness of beings in a concealed way and is thus the *secret* of the history of being, for the first time gifts the experience of the [256] thinking responsive to the history of being, a passage to freedom. The truth of being itself essences as freedom.

If the lack of urgency is the most extreme urgency and exists, as if it just did not exist, then human capacity must first be steered into the lack of urgency [*Notlosigkeit*]. Only then is the urgency able to urge in the essential realm of the human being. To experience this as such is necessity [*Notwendigkeit*]. Let us grant that necessity is the urgency [*Not*] of being as such. Let us also grant that being as such is already and exclusively only entrusted to thinking. Then the subject matter of being, that it is the being of beings in its unconcealedness, passes over to thinking. Being itself in its unconcealedness and thus unconcealedness itself must first become questionable for thinking. This must happen in the age of metaphysics, which debases being into value. For, the dignity of being does not consist in being considered a value, even if it be the highest value. Rather, the dignity of being consists in *being* the freedom, which frees all beings as such into itself, that remains for thinking that which is to be addressed in thinking. The fact that beings exist as if being were not the unrelenting and the one requiring accommodation, as if it were not the urgency of the truth itself that urges, is the dominance of the lack of urgency, which is reinforced in the metaphysics that has reached consummation.

Appendix

[259] ADDENDUM TO: THE ESSENCE OF NIHILISM

I.

1.
To pp. 201–208f.

How can it happen that being itself becomes question-worthy? Only in such a way that "it," being as such, is first cleared up. When that happens, being manages to become unconcealed, which is how it itself essences. In this way, the essence of unconcealedness itself first becomes question-worthy. However, the question concerning the essence of truth is now no longer a metaphysical one, i.e., the one that concerns certainty as the assurance of the possibility of cognition.

The question concerning the essence of truth is the question concerning being itself.

Being is that which is to be addressed in thought as being itself – no longer as the transcendent, which is how and only how being remains related to beings. This is how it is taken back to beings and in accordance with the type of metaphysical thinking, (concept – productive) represented as the *most universal* of beings and as the highest being, i.e., as ἀρχή – as principle – ground.

It is to be addressed in thought no longer as ground. We therefore need to reflect upon the essence of ground in unison with transcendence and this in reference to the essence of metaphysics, whose fundamental question is called such because it is the question concerning the ground – in the form of the what-question and with regard to beings as such.

"Why are there beings at all rather than nothing?" *But* now *this question*, where it is asked in accordance with the essence of metaphysics, is thought differently.

The essence of metaphysics and that means, metaphysics as history – metaphysics in its history.

212   *Appendix*

[260] 2.
Characterizing Thinking from (*Being and Time*)
in terms of the History of Being

The oldest appreciation of being from the earliest history of its unveiling: μελέτα τὸ πᾶν* – in the midst of the age of the most extreme rationality, which is infatuated with irrationality and says that the thinking of the *alien* is what is alien to thinking.

Thinking of *being*, i.e., first of all "essence" of truth, *essence of metaphysics*; thinking this essence historically.

Destiny – that captures – what essences [*Wesende*] as the arrival – of what was [*Ge-wesen*].

Metaphysics in its consummation – the reigning omission, i.e., the consummated metaphysics of nihilism.

Nietzsche – metaphysics – nihilism – value.

3.
Manufacturing Human Dignity!

Assurance of a dignified human life on earth. From which essential space are human beings accorded their essence and which one?

Are they, where they are now, worthy of this essence and its dignity?

In order to advocate for the maintenance of human dignity, is it enough to go without engaging with the essential provenance of this dignity and the relationship to the human essence that reigns from it.

Is it enough to manufacture a standard of living and assure it? Assure it from where and through what? Assurance to what end? Is it enough to preach supernatural purpose to oppose this assurance of a standard of living and to essentially replace it? Both are inaccessible and yet both only move in the sphere of the accomplishments of the *human beings* of this epoch, which is already something different from what they imagine on the basis of the prevailing ideas.

* {TN: In *Nietzsche III*, 5, Heidegger translates this saying attributed to Periander of Corinth, son of Cypelsus as "Take into care, beings as a whole." An alternative translation: "Practice is all," in *Early Greek Philosophy II: Beginnings and Early Ionian Thinkers, Part I*, ed. and trans. André Laks and Glenn W. Most (Cambridge, MA: Harvard University Press, 2016), 147.}

[261] 4.
The Essence of Nihilism
Nihilism – Question of Being – Metaphysics – History of Being[1]

Nihilism cannot be discussed as an isolated phenomenon. The essence of nihilism is to be thought entirely only from the fundamental experiences within the still veiled happening of the overcoming of metaphysics that enters into world history itself. Thus, a sufficient experience of the essence of nihilism must reflect upon the essence of metaphysics. Offering a metaphysical concept deployed by metaphysics does not suffice for this purpose. With the essence of metaphysics, we need also [to reflect upon] all the "metaphysics of metaphysics." Today, we also have to think metaphysics itself, especially in its final form, which concerns and supports the contemporary age from the ground up. This is Nietzsche's metaphysics. Nihilism, in the entirety of its essence, specifically enters into the horizon of metaphysics. Nietzsche's metaphysics thinks nihilism for the first time. But it *thinks* it metaphysically. Nietzsche does not yet think the essence of nihilism (cf. Lecture Summer Semester 1940,[2] *Nietzsche III* 1940[3])

[262] 5.
What is Alien to Thought
A Moment in the History of Being!

What is greater today –
Ill-will toward thinking
or false satisfaction in thinking
or misleading in thinking
or fear of thinking
or incapacity to think (by which we do not mean the personal inability to engage in the activity of thinking)
or are they all equally great because they are the same?
The consequence of an omission of the truth of being – the dis-inclination [*Un-mögen*] of being.

[1] The following text is struck out in the manuscript.
[2] *Nietzsche: Der europäische Nihilismus*, Freiburg Lecture II, Trimester 1940, GA 48, ed. P. Jaeger, (Frankfurt am Main: Klostermann, 1986). {TN: See footnote 2 to section 30 of *The Overcoming of Metaphysics*.}
[3] *Nietzsches Metaphysik*, Freiburg lecture announced for Winter Semester 1941/42, but not held, ed. P. Jaeger, GA 50 (Frankfurt am Main: Klostermann, 1990). {TN: See the long note in footnote 1 of section 78 of *The Overcoming of Metaphysics*.}

6.
The Path "through" the Essence of Metaphysics

Even here – in relation to metaphysics – what is needed, not against, but toward its essence, *traversing* through this essence as the enduring leap; and this is indeed the *shortest* path to successfully approach what is proper to the essence of nihilism. But even this can be prepared from [the] history of thinking *alone* and only from being occasioned, quite certainly, by being itself.

Now it is from the experience of its essence that metaphysics, and that is to say, its history appears to be the inescapable region, in which the path of the thinking responsive to the history of being runs, even though it is no longer metaphysical.

Cf. the phenomenological "destruction" in *Being and Time* and the treatise *What is Metaphysics?* In this way metaphysics must *stand* simultaneously in the no and the yes!

How it is that the essence of metaphysics is cleared up only gradually in the thinking responsive to the history of being and lays claim to thinking– (not [263] as the reflection of metaphysics upon metaphysics), but rather as the essencing from the essence of truth itself.

II.
THE FUNDAMENTAL EXPERIENCE IN
BEING AND TIME

1.

How and when was thinking affected by the *essence of nihilism*? (p. 189)? When the experience of the forgottenness of being occurred. This was the experience on which the question concerning the truth of being rests. (The fundamental experience of *Being and Time*) It is expressed in the language of metaphysics – as the repetition [*Wiederholung*] of the question: τί τὸ ὄν? What does a being as such mean, i.e., *what does being itself mean*; but this *simple step*, which lies in this "i.e.," is what is decisively other, which neither Plato nor metaphysics since Plato nor the thinking before him asked.

The re-trieval [*Wieder-holung*] of the question of being.

2.
Conclusion: What is Metaphysics?

What does the question ask, not metaphysically, but thought from the essence of metaphysics?

What does the question ask, when it stands at the conclusion of a reflection, which asks: What is metaphysics, which thus asks after the essence of metaphysics and in so doing *asks* after the nothing?

It no longer asks after beings as such, referring back to beings, but approaches being itself in questioning.

[265] 3.
The Proper Essence of Nihilism and Fundamental Experience
The Nature of the Overcoming

The essence of nihilism is the concealment of being itself stemming from the being of beings in such a way that being is forgotten in its truth. As a consequence of having forgotten being itself, the differentiation between beings and being as the differentiation bearing all metaphysics as ontology in the broadest sense of the term, is forgotten. As a consequence of this forgottenness the ontological difference (*Differenz*) as the distinction between being and beings remained unthought.

As a consequence of this unthought difference, the question concerning being itself remains unasked. As a consequence of this lack of questioning [*Fraglosigkeit*] with respect to being itself, the question concerning the truth of being in the sense of the question concerning the being of truth remains unthinkable. As a consequence of this unthinkability, the question posed by *Being and Time* remained necessarily incomprehensible in the age of the self-consummating metaphysics. As a consequence of this non-comprehension, one finds "nihilism" in the place where we perhaps take the first step of thinking in the direction of overcoming metaphysics, as it is rooted in the history of its essence.

One keeps bickering over names, orientations, standpoints, and cares little about the matter of thinking.

Yet, it is not a question here of the validity and recognition of a philosophy, but of having an ear for the voice of beyng. Thinking cannot produce such an ear. Having an ear [*Gehör*] comes from belonging [*Gehören*].

4.
The Essence of Nihilism

is what is thought in *Being and Time* from the question concerning the truth of being, which is determined as the falling into beings.[a] [266] This *fall* is neither meant morally nor theologically as the secularized fall into sin. Fall means that the human being falls prey to beings only to determine these beings from a general representation, which is said to be the being of beings. The fall which is to be thought this way is

---

[a] In the way the truth of being is the ontological *movement-concept* of Da-sein (*Being and Time*, § 38).

the presupposition for the possibility of ascending [*Steigen*] in the sense of *transcending* [*Überstieg*], which thinks the being of beings from the standpoint of beings. (*Being and Time*, 167–168f.)*

Falling and transcending in their belonging-together. The understanding of being. Facticity, existence – throwness, existence, falling. (*Being and Time*, 262)

5.
Cf. Nietzsche's Words (Comment on p. 145)

The question concerning the essence of nihilism must indeed have to do with the nihil – the nothing, if the name is to make sense and this sense is to be thought rigorously. The question concerning the nothing emerging from the question posed by *Being and Time* (cf. there § 40 and § 58). Only folly and ill-will, superficiality of reading and hearing or the good-hearted incapacity to think can hold and disseminate the view that reflection upon the nothing perpetuates the intention to proclaim the nothing, in the sense of nihilating pure and simple, as the ultimate sense of the world. Perhaps one day some thoughtful ones will work out the simple thought that in order to overcome the nothing on its own grounds, and not in order simply to rebut mere views, what might very well be needed is to give some thought to the nothing beforehand.

[267] 6.
The Essence of Nihilism and the Fundamental Experience in *Being and Time*

The reflection upon the essence of nihilism stems from the experience on which the thinking in *Being and Time* is based. This experience consists in the growing perplexity from this one happening, which in certain aspects is perhaps also self-clarifying. This is the perplexity that in the history of Western thought, indeed from its inception, beings were thought in their being and yet being itself in its truth and this truth itself in its being remained unthought. As what can possibly be experienced, this truth is not only refused to thinking, but Western thinking in the form of metaphysics specifically, yet unknowingly, veils this one happening of the refusal of truth of being itself.

* {TN: Martin Heidegger, *Being and Time*, trans. Joan Stambaugh (Albany: SUNY Press, 1996).}

[269] Editor's Afterword

The two present treatises *The Overcoming of Metaphysics* (1938/39) and *The Essence of Nihilism* (1946–48) are appearing here for the first time in their entirety from the posthumous works as Volume 67 of the *Gesamtausgabe*.

When Martin Heidegger put together the first pamphlet for the announcement of the *Gesamtausgabe* in 1974, he envisaged one volume each for the two treatises. However, during review, it emerged that the scale of the manuscripts was really too small for two separate volumes. The administrators of the posthumous works of the *Gesamtausgabe*, Hermann Heidegger and Friedrich Wilhelm von Hermann decided, for this reason, to bring the two essays together in one volume. Even if the texts do not go together temporally and formally, they can be brought together in a single volume, because they cover a common thesis from the standpoint of different questions, that nihilism is the essence of metaphysics in its relation to the history of being. In this regard, the two treatises complement each other, resulting in the overarching title *Metaphysics and Nihilism* being chosen for this volume.

The Overcoming of Metaphysics originated in 1938/39. What we have here is a text that temporally and in terms of its subject matter belongs to the neighborhood of a series of treatises, which Heidegger composed in connection with the *Contributions to Philosophy (Of the Event)*. Even the present text is oriented in terms of content and form to the *Contributions*.

The manuscript is composed of one main part and two sequels. The first sequel is divided into five parts, the second sequel into three parts. The text itself consists of 164 sections of varying length, each with its own sub-heading. All of the text-sections have been numbered serially by the editor.

The main part consists of handwritten pages, 122 in number in the DIN* A5 format. The two sequels [270] consist of 190 pages, again in the DIN A5 format. Yet, here in this manuscript we have numbered the text-sections instead of the pages. The text-section no. 130 is only available as a typescript with handwritten corrections and additions.

The editor had at his disposal a typewritten transcription of the whole of the handwritten text, and one more carbon copy of the transcription of the main part and the first sequel.

The typewritten transcription was produced by Heidegger's brother Fritz Heidegger immediately after the manuscript was finished. For, Heidegger makes a note on the first page of the typescript that the main part was checked against the original on July 28,1940. The two sequels composed later were checked against the original on May 4, 1941, as a similar note on the first page of the transcription of the first sequel suggests. The transcriptions of the main part and the two sequels were serially numbered according to their pages independently of each other. The main part comprises 60 and the two sequels taken together comprise 81 pages.

In the typewritten transcription and also in some places in the carbon copy, Heidegger himself inserted some textual amendments as well as shorter and longer additions and marginal notes.

All the handwritten revisions and additions were transcribed for the production of the manuscript. The additions were able to be incorporated into the text with the help of the insertion signs placed by Heidegger. The other marginal notes, which could not be syntactically integrated with the text, were rendered as footnotes.

In order to demarcate these marginal notes from the bibliographical details, we differentiated two kinds of footnotes. The footnotes provided with a number contain bibliographical details about his own texts as well as citations and references to other authors. The footnotes with a small alphabet [271] render the mentioned marginal notes.

*

The overcoming of metaphysics is, for Heidegger, the decisive historical moment, in which metaphysics is experienced as the history of the abandonment by being and overcome at the same time. The abandonment of beings by being reveals itself in the final and most extreme intensification of metaphysics as the "unconditional predominance of manipulation." Manipulation means here the all-dominating

---

* {TN: Deutsche Institute für Normung [German Standards Institute].}

producibility of beings. Through this, it is manifest that the being of beings in metaphysics is grasped as the production from a highest cause or a highest ground. Being itself remains unthought here because in this grounding, being is only explained in its being again through another highest being. From this experience rooted in the history of being, the present treatise derives its task of thinking through the truth of beyng as "abyss" and "event" on the basis of the overcoming of the metaphysical grounding of being.

Heidegger published some sketches of this treatise in a revised form in 1954 in the collected volume *Lectures and Essays* under the title "Overcoming Metaphysics."

*

Even the second treatise: *The Essence of Nihilism* is linked to the fundamental thought of "overcoming," and indeed, from the standpoint of the manipulation that conditions it, which is a condition related to the history of being.

This treatise originated in the years 1946–1948. What we have here is a text that is written out continuously comprising originally 86 serially numbered manuscripts, of which [272] we are missing the first 20 pages. In its place Heidegger inserted manuscript pages marked with the small alphabet (a) in which he gives a short introduction to the treatise which begins abruptly.

As is mentioned in this introduction, the treatise concerns the attempt to indicate the essence of nihilism through Nietzsche's words "God is dead." The killing of God springs from the will to power as the most extreme form of manipulation. The being of beings is here grasped as the positing of value originating from the will to power. In this positing of being as value, it become absolutely clear that being itself remained unthought in metaphysics. Metaphysics is accordingly the history, in which there is "nothing" with respect to being itself and fundamentally speaking, metaphysics as such is the proper nihilism.

Parts of this treatise were already published by Heidegger. The final two-thirds of the text (pp. 204–256 [167–208]) appeared in a revised form under the title "Nihilism as Determined by the History of Being" in the second volume of the two-volume Nietzsche from 1961 (Nietzsche II. Gesamtausgabe Vol. 6.2, 301–361)[*]

---

[*] {TN: Translated into English as "Nihilism as Determined by the History of Being," *Nietzsche IV: Nihilism*, trans. Frank Capuzzi, ed. David Farrell Krell (San Francisco: HarperOne, 1991), 197–250.}

In addition to this, as it is explicitly noted in the typewritten transcription of the manuscript completed by Fritz Heidegger, four pages
of this text (188–191 [154–157]) were included in the treatise "God is
Dead," which appeared in 1950 in *Off the Beaten Track* (Off the Beaten
Track. Gesamtausgabe Vol. 5, 244–248).

The addenda in the appendix contain some selected sketches on *The
Essence of Nihilism*. Here, we see in the second part that the engagement with the essence of nihilism is based on the fundamental experience of *Being and Time*, i.e., on the experience of the forgottenness of
being.

*

[273] I thank Dr. Hermann Heidegger for the trust he has shown in
me through the transcription of this volume as well as for collating
the parts of the handwritten portions that were transcribed by me. I
am particularly grateful to Prof. Friedrich-Wilhelm von Herrmann,
who always stood helpfully by my side during the all the editorial questions. I am equally thankful to Dr. Hartmut Tietjen for his help in the
selection of the addenda and for his conscientious final revisions. For
the careful correction of the printed text, I further thank Dr. Peter
von Ruckteschell. Last but not the least, I would like to also thank Dr.
Walter Biemel and the doctoral candidate Mr. Manfred Hölscher M.A.
for their help in deciphering the text.

Würselen, in August 1998
Hans-Joachim Friedrich

Printed and bound by CPI Group (UK) Ltd, Croydon, CR0 4YY

09/06/2025

14685747-0001